MCSE Exam Notes™:
NT® Workstation 4

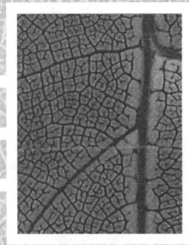

Gary Govanus and
Robert King

San Francisco • Paris • Düsseldorf • Soest

Associate Publisher: Guy Hart-Davis
Contracts and Licensing Manager: Kristine Plachy
Acquisitions & Developmental Editor: Neil Edde
Editor: Davina Baum
Technical Editor: Jim Cooper
Book Designer: Bill Gibson
Graphic Illustrator: Michael Gushard
Electronic Publishing Specialist: Robin Kibby
Production Coordinator: Rebecca Rider
Indexer: Nancy Guenther
Cover Design: Archer Design
Cover Illustrator/Photographer: FPG International

Screen reproductions produced with Collage Complete.
Collage Complete is a trademark of Inner Media Inc.
SYBEX, Network Press, and the Network Press logo are registered trademarks of SYBEX Inc.
Exam Notes is a trademark of SYBEX Inc.

Library of Congress Card Number: 98-85469
ISBN: 0-7821-2290-6

Manufactured in the United States of America

10 9 8 7 6 5 4 3 2 1

Microsoft
CERTIFIED PROFESSIONAL
Approved Study Guide

November 1, 1997

Dear SYBEX Customer:

Microsoft is pleased to inform you that SYBEX is a participant in the Microsoft®
Independent Courseware Vendor (ICV) program. Microsoft ICVs design, develop,
and market self-paced courseware, books, and other products that support Microsoft
software and the Microsoft Certified Professional (MCP) program.

To be accepted into the Microsoft ICV program, an ICV must meet set criteria. In
addition, Microsoft reviews and approves each ICV training product before
permission is granted to use the Microsoft Certified Professional Approved Study
Guide logo on that product. This logo assures the consumer that the product has
passed the following Microsoft standards:

- The course contains accurate product information.
- The course includes labs and activities during which the student can apply
  knowledge and skills learned from the course.
- The course teaches skills that help prepare the student to take corresponding
  MCP exams.

Microsoft ICVs continually develop and release new MCP Approved Study Guides.
To prepare for a particular Microsoft certification exam, a student may choose one or
more single, self-paced training courses or a series of training courses.

You will be pleased with the quality and effectiveness of the MCP Approved Study
Guides available from SYBEX.

Sincerely,

Holly Heath
ICV Account Manager
Microsoft Training & Certification

MICROSOFT INDEPENDENT COURSEWARE VENDOR PROGRAM

To my best friend and my wife, Bobbi.

—Gary

To my wife Susan.

—Bob

Acknowledgments

People keep trying to teach me patience. Someday it may take! There are many people who have been tried severely during the writing of this book, and I'd like to thank them all: my loving wife Bobbi; my two daughters, Dawn and Denise; Brandice and CJ for giving up time with their grandfather; Mom and Dad for understanding why we couldn't visit; Neil Edde, for giving Bob and me the chance; Davina Baum, our editor, for nursing us through; Jim Cooper, our technical editor, for making sure we didn't lie to you; Production Coordinator Rebecca Rider; Electronic Publishing Specialist Robin Kibby; and Designer Bill Gibson, for all the hard work they put in over the course of this project. To all, thank you.

—Gary Govanus

I always thought that writing a book would be easy—it's just teaching on paper, right? Little did I know just how much sacrifice would be involved. Unfortunately most of the sacrifices were made by my family. For that (and more), thanks first go to my wife, Susan, and my daughter, Katie.

I'd also be remiss if I didn't thank the guys at The Endeavor Group in Reno (www.endeavor-net.com) who donated a couple of their great computers to my home lab so I could test before I typed.

Lastly, thanks to the fine folks at Sybex for giving me the opportunity to write this book.

—Bob King

Table of Contents

Introduction

If you've purchased this book, you are probably chasing one of the Microsoft professional certifications: MCP, MCSE, or MCT. All of these are great goals, and they are also great career builders. Glance through any newspaper and you'll find employment opportunities for people with these certifications—these ads are there because finding qualified employees is a challenge in today's market. The certification means that you know something about the product, but, more importantly, it means you have the ability, determination, and focus to learn—the greatest skill any employee can have!

You've probably also heard all the rumors about how hard the Microsoft tests are—believe us, the rumors are true! Microsoft has designed a series of exams that truly test your knowledge of their products. Each test not only covers the materials presented in a particular class, it also covers the prerequisite knowledge for that course. This means two things for you—that first test can be a real hurdle and each test *should* get easier since you've studied the basics over and over.

This book has been developed in alliance with the Microsoft Corporation to give you the knowledge and skills you need to prepare for one of the key exams of the MCSE certification program: *Implementing and Supporting Microsoft Windows NT Workstation 4.0* (Exam 70-073). Reviewed and approved by Microsoft, this book provides a solid introduction to Microsoft networking technologies and will help you on your way to MCSE certification.

Is This Book for You?

The MCSE Exam Notes books were designed to be succinct, portable exam review guides that can be used either in conjunction with a more complete study program (book, CBT courseware, classroom/lab environment) or as an exam review for those who don't feel the need for more extensive test preparation. It isn't our goal to "give the answers away," but rather to identify those topics on which you can expect to be tested and to provide sufficient coverage of these topics.

Perhaps you've been working with Microsoft networking technologies for years now. The thought of paying lots of money for a specialized MCSE exam preparation course probably doesn't sound too appealing. What can they teach you that you don't already know, right? Be careful, though. Many experienced network administrators have walked confidently into test centers only to walk sheepishly out after failing an MCSE exam. As they discovered, there's the Microsoft of the real world and the Microsoft of the MCSE exams. It's our goal with these Exam Notes books to show you where the two converge and where they diverge. After you've finished reading through this book, you should have a clear idea of how your understanding of the technologies involved matches up with the expectations of the MCSE test makers in Redmond.

Or perhaps you're relatively new to the world of Microsoft networking, drawn to it by the promise of challenging work and higher salaries. You've just waded through an 800-page MCSE study guide, or taken a class at a local training center. Lots of information to keep track of, isn't it? Well, by organizing the Exam Notes books according to the Microsoft exam objectives, and by breaking up the information into concise manageable pieces, we've created what we think is the handiest exam review guide available. Throw it in your briefcase and carry it to work with you. As you read through the book, you'll be able to identify quickly those areas you know best and those that require more in-depth review.

NOTE The goal of the Exam Notes series is to help MCSE candidates familiarize themselves with the subjects on which they can expect to be tested in the MCSE exams. For complete, in-depth coverage of the technologies and topics involved, we recommend the MCSE Study Guide series from Sybex.

How Is This Book Organized?

As mentioned previously, this book is organized according to the official exam objectives list prepared by Microsoft for the *Implementing and Supporting Microsoft Windows NT Workstation 4.0* exam. The chapters coincide with the broad objectives groupings, such as Planning, Installation and Configuration, Monitoring and Optimization, and Troubleshooting. These groupings are also reflected in the organization of the MCSE exams themselves.

Within each chapter, the individual exam objectives are addressed in turn. And in turn, the objectives sections are further divided according to the type of information presented.

Critical Information

This section presents the greatest level of detail about information that is relevant to the objective. This is the place to start if you're unfamiliar with or uncertain about the technical issues related to the objective.

Necessary Procedures

Here you'll find instructions for procedures that require a lab computer to be completed. From installing operating systems to modifying configuration defaults, the information in these sections addresses the hands-on requirements for the MCSE exams.

Exam Essentials

In this section, we've put together a concise list of the most crucial topics of subject areas that you'll need to comprehend fully prior to taking the MCSE exam. This section can help you identify those topics that might require more study on your part.

Key Terms and Concepts

Here we've compiled a mini-glossary of the most important terms and concepts related to the specific objective. You'll understand what all those technical words mean within the context of the related subject matter.

Sample Questions

For each objective, we've included a selection of questions similar to those you'll encounter on the actual MCSE exam. Answers and explanations are provided so you can gain some insight into the test-taking process.

NOTE For a more comprehensive collection of exam review questions, check out the MCSE Test Success series, also published by Sybex.

How Do You Become an MCSE?

Attaining Microsoft Certified Systems Engineer (MCSE) status is a challenge. The exams cover a wide range of topics and require dedicated study and expertise. This is, however, why the MCSE certificate is so valuable. If achieving the MCSE were too easy, the market would be quickly flooded by MCSEs and the certification would become meaningless. Microsoft, keenly aware of this fact, has taken steps to ensure that the certification means its holder is truly knowledgeable and skilled.

To become an MCSE, you must pass four core requirements and two electives.

Client Requirement

70-073: Implementing and Supporting Windows NT Workstation 4.0 or

70-064: Implementing and Supporting Microsoft Windows 95

Networking Requirement

70-058: Networking Essentials

Windows NT Server 4.0 Requirement

70-067: Implementing and Supporting Windows NT Server 4.0

Windows NT Server 4.0 in the Enterprise Requirement

70-068: Implementing and Supporting Windows NT Server 4.0 in the Enterprise

Electives

Some of the more popular electives include:

70-059: Internetworking Microsoft TCP/IP on Microsoft Windows NT 4.0

70-087: Implementing and Supporting Microsoft Internet Information Server 4.0

70-081: Implementing and Supporting Microsoft Exchange Server 5.5

70-026: System Administration for Microsoft SQL Server 6.5

70-027: Implementing a Database Design on Microsoft SQL Server 6.5

70-088: Implementing and Supporting Microsoft Proxy Server 2.0

70-079: Implementing and Supporting Microsoft Internet Explorer 4.0 by Using the Internet Explorer Administration Kit

---

TIP   This book is a part of a series of MCSE Exam Notes books, published by Network Press (SYBEX), that covers four core requirements and your choice of several electives—the entire MCSE track!

Where Do You Take the Exams?

You may take the exams at any one of more than 800 Sylvan Prometric Authorized Testing Centers around the world. For the location of a testing center near you, call (800) 755-EXAM (755-3926). Outside the United States and Canada, contact your local Sylvan Prometric Registration Center. You can also register for an exam with Sylvan Prometric via the Internet. The Sylvan site can be reached through the Microsoft Training and Certification site or at http://www.slspro.com/msreg/microsoft.asp.

To register for a Microsoft Certified Professional exam:

1. Determine the number of the exam you want to take.

2. Register with Sylvan Prometric. At this point, you will be asked for advance payment for the exam. At this writing, the exams are $100 each. Exams must be taken within one year of payment. You can schedule exams up to six weeks in advance or as late as one working day prior to the date of the exam. You can cancel or reschedule your exam if you contact Sylvan Prometric at least two working days prior to the exam. Same-day registration is available in some locations, although this is subject to space availability. Where same-day registration is available, you must register a minimum of two hours before test time.

3. After you receive a registration and payment confirmation letter from Sylvan Prometric, call a nearby Sylvan Prometric Testing Center to schedule your exam.

When you schedule the exam, you'll be provided with instructions regarding appointment and cancellation procedures, ID requirements, and information about the testing center location.

NOTE Beginning in June 1998, MCPS and MCSE candidates in the U.S. and Canada will be able to sign up to take the exams from Virtual University Enterprises (VUE) as well as Sylvan Prometric. To enroll at a VUE testing center, call toll-free in North America: (888) 837-8616, or visit www.vue.com/student-services.

What the NT Workstation 4.0 Exam Measures

The people who write the exams for Microsoft want to make sure that you are a very well-rounded network administrator. The MCSE designation is kind of a Liberal Arts degree in Networking; that is, you need to know something about multiple topics.

That philosophy shows in the NT Workstation 4.0 exam and in the way the questions are worded. As you study, try to think like an exam writer. What would you write questions about?

- Is there some special terminology that Microsoft uses?

- Are there tips presented on things like troubleshooting?

- Is there a specific way of doing something, stressed over and over?

- Is there something about the subject that is very specific, like minimum requirements or command line switches?

The NT Workstation 4.0 exam measures how well you understand the underlying concept related to NT Workstation, as well as how well you know the procedures involved. Also, you should know the reasoning behind procedures. If you know the subject matter and can understand and support the product, you should do great on the exam.

How Microsoft Develops the Exam Questions

Microsoft's exam development process consists of eight mandatory phases. The process takes an average of seven months and contains more than 150 specific steps. The phases of Microsoft Certified Professional exam development are listed here.

Phase 1: Job Analysis

Phase 1 is an analysis of all the tasks that make up the specific job function based on tasks performed by people who are currently performing that job function. This phase also identifies the knowledge, skills, and abilities that relate specifically to the certification for that performance area.

Phase 2: Objective Domain Definition

The results of the job analysis provide the framework used to develop exam objectives. The development of objectives involves translating the job function tasks into a comprehensive set of more specific and measurable knowledge, skills, and abilities. The resulting list of objectives, or the objective domain, is the basis for the development of both the certification exams and the training materials.

NOTE The outline of all Exam Note books is based upon the official exam objectives lists published by Microsoft. Objectives are subject to change without notification. We advise that you check the Microsoft Training & Certification Web site (www.microsoft.com\train_cert\) for the most current objectives list.

Phase 3: Blueprint Survey

The final objective domain is transformed into a blueprint survey in which contributors—technology professionals who are performing the applicable job function—are asked to rate each objective. Based on the contributors' input, the objectives are prioritized and weighted. The actual exam items are written according to the prioritized objectives. The blueprint survey phase helps determine which objectives to measure, as well as the appropriate number and types of items to include on the exam.

Phase 4: Item Development

A pool of items is developed to measure the blueprinted objective domain. The number and types of items to be written are based on the results of the blueprint survey. During this phase, items are reviewed and revised to ensure that they are:

- Technically accurate

- Clear, unambiguous, and plausible

- Not biased toward any population, subgroup, or culture

- Not misleading or tricky

- Testing at the correct level of Bloom's Taxonomy

- Testing for useful knowledge, not obscure or trivial facts

Items that meet these criteria are included in the initial item pool.

Phase 5: Alpha Review and Item Revision

During this phase, a panel of technical and job function experts reviews each item for technical accuracy, then answers each item, reaching consensus on all technical issues. Once the items have been verified as technically accurate, they are edited to ensure that they are expressed in the clearest language possible.

Phase 6: Beta Exam

The reviewed and edited items are collected into a beta exam pool. During the beta exam, each participant has the opportunity to respond to all the items in this beta exam pool. Based on the responses of all beta participants, Microsoft performs a statistical analysis to verify the validity of the exam items and to determine which items will be used in the certification exam. Once the analysis has been completed, the items are distributed into multiple parallel forms, or versions, of the final certification exam.

Phase 7: Item Selection and Cut-Score Setting

The results of the beta exam are analyzed to determine which items should be included in the certification exam based on many factors, including item difficulty and relevance. Generally, the desired items are answered correctly by 25 to 90 percent of the beta exam candidates. This helps ensure that the exam consists of a variety of difficulty levels, from somewhat easy to extremely difficult.

Also during this phase, a panel of job function experts determines the cut score (minimum passing score) for the exam. The cut score differs from exam to exam because it is based on an item-by-item determination of the percentage of candidates who would be expected to answer the item correctly. The experts determine the cut score in a group session to increase the reliability.

Phase 8: Live Exam

Once all the other phases are complete, the exam is ready. Microsoft Certified Professional exams are administered by Sylvan Prometric.

Tips for Taking Your NT Workstation Exam

Here are some general tips for taking your exam successfully:

- Arrive early at the exam center so you can relax and review your study materials, particularly tables and lists of exam-related information.

- Read the questions carefully. Don't be tempted to jump to an early conclusion. Make sure you know *exactly* what the question is asking.

- Don't leave any unanswered questions. They count against you.

- When answering multiple-choice questions you're not sure about, use a process of elimination to get rid of the obviously incorrect questions first. This will improve your odds if you need to make an educated guess.

- Because the hard questions will eat up the most time, save them for last. You can move forward and backward through the exam.

- This test has many exhibits (pictures). It can be difficult, if not impossible, to view both the questions and the exhibit simulation on the 14- and 15-inch screens usually found at the testing centers. Call around to each center and see if they have 17-inch monitors available. If they don't, perhaps you can arrange to bring in your own. Failing this, some have found it useful to quickly draw the diagram on the scratch paper provided by the testing center and use the monitor to view just the question.

- Many participants run out of time before they are able to complete the test. If you are unsure of the answer to a question, you may want to choose one of the answers, mark the question, and go on— an unanswered question does not help you. Once your time is up, you cannot go on to another question. However, you can remain on the question you are on indefinitely when the time runs out. Therefore, when you are almost out of time, go to a question you feel you can figure out—given enough time—and work until you feel you have got it (or the night security guard boots you out!).

- You are allowed to use the Windows calculator during your test. However, it may be better to memorize a table of the subnet addresses and to write it down on the scratch paper supplied by the testing center before you start the test.

Once you have completed an exam, you will be given immediate, online notification of your pass or fail status. You will also receive a printed Examination Score Report indicating your pass or fail status and your exam results by section. (The test administrator will give you the printed score report.) Test scores are automatically forwarded to Microsoft within five working days after you take the test. You do not need to send your score to Microsoft. If you pass the exam, you will receive confirmation from Microsoft, typically within two to four weeks.

Contact Information

To find out more about Microsoft Education and Certification materials and programs, to register with Sylvan Prometric, or to get other useful information, check the following resources. Outside the United States or Canada, contact your local Microsoft office or Sylvan Prometric testing center.

Microsoft Certified Professional Program—(800) 636-7544
Call the MCPP number for information about the Microsoft Certified Professional program and exams, and to order the latest Microsoft Roadmap to Education and Certification.

Sylvan Prometric testing centers—(800) 755-EXAM
Contact Sylvan to register to take a Microsoft Certified Professional exam at any of more than 800 Sylvan Prometric testing centers around the world.

Microsoft Certification Development Team—Web: *http://www.microsoft.com/Train_Cert/mcp/examinfo/certsd.htm*
Contact the Microsoft Certification Development Team through their Web site to volunteer for participation in one or more exam development phases or to report a problem with an exam. Address written

correspondence to: Certification Development Team; Microsoft Education and Certification; One Microsoft Way; Redmond, WA 98052.

Microsoft TechNet Technical Information Network—(800) 344-2121
This an excellent resource for support professionals and system administrators. Outside the United States and Canada, call your local Microsoft subsidiary for information.

How to Contact the Authors

Gary Govanus can be reached at ggovanus@psconsulting.com.

Bob King can be reached at bking@royal-tech.com.

How to Contact the Publisher

Sybex welcomes reader feedback on all of their titles. Visit the Sybex Web site at www.sybex.com for book updates and additional certification information. You'll also find online forms where you can submit your own comments or suggestions regarding this or any other Sybex book.

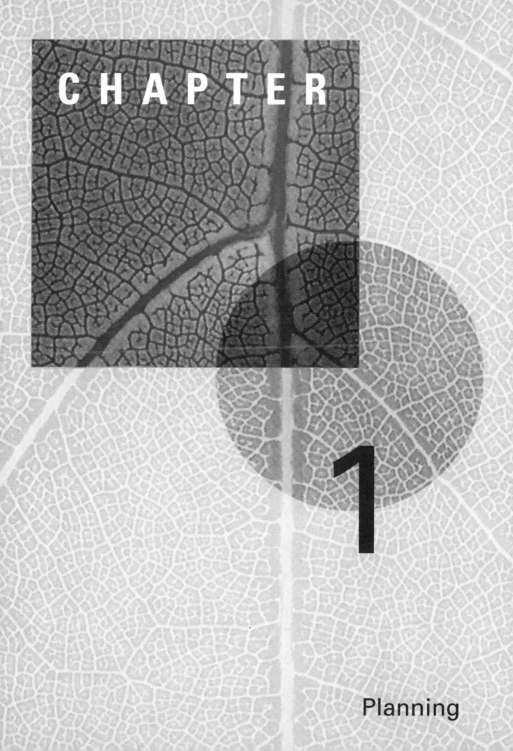

CHAPTER

1

Planning

Microsoft Exam Objectives Covered in This Chapter:

▶ **Create unattended installation files.** *(pages 3 – 16)*

▶ **Plan strategies for sharing and securing resources.** *(pages 16 – 22)*

▶ **Choose the appropriate file system to use in a given situation. File systems and situations include:** *(pages 22 – 29)*
- NTFS
- FAT
- HPFS
- Security
- Dual-boot systems

S omeone once said that proper planning prevents poor performance. Now, let's face it, planning is not usually one of the strengths of most front-line computer people, who are more of the "There's a problem, let's fix it" kind of people. Sometimes this quick-fix attitude can be a detriment: Rolling out a major NT Workstation installation would definitely be one of those times where planning is of paramount importance.

Implementing a new desktop operating system is not an easy process. It has major implications, even if you are discussing changing the operating system of just your desktop computer, not to mention an entire organization. Sometimes, the reasons for the change are irrefutable, and once the final decision has been made, it is up to you to implement the decision. Mastering the objectives covered in this chapter will make the projected rollout run smoother with much less work.

If you are faced with the task of rolling a new desktop out to 10, 25, 250, or 2,500 users, the task can be a bit overwhelming. The objectives covered in this chapter break down how to do the job, and give you some tips and hints to make your life easier. The first BIG hint will come as part of the discussion on creating unattended installation files. If you have a "corporate standard" computer that is configured the same way for everyone, why should you have to sit there and provide the same answers to the same questions time after time? There are several ways around the tedium.

Once you have NT deployed to the desktop, you need to understand the whole reason behind networks: the sharing of resources and information. If a user is sharing the information on their computer with others, they are going to want some reassurance that the data will be safe from unauthorized access. The same is true with the hardware resources on your network. The chances that the Human Resources department will want every Tom, Dick, and Harriet printing to the printer that is loaded with payroll checks is slim to none.

If you decide that security is an issue, implementing it is part of a multi-tiered process. An important factor in that process is the way your disk drives access information, that is, the basic file system the computer will use. NT is capable of using the New Technology File System (NTFS), the File Allocations Tables (FAT), and the CD File System (CDFS). Each of these file systems has advantages and disadvantages.

The NT Workstation test places a strong emphasis on knowing when to use NT and when to stick with Windows 95. There will also be some questions (though usually not very direct) on the types of file systems used and when to use each. There are even some questions on how to do an automated configuration. You have a lot to learn for the very first objective. Good luck!

Create unattended installation files.

An unattended installation means that you can install NT Workstation to a desktop without having to be there and enter information every step of the way. By utilizing two or three tools, you can set up a system to roll out a large number of desktop units with little or no user input during the installation process.

Now this is a double-edged sword. While it sounds like a good deal for someone who is about to roll out several hundred new desktops, there are some *gotcha*'s. First of all, the systems must all be configured in the same way. As you will see, one slightly different setting can throw a monkey wrench into the works. Also, there is some serious setup to get to the point that you can run an unattended installation on multiple machines.

An unattended installation can be the next best thing to sliced bread for an administrator who is rolling out a large number of desktops. For the administrator who has to do five or ten workstations, the work involved in setting up and configuring an unattended install may not be worth it. Besides, there are more and more third-party utilities that make this a really easy process without all the grunt work. While this may or may not be something you will use, it will be something you will be tested on, so read on, my friend.

Critical Information

Before you have visions of walking into your boss's office one afternoon to say that in the last four hours you configured 2,000 workstations, remember that there is some groundwork that needs to be laid. Actually, there are several steps to take. You can use an *unattended answer file* to handle the routine questions that NT asks, plus you can use a *uniqueness database file* (UDF) to handle the not-so-routine questions. Finally, after NT has been configured as the operating system of choice, you can complete the installation by using the *SYSDIFF utility* to download a complete application suite to the desktop.

Here is how it works. You should start by looking at the computers you are going to configure and making some notes about how you are going to configure them. You may want to look at the NT Workstation installation CD and find the file named UNATTEND.TXT, located in the \i386 folder. This is a sample of the file you will be customizing to provide you with the starting point of your "simple" install.

TIP   At first glance, preparing an unattended installation may not look all that easy, but if you are configuring lots of workstations, the time invested is well worth it.

Looking at the UNATTEND.TXT file, you will see some generic questions. For instance, in the first section, you will be asked if this is an OEM (Original Equipment Manufacturer) installation, if you want to confirm hardware, if it is an NT upgrade, whether you are upgrading from Windows 3.1, and where to put the root folder. The next section provides some unique information on the user: the user name, the organization name, and a computer name. You get the idea—all the generic information that you would be entering time after time after time if you did this without the unattended files. You will also be prompted for information on the Display setting, time zones, network installation, protocols, and DHCP.

Since this is such routine information, there must be some way to automate the creation of the UNATTEND.TXT file. Actually, there is, but it is going to cost you some bucks. The Setup Manager is a graphical utility that comes on the Windows NT Resource Kit CD, which is pricey.

NOTE   The UNATTEND.TXT file on the NT Workstation installation CD shows a small number of the options you can configure. For more information, refer to the Microsoft TechNet CD.

But, you ask, keen of eye and all-knowing in the ways of installations, that is all fine and good for some of the information, but what about all that stuff that is unique to the computer? For that, you can create a uniqueness database file, or UDF.

The UDF contains information that is unique to each system. You can create the UDF with any text editor, and it will contain information that must be unique per computer: things like the user's full name, the organization name, and the computer name. These instructions are contained in sections defined as UniqueIDs. Once the UDF file is completed, you can use these two pieces—the UNATTEND.TXT file and the UDF file—to do an unattended install.

NOTE Samples of the UNATTEND.TXT file and the UDF will be handled as part of the Necessary Procedures section of this objective.

Here's a scenario to illustrate the point. You have to install 10 machines that contain exactly the same hardware. You have invested in the resource kit, so you fire up Setup Manager and create a generic unattended installation file called UNATTEND.TXT. In addition, you have brushed off your typing skills and created a uniqueness database file that contains information on all 10 new owners of these machines. This work of art is named UDF10.TXT. Each user has its own UniqueID, numbered 1 to 10. The unattended answer file and the uniqueness database file have been installed out to a network share that is assigned a drive letter of J:. In addition to the two text files, you have also copied the \i386 folder from the Windows NT Workstation installation CD. When you are ready to install your first workstation, you boot the workstation, configure the share to point to J:, and then from a command prompt, type in the following syntax:

```
winnt /s:f:\ /u:UNATTEND.TXT /UDF:id1,udf10.txt
```

As NT begins to install, all information will be taken from the source subdirectory (`/s:f:\`). Information will be filtered in from the UNATTEND.TXT file (`/u:UNATTEND.TXT`) and unique information will come for user 1 from the UDF10.TXT file (`/UDF:id1,udf10.txt`).

The NT operating system will now be installed using all the parameters you passed to it from the two files. The workstation configuration is far from completed, however. After all, you have to configure it to run Microsoft Office, along with several proprietary applications that may take you an additional four or five hours to install on each machine. SYSDIFF to the rescue!

The SYSDIFF Utility

SYSDIFF is a utility that is used to take a snapshot of the machine after the installation of the operating system, but before the installation of any applications. Once the snapshot has been taken, all the applications are installed and configured on the model machine. After that configuration is completed, then SYSDIFF is run again, this time in *difference mode*. SYSDIFF looks at the machine and finds and records the differences between the state of preliminary NT installation and the current state of the computer. This information is then saved to a *differences file*. When SYSDIFF is run on the next machine, it will apply the data from the difference file to another Windows NT installation, completing the automated installation of the workstation.

WARNING   SYSDIFF will only work on computers of the same hardware configuration.

SYSDIFF can also be used to create an INF file and installation data from the difference file. This information can be saved to the server-based installation share, and these changes can be applied to any installations done from this share.

Necessary Procedures

Three components are necessary to the unattended process:

- The UNATTEND.TXT file
- The UDF file
- The SYSDIFF utility

The UNATTEND.TXT File

This sample file is taken directly from the Windows NT 4.0 Workstation CD. It is in the \i386 folder.

NOTE The UNATTEND.TXT file can be edited using any text editor
to provide for generic input specific to your site.

Let's see how you may need to configure this file. You are going to be
installing Windows NT on a workstation, but you do not want to
hang around while the files are being copied. You know it will be a
clean installation with no upgrades, but you will be changing the
default location of the root directory to \WIN instead of \WINNT;
after all, old habits die hard. In addition, the workstation has a VGA
card in it, and the display will be 800×600 instead of the default
640×480. You want the system to detect the network cards and
install the TCP/IP protocol. Finally, you want the computer to join the
PSMain domain to accept DHCP.

What needs to be changed from the boilerplate file? Let's take a quick
look at it section by section.

[Unattended]

```
OemPreinstall = no
ConfirmHardware = no
NtUpgrade = no
Win31Upgrade = no
TargetPath = WINNT
OverwriteOemFilesOnUpgrade = no
```

From this section, in looking at the instructions, the only section that
will have to be edited is the TargetPath:. WINNT should be changed
to WIN.

[UserData]

```
FullName = "Your User Name"
OrgName = "Your Organization Name"
ComputerName = COMPUTER_NAME
```

Here a number of changes need to be made. In this case, the installing
user and organization name will have to be replaced with the corporate standards. In place of "Your User Name", enter something

descriptive like Dilbert. For the OrgName line, put in the name of your organization—let's say it's ACME Blasting Co. The ComputerName needs to be a unique entry in the Domain. Let's say Wally.

NOTE   Since you weren't told to change the time zone the [GUIUnattended] section will stay the same.

[Display]

```
ConfigureAtLogon = 0
BitsPerPel = 16
XResolution = 640
YResolution = 480
VRefresh = 70
AutoConfirm = 1
```

Get out the user manual for the display and see if you have to change bits per pixel or VRefresh. Otherwise, just change the XResolution to 800 and the YResolution to 600, and the [Display] section is finished.

[Network]

```
Attend = yes
DetectAdapters = ""
InstallProtocols = ProtocolsSection
JoinDomain = Domain_To_Join
```

This section is not very self-explanatory. The first choice—Attend = yes—means that the system will slip back into interactive mode (you get to push buttons) when it hits the section on installing the Network adapter card. If you change this to no you will have to add sections to the file that will allow the installation to configure the installed network adapter card.

DetectAdapters and InstallProtocols can be changed to point to a user-defined section name. If you are installing multiple 3Com 575 cards in each machine, you may create a section called [3C575]. If DetectAdapters is left at " ", the system will attempt to detect and install the first network adapter card it finds. If you are installing multiple protocols, you would configure a section for the protocols.

WARNING Make sure that there is no space between the two quotation marks ("") in the **DetectAdapters** section. Also, if the **InstallProtocols** and the **DetectAdapter** keys are not present, the system will default to interactive mode.

Here is an example of the section after you have customized it.

```
[Network]
Attend = no
DetectAdapters = 3c575
InstallProtocols = TCPIPSection
JoinDomain = PSMAIN
CreateComputerAccount=BrandiceC, DeniseB

[3C575]
DetectCount=1
IRQ=3
IOBaseAddress=0x300
IOChannel=auto
Transceiver=auto

[TCPIPSection]
TC=TCPIPParams

[TCPIPParams]
DHCP=Yes
DNSServer=192.1.1.2, 192.1.1.3, 192.1.1.4
WINSPrimary=111.2.2.2
DNSName=PSCONSULTING.COM
```

When the unattended installation is completed using the UNATTEND .TXT file, the system files will be installed in the WIN folder instead of the WINNT folder. The user who installed the system is named Dilbert, and he works for the ACME Blasting Co. The computer is named Wally. Since you did not mess with the default time zone, it is set for the Pacific time zone. The display will be an 800×600 VGA display. There will be a 3Com 575 Ethernet adapter installed with an IRQ of 3 and a base I/O address of 300. The IO Channel and the transceiver will be automatically selected. The system will have TCP/IP configured to use Dynamic Host Control Protocol. It will receive the Domain Name Service from the host at address 192.1.1.2, 192.1.1.3, or 192.1.1.4. The Windows Internet Name Service or WINS will be handled by the host at 111.2.2.2. The computer will be added to the Domain Name Service of PSCONSULTING.COM.

SEE ALSO For more complete coverage of all the sections available in the unattended answer file, refer to the *MCSE: NT Workstation 4 Study Guide* by Charles Perkins, Matthew Strebe, and James Chellis (Sybex, 1998), or Microsoft's *NT Workstation Resource Kit.*

The Uniqueness Database File (UDF)

The following is a sample to create five different computers. This file is created using a text editor and saved in plain text format. In the case above, there was still some information on user data that needed to be added to the UNATTEND.TXT file. You can configure the UDF file to provide that information, as shown below.

In the section above, the example showed you entering information into the [UserData] section. You could choose to use a UDF file that lays out the information for multiple users, and this information would be used in order during the installations. For example, the first installation would use the information from the UNATTEND.TXT file until it came to the [UserData] section. At that point it would jump to the UDF file and grab the information about the first user. When it had input Gary Govanus at Paradigm Shift using a computer

name of PS1, it would go back and get more information from the
UNATTEND.TXT file. Here is the layout of a customized UDF file.

```
;UDF file to complete installation of 5 new computers
;
;
[UniqueIds]
u1 = UserData
u2 = UserData
u3 = UserData
u4 = UserData
u5 = UserData
[u1:UserData]
FullName = "Gary Govanus"
OrgName = "Paradigm Shift"
ComputerName = PS1
[u2:UserData]
FullName = "Bob King"
OrgName = "Royal Technologies"
ComputerName = RT1
[u3:UserData]
FullName = "Bobbi Govanus"
OrgName = "For Your Instructors"
ComputerName = FYI1
[u4:UserData]
FullName = "Susan King"
OrgName = "Nursing Specialities"
ComputerName = NS1
[u5:UserData]
FullName = "Brandice Carpenter"
OrgName = "Paradigm Shift"
ComputerName = PS2
```

The SYSDIFF Utility

The System Difference, or SYSDIFF, utility is found on the Windows NT
Workstation 4.0 CD. To install the tool, simply copy *<driveletter>*:\
support\deptools\i386\SYSDIFF.EXE and SYSDIFF.INF to a directory on your hard drive.

The syntax of a SYSDIFF command line is as follows:

```
SYSDIFF.EXE [/snap | /diff | /apply | /dump | /inf] [/
log:log_file]
```

The individual components of this line are explained below:

/snap   When you run SYSDIFF the first time, it takes a snapshot of the Windows Registry, the file systems, and the directories. The information is stored in a snapshot file.

/diff   Once the model machine has been completely configured, SYSDIFF is run again. This time the utility records any changes made to the file system, the directories and the registry. This information is stored in a difference file.

/apply   On the next computer that is installed, SYSDIFF applies the differences, simplifying the application installation process.

/dump   Generates a file that allows you to look at the details of the difference file.

/inf   SYSDIFF can automatically create an INF file and installation data based on the differences file. This can be applied to a server-based share and the differences will be applied to any further Windows NT installations made from that share.

/log   Location of the log file.

Exam Essentials

When studying for the exam, you should concentrate on what each of the files and utilities do. Don't memorize all the settings for the files. Even the Microsoft exam writers didn't get into that much detail!

Know what an unattended answer file is used for during automated installations.   The unattended answer file (UNATTEND .TXT) provides answers to some or all of the user prompts during setup. The answer file can be used for hardware settings or system settings.

Know the function of a uniqueness database file (UDF) during an automated installation. The UDF provides information about individual users or computers.

Know the function of SYSDIFF. SYSDIFF can be used to take before and after snapshots of a workstation that is going through an installation. SYSDIFF can then be used to apply those same changes to another workstation. SYSDIFF can also be used to create an INF file to further automate the installation process.

Know what files or utilities are needed to take a workstation completely through the automated installation process, including the installation of applications. You would need to customize an unattended answer file (UNATTEND.TXT) and a uniqueness database file (UDF), and to run SYSDIFF.EXE.

Know the minimum number of unattended answer files and UDF files required to complete the automated installation of different types of hardware configurations. You would need one UNATTEND.TXT per type of hardware configuration. You could use the same UDF file for all the configurations.

Key Terms and Concepts

DHCP (Dynamic Host Control Protocol): A protocol used for the dynamic assignment of TCP/IP addresses.

DNS (Domain Name Service): A service that resolves Internet names to TCP/IP addresses.

SYSDIFF: A utility found on the Installation CD in the \support\deptools\i386 directory. This utility can be used to aid in the installation of suites of applications on a workstation.

TCP/IP (Transmission Control Protocol/Internet Protocol): A suite of communication protocols used to enhance communications between computers.

UNATTEND.TXT (Unattended answer file): A sample of this plain-text file is found on the Installation CD in the `<driveletter>`:\i386 directory.

Uniqueness Database File (UDF): File created with a text editor to provide unique entries for a large number of different installations.

WINS (Windows Internet Name Service): A service that resolves computer names to TCP/IP addresses.

Sample Questions

1. What is an unattended answer file used for during automated installations?

   A. It provides specific information about that particular computer, including things like the system serial number.

   B. It answers some or all user-supplied information during an NT Workstation setup.

   C. It installs and configures software application suites.

   D. It provides a way to automate hardware installation.

   Answer: B. The unattended answer file provides some or all of the user-supplied information during a Windows NT Workstation setup.

2. What is the function of a uniqueness database file (UDF) during an automated installation?

   A. It provides specific information about that particular computer, including the user name.

   B. It answers some or all user-supplied information during NT Workstation setup.

   C. It installs and configures software application suites.

   D. It provides a way to automate hardware installation.

   Answer: A. It supplies information about that specific computer, including things like the user name.

3. What is the function of the SYSDIFF utility during an automated installation?

A. It provides specific information about that particular computer, including things like the system serial number.

B. It answers some or all user-supplied information during NT Workstation setup.

C. It installs and configures software application suites.

D. It provides a way to automate hardware installation.

Answer: C. It helps to install and configure software application suites by taking a snapshot of the system before and after installation. It then creates a difference file to use for the next workstation installation.

4. Which files or utilities are needed to take a workstation completely through the automated installation process?

A. UNATTEND.TXT

B. SYSDIFF.EXE

C. Uniqueness database file

D. Regedit

Answer: A, B, and C. To complete the unattended installation, you can use the UNATTEND.TXT file, the SYSDIFF.EXE utility and the uniqueness database file.

Plan strategies for sharing and securing resources.

Microsoft Windows NT has numerous tools to share and protect data on your network. We'll take a close look at those procedures in Chapter 3, *Managing Resources*. For now, we'll limit our discussion to the pre-installation planning that must go into any NT installation.

Critical Information

Before planning your data structure, you will need to gather two critical lists. The first should be a list of system users, and the second should be a list of the data and applications that will be stored on your network. The process of gathering this information can be difficult—you will have to talk to representatives of each department, and possibly even do a series of interviews with key employees. Some of the questions you should ask are:

- What information is critical to your function?

- Who should have access to this data?

- What applications do you use?

- Are there any special hardware or licensing issues with that software?

Based upon the answers to these questions, you can begin to build a list of resources that will be shared across the network, and who will need access to those resources. After gathering this data, build a table that lists the data and applications across the top and the users down the side. You can then document what resources each user will need. Figure 1.1 shows a spreadsheet from a recent installation.

FIGURE 1.1: Planning resources

Users	**Applications**						**Data**		
	Win3.1	Win95	WinNT	Word	Excl	Access	Accounting	Research	Sales
Bking			x	x	x	x		x	
Sking		x		x	x		x		
Kking	x			x	x				x
Ggovanus			x	x	x	x		x	
Bmalone			x		x	x		x	
Jgibson			x	x	x	x		x	
Dkarpinski		x		x	x				x
Ekarpinski		x		x	x			x	
Danderson	x			x	x	x	x		

Once your data is gathered and you've organized it, the next step is to look for logical groupings of users. Be aware that it is usually easier to manage a system where most permissions are managed through groups rather than through individual assignments.

TIP Managing groups of users is much easier than working with each individual. Think about taking your local third grade class to the zoo. There would be two approaches you could take. One way would be to tell each child which exhibits he or she could visit, another way would be to take the entire class as a group through the park. It's hard to imagine who would choose the former method: Without even discussing the dangers involved, just keeping track of where each child could go and when they could go there would drive you crazy! This is not to suggest that administrating a network is similar to dealing with third-graders... although every company is different!

Once you've decided how to group your users, you can add these groups to your overview, as shown in Figure 1.2.

F I G U R E 1.2: Planning resources using logical groupings

Users	Win3.1	Win95	WinNT	Word	Excl	Access	Accounting	Research	Sales
Word users				X					
Excel users					X				
Access users						X			
Accounting							X		
Research								X	
Sales									X
Bking			X	X	X	X		X	
Sking		X		X	X		X		
Kking	X			X	X				X
Ggovanus			X	X	X	X		X	
Bmalone			X		X	X		X	
Jgibson			X	X	X	X		X	
Dkarpinski		X		X	X				X
Ekarpinski		X		X	X			X	
Danderson	X			X	X	X	X		

Now you are ready to start planning rules for resource access. While each environment will be different, there are a few general guidelines that you should consider. In general, there are two types of files that users will need to access—application and data. Each type has its own set of guidelines.

Network Applications

Microsoft suggests that applications not be stored on the same volume as your operating system and boot files. If you keep them separate, in the event that you have to reinstall NT, there is a good chance that the application volume will not have to be restored. Some other guidelines include:

- Make any permission assignments *before* you share the resource. This prevents unauthorized access during the period between sharing and securing.

- Make executable files read-only for all users.

- Create and share a common applications folder. Within that folder, create a folder for each application. This allows you to set permissions on the upper folder that can be applied to each of the lower folders automatically.

- If licensing issues require it, you can then remove permissions from selected lower-level application folders on a case-by-case basis— allowing only the appropriate users access to the applications.

- If your software is licensed on a simultaneous users basis, meaning that access is limited to a certain number of users at one time, share the appropriate folder and limit the number of users who can connect to it.

- Remember to assign the Administrators group full control to the application directory, and remove the Full Control permission from the Everyone group.

- Remember to assign the Change permission to whomever will be responsible for maintaining each application.

Network Data Folders

Microsoft suggests that data folders also be kept on a separate volume from your operating system and boot files. This allows you to easily configure your backup software to back up only data, since the operating system and applications rarely change. Some other guidelines include:

- Make any permission assignments *before* you share the resource. This prevents unauthorized access during the time between sharing and securing.

- Analyze the type of access the users will need. If users need to edit the data, make sure they have the appropriate permissions.

- Organize your data for ease of access and management. Create a main folder to store all shared data folders.

- Assign permissions to each subfolder as appropriate.

WARNING   Remember human nature—it is much easier to give higher permissions later than it is to take away rights that someone has grown used to!

Exam Essentials

Networks would not be used in today's businesses if the information they stored could not be made secure. This objective is concerned with the planning necessary to ensure that data is accessible, but only to those who are supposed to have access.

Understand the reasoning behind not placing shared resources on the system/boot volume.   If the operating system needs to be reinstalled due a problem with the system volume, you might lose all data on that volume. By placing your shared resources on another volume, you might avoid having to restore it during the reinstallation process.

Understand the issues involved in sharing data on the network.
Place data on a separate volume, assign permissions before sharing
the folder, and organize the data for ease of access and management.

**Understand the issues involved in sharing applications on the
network.** Place data on a separate volume, assign permissions
before sharing the folder, use the read-only attribute where appropriate, remember licensing issues, and analyze permissions carefully.

Key Terms and Concepts

Licensing based upon simultaneous usage: A software package
sold under the pretext that only a certain number of users will use
the product concurrently.

Permissions: A set of rights granted to users and groups that controls the actions they can take on a file or within a directory. For
a more detailed discussion, see Chapter 3.

Share Point: A directory that has been made accessible to users
over the network.

Sample Questions

1. You are creating a shared resource strategy for your company.
   Which of the following suggestions would you include?

   A. Place all data and system files on one volume for easy backup.

   B. Place your system/boot files on a separate volume from your
   data for easy backup.

   C. Create all shares, copy in any data, and then assign
   permissions.

   D. Create each share, assign permissions, and then copy in any
   available data.

   Answer: B, D. Separating your data from the system files makes
   backup easier to configure and can also help during a disaster

recovery. Assigning permissions before the data is placed in a share point ensures that there is no accidental access by users.

2. When planning your data structure, which of the following is true?

   A. Place everything on one partition to ease and speed access.

   B. Separate your data from the NT system files.

   C. Store all data on local workstations.

   D. The NT Data Placement Wizard will automatically build your structure for you.

   Answer: B. Keeping your data on a separate volume eases administration and protects your data in the event that you have to reinstall NT.

Choose the appropriate file system to use in a given situation. File systems and situations include:

- NTFS
- FAT
- HPFS
- Security
- Dual-Boot systems

The file system controls the mechanics of how a file is written to, or read from, the physical hard drive. Microsoft Windows NT supports multiple file systems—each of which has strengths and weaknesses. As an MCSE you will be required to choose the file systems that will be used on your NT computers based upon the needs of your business.

Critical Information

NT supports four different file systems:

- NTFS (New Technology File System)
- FAT (File Allocation Table)
- HPFS (High Performance File System)

NOTE Although you cannot create or manage an HPFS partition on NT 4, you can still mount it. This comes in handy during an upgrade.

- CDFS (CD-ROM file system)

NOTE Since CDFS is a specialized file system used for CD-ROMs, it will not be discussed here.

NTFS

NTFS is the file system specifically designed to be used on a Windows NT–based computer. It offers many advantages over the older FAT file system. NTFS offers the following:

- File and directory-level security
- Support of larger file and partition sizes. Theoretically, both the maximum file and partition size is 16 exabytes. Functionally, with today's hardware, the limit is 2 terabytes.
- Support for file compression
- A recoverable file system. It uses a transaction log for disk activity. The log file can be used to redo or undo operations that failed.
- Bad-cluster remapping. If a write error occurs, the file system will move the data to another sector of the disk.

- Support for Macintosh files. (You must install Services for Macintosh.)

- Support for POSIX.1-compliant software

- Reduced file fragmentation

There are only two small drawbacks to NTFS: Since it has a fairly high overhead (about 50MB), floppy disks cannot be formatted with NTFS; also, NTFS does not support removable media. When using removable media formatted with NTFS, you must restart the computer to change disks.

FAT

The FAT file system has been in use since the earliest days of DOS computers. FAT has minimal overhead (less than 1MB) and is the most efficient file system for partitions smaller than 400MB. Since it is the only file system that both DOS (or Windows 95) and Windows NT have in common, the system partition must be a FAT partition on dual-boot machines. RISC-based computers will only boot from a FAT partition, so all RISC systems must have a small FAT partition to hold boot files.

On the down side, performance decreases as the number of files in a partition increases due to the way files are tracked. Another drawback is that the FAT file system has no features to prevent file fragmentation, another problem that can affect performance. Lastly, as a security feature, Windows NT prevents a deleted file from being undeleted, but on a FAT partition (if the computer is booted to DOS) undelete tools might be able to recover deleted files. There is also no file or directory-level security available on a FAT partition. The only security would be that available through directory-level sharing. We'll discuss security issues in more detail later in this section.

The version of the FAT file system included with Windows NT has been enhanced to support long filenames. Filenames adhere to the following criteria:

- Names can be up to 255 characters (including the full path).

- Names must start with a letter or number and can include any characters except: "∧[];:=,^*?.

- Names can include multiple spaces.

- Names can include multiple periods.

- Names preserve case but are not case sensitive.

TIP   As an aid to troubleshooting, many administrators will create a FAT partition and place the NT boot files there. In the event of a problem they can then boot to DOS, and access the files on the partition— replacing corrupt files or using DOS based disk diagnostic tools.

HPFS

HPFS is the native file system used by OS/2. Earlier versions of Microsoft Windows NT allowed the management of HPFS partitions on an NT server. This capability was provided primarily to ease the migration from OS/2 to NT. NT version 4.0 no longer supports the ability to manage HPFS partitions.

TIP   HPFS was covered in the MSCE exams for earlier versions of NT, but is not being heavily covered in the NT 4.0 exams. This objective may actually be a holdover from earlier exams.

The key features of the HPFS environment follow:

- Long filenames are supported—up to 254 characters.

- Names preserve case but are not case sensitive.

- Any characters can be used except the following: ?"∧*|:.

- HPFS does not create a "short" or DOS-compatible filename for each file. This could impact accessibility from some applications.

- HPFS partitions cannot be protected by local file or directory-level security.

- Performance might suffer on drives larger than 400MB.

Security

Security will be discussed in detail in Chapter 3, but during the planning stage you should be aware of the differences between the various supported file systems. You might encounter a test question that concerns making choices based upon a set of business needs. The bottom line is that Microsoft seems to believe that NTFS is the choice for most installations. They might, however, slip in a question where the particular description leads to another file system.

First, let's define *local file and directory-level security*. On an NT system, this phrase can only be applied to an NTFS partition. It implies that security will be applied to file access of a user sitting at the computer upon which the files are stored. This differs from *share security*, which can be used on all file systems. Share security applies only to users who are accessing a directory over the network.

The following three items should give you enough detail to make an informed decision.

HPFS   Will never be the file system of choice unless you are in the process of upgrading an OS/2 computer to Windows NT. HPFS on NT provides no mechanism for local file or directory level security.

FAT   Does not provide local or file level security. Anyone who successfully logs in at a computer can access any file stored on a FAT partition. Share security still applies at the directory level. About the only benefit to FAT over NTFS is the fact that a FAT partition can be accessed by DOS. In the event of problems, you can boot to a DOS disk and access any data on the partition.

WARNING   Of course, this also means that anyone can do the same thing; in other words, a FAT partition is an open door for data thieves.

NTFS   Provides security at the local file and directory level. NTFS also has various tools that protect data from disaster—bad-cluster remapping and a log file to recover from interrupted transactions.

Dual-Boot Systems

Microsoft is very specific in recommending that you do not dual-boot your Windows NT computer with another operating system. Since this is not a supported configuration, you are pretty much on your own as far as troubleshooting any problems.

With that said, there will be times where you are forced to dual-boot between NT and either DOS or Windows 95. You might have a legacy software package that won't work with NT, or you might need to set up a machine in your testing lab to serve multiple functions. The setup process will be discussed in Chapter 2. For now you should know that there is only one file system that creates partitions that can be read by DOS, Windows 95, *and* Windows NT—the FAT file system. If you intend to dual-boot your computer you will have to boot to a FAT partition.

Exam Essentials

Know the file systems supported by Windows NT.   These are FAT, NTFS, HPFS, and CDFS.

Know the advantages of NTFS.   File and directory-level security, support of larger file and partition sizes, support for file compression, a recoverable file system, bad-cluster remapping, support for Macintosh files, support for POSIX.1-compliant software, reduced file fragmentation.

There are only two small drawbacks to NTFS: Since it has a fairly high overhead (about 50MB), floppy disks cannot be formatted with NTFS; also, NTFS does not support removable media. When using removable media formatted with NTFS, you must restart the computer to change disks.

Know the drawbacks of the FAT file system.   Names can be up to 255 characters (including the full path), they must start with a letter or number and can include any characters except: "∧[];:=,^*?, they can include multiple spaces, they can include multiple periods, and they preserve case but are not case sensitive.

Understand when the HPFS file system might be used.   HPFS might be used during the migration from OS/2 to NT.

Be able to compare the security issues of FAT and NTFS.   FAT does not provide local or file level security. Anyone who successfully logs in at a computer can access any file stored on a FAT partition. Share security still applies at the directory level. About the only benefit of FAT over NTFS is the fact that a FAT partition can be accessed by DOS. In the event of problems, you can boot to a DOS disk and access any data on the partition.

NTFS provides security at the local file and directory level. NTFS also has various tools that protect data from disaster—bad-cluster remapping and a log file to recover from interrupted transactions.

Key Terms and Concepts

Bad-cluster remapping: A process used by the operating system to mark bad sections on a hard drive so that they are not used to store data.

Dual-boot system: A computer that can boot to multiple operating systems.

FAT (File Allocation Table):   A file system first developed for DOS. It is very fast and efficient on small disks but loses performance as disk size increases.

HPFS (High Performance File System):   A file system developed for OS/2.

Local File and Directory-Level Security: Security that applies to a user logged in at a computer and accessing files stored on that computer.

NTFS (New Technology File System):   A file system designed for the NT operating system.

Partition: A physical section of a hard disk set aside for a particular operating system.

POSIX.1 compliance: POSIX is a set of specifications concerned with how some Unix programs access files. NT is compliant with the POSIX.1 standards.

Share Security: Security that applies to a user accessing files over the network.

Sample Questions

1. Which of the following file systems offer local file and directory level security?

   A. NTFS

   B. FAT

   C. HPFS

   D. CDFS

   Answer: A. While network access to any of these file systems can be secured, only NTFS offers security against an individual with direct access to the computer.

2. You are building a test computer for your company lab. The computer will boot to DOS, Windows 95, and Windows NT. Which of the following file systems will be mandatory?

   A. NTFS

   B. FAT

   C. HPFS

   D. CDFS

   Answer: B. The FAT file system is the only choice that all of these operating systems can read.

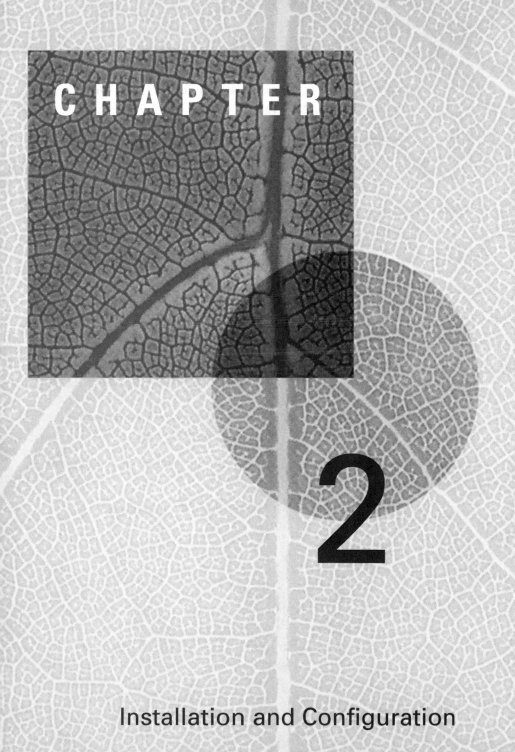

CHAPTER

2

Installation and Configuration

Microsoft Exam Objectives Covered in This Chapter:

▶ **Install Windows NT Workstation on an Intel Platform in a given situation.** *(pages 33 – 51)*

▶ **Set up a dual-boot system in a given situation.** *(pages 51 – 55)*

▶ **Remove Windows NT Workstation in a given situation.** *(pages 56 – 59)*

▶ **Install, configure, and remove hardware components for a given situation. Hardware components include:** *(pages 60 – 82)*
- Network adapter drivers
- SCSI device drivers
- Tape device drivers
- UPS
- Multimedia devices
- Display drivers
- Keyboard drivers
- Mouse drivers

▶ **Use Control Panel applications to configure a Windows NT Workstation computer in a given situation.** *(pages 82 – 91)*

▶ **Configure server-based installation for wide-scale deployment in a given situation.** *(pages 91 – 97)*

▶ **Upgrade to Windows NT Workstation 4.0 in a given situation.** *(pages 98 – 103)*

These objectives cover the procedures necessary to install and configure NT Workstation, not only on one system, but on a large number of computers. As you scan this list, you can see there's a lot of work that needs to be done. For a computer to be useful, it must provide services to its customers in an easy-to-use format. The company's newest employee should be able to sit down and be productive *immediately*. Using the information in this chapter will help you reach that goal and will make your life much less stressful. Some administrators have anxiety attacks at the mere thought of taking the top off of a computer to add a new component. This chapter will help relieve that anxiety.

For the most part, the preliminary work has been completed. You have decided how your network is going to serve your customers, and what part sharing resources from a workstation level will play. Be sure not to put those working papers away: As you go through the workstation installation and configuration process, you will be referring to your notes many times.

Since the difficult decisions have been made, it's time to get on to the real work, that is, hooking client workstations to the network. Installation and configuration is not a one-time thing, it is an ongoing process. As your network grows, you will deal with more and more users, and they will demand more and more services.

In the first chapter, you developed a task list of things to do to configure each workstation that will be running NT Workstation. By the end of this chapter, you will see how you can change and adapt that configuration to meet the demands of everyday life. Each workstation has to meet the end user's individual needs.

NOTE Microsoft's testing philosophy has revolved around testing "real world" tasks and concepts. The objectives in this section epitomize that philosophy.

Install Windows NT Workstation on an Intel-based platform in a given situation.

This objective is a behind-the-scenes look at what happens during the installation process. This section is proactive. It describes how the installation process is going to work and what NT will be doing each step along the way. Some installations fail. It is far easier to troubleshoot problems if you know what is supposed to happen next, rather than be left in a fog.

Critical Information

NT Workstation 4 can be installed on a variety of platforms, including the Intel *x*86 or Pentium-based platforms and RISC-based computers. As a matter of fact, NT 4 will run on the MIPS R4x00-based microprocessor or higher, as well as the Digital Alpha AXP-based microprocessor. This book (and the exam) concentrates on the Intel platform.

There are some minimal hardware requirements for NT Workstation 4 that must be met before the installation begins. These are:

- 12MB of RAM
- VGA-level video support
- Keyboard
- IDE, EIDE, SCSI, or ESDI hard disk
- 486/33 processor or better
- CD-ROM drive, 1.44MB or 1.2MB floppy disk drive, or active network connection
- Mouse or Pointing Device

Now, let's be really honest here. The fact that you grabbed this book rather than some of the others implies you have worked with NT. You *know* a 486/33 with 12MB of RAM just would not cut it in your home lab, much less in a production environment. Microsoft agrees and comes out with a "suggested minimum" list that looks a little better:

- 486DX2/50 processor or better
- 32MB of RAM
- 28.8 v.34 external modem, for remote debugging and troubleshooting
- Windows NT–compatible CD-ROM drive

Again, this machine will never be described as one that is really fast, but it will at least come up and the services will start. The folks from Redmond also forgot to mention a Network Interface Card (NIC). If your workstation is going to attach to the network, you must have one of those, and it must be on the Microsoft NT Hardware Compatibility List (HCL). You can find the HCL on Microsoft's Web page.

How much disk space will an NT Workstation and Server installation take? That will depend on the accessories that you install, but you should start with the following:

- Standard Installation: 124MB of free disk space

- WINNT /b: 124MB of free disk space

- Copying i386 folder to hard disk: 223MB of free disk space

NOTE Don't worry if you are not familiar with the WINNT /b command. The command line switches for the NT Installation Wizard will be covered later in this chapter.

These disk space requirements assume a standard hard disk controller, not an Enhanced IDE (EIDE) hard disk controller. If you are using a hard disk controller that uses a translation mode for addressing the hard disk drive, increase the above sizes by 80MB.

NOTE Some 486 computers have an idea that Integrated Device Electronics (IDE) drives can be a maximum of 504MB in size. It wasn't that long ago that 504MB was a LARGE drive. Translation mode means you are faking out the system. The inner workings of the computer may think that the new Extended Integrated Device Electronics (EIDE) drive is only 504MB in size when in reality it might be 5 gigabytes in size.

Make sure the disk is partitioned and formatted. Here are the recommendations from Microsoft on the disk configurations:

- The root folder (the folder where you are going to install NT 4) should be on a disk formatted with either the FAT translation or NTFS from NT version 3.51 or NT 4. If you are using NTFS, the drive can be compressed. NT will not install on a hard drive that has been compressed with any other utility.

TIP If you are using an IDE drive, do not format it using Windows 95 FAT32 file system. NT 4 does not recognize FAT32 and will not install on a FAT32 partition.

- If your target drive does use address translation, it should use one of the following:
  - Logical Block Addressing (LBA)
  - ONTrack Disk Manager
  - EZDrive
  - Extended Cylinder Head Sector

These are the translations methods supported by NT 4. If you make sure your BIOS and your hard drive support these, you should be in good shape.

NOTE If you are unsure of the translation method used for your drive, try to find the manual for the disk. If you are unsuccessful, check the Internet and the drive maker's Web site. As a last resort, do an Internet search on the make and model number. The appropriate specifications are out there somewhere.

Keep in mind that these are the recommended *minimum* requirements. NT will make use of all of the tools you give it, so give it as much as you can. The more advanced the processor and the more memory given to the server, the better.

Now that you know what NT demands in the way of hardware, it is time to examine what is going to happen during the installation process.

If you have installed NT Workstation, you know that there are several ways you can install the operating system. Microsoft has three pre-configured setup scenarios for you, as well as the Custom option. Selecting the Custom option gives you the right to make all the decisions necessary to install NT just the way you want it. The three pre-configured options give you access to different features of NT.

Table 2.1 lays out what components are available with which option. The Compact option is designed to save disk space, so it does not give you any optional components. Portable is used for laptops; it is not as spartan as Compact, but you can choose to leave just about everything off. If you want messaging or games, the only way to get them is to chose Custom.

T A B L E 2.1: Characteristics of Setup Options

	Typical	Portable	Compact	Custom
Accessibility Options	Yes	Yes	None	All options
Accessories	Yes	Yes	None	All options
Communication	Yes	Yes	None	All options
Games	No	No	None	All options
Multimedia	Yes	Yes	None	All options
Windows Messaging	No	No	None	All options

There are seven stages in the setup:

- Text Mode
- Disk Configuration
- Graphic Mode
- Virtual Memory Configuration
- Printer Configuration
- Network Configuration
- Final Stages

Text Mode

Let's assume that you have booted the target computer to the WINNT Setup Boot Disks that came with the operating system. Booting to these setup floppies will load SETUPLDR, the Windows NT setup utility. SETUPLDR needs to know more about your system, so it kicks off NTDETECT.COM, which goes out and looks at the hardware installed in the computer. Once NTDETECT has finished its work, SETUPLDR shuts it down and starts SETUPAPP.EXE.

SETUPAPP is nosy, it wants to know what you want to do. Are you going to specify what needs to be installed, or is the setup program? This is where you get to choose which of the hardware detection routines you will use.

Are there any SCSI devices in the system? If there are, does NT already have the driver for the disk drive or CD-ROM, or do you have to provide it from a manufacturer's disk? Once the SCSI issue is resolved, there are other devices to discover. NT will look at machine type, display adapter, mouse, and keyboard information.

NOTE Much of the information that NT discovers here can be updated or changed later. See the objective on installing, configuring, and removing hardware components, later in this chapter.

Once hardware discovery has been completed, NT loads all the drivers it needs to run the computer in an installation mode. Now it is time to find out where you want to put NT, so the system checks the hard drive to see if this will be a Windows 3.1 upgrade. NT looks for WIN.COM, and, if it finds it, the installation program will ask if you want to use the <drive letter>:Windows\System 32 directory. Otherwise, it will prompt you for the location where you want the system files copied. The default is the WINNT folder.

Disk Configuration

If no installation of Windows 3.1 is found, the installation process needs to find out about the hard disks in the computer. You will be shown a list of available partitions and free space. Here, you can create, delete, format, or determine file systems for any given area of disk space.

NOTE   If the drive is formatted with the IBM OS/2 high performance file system (HPFS) you will be prompted at this point to convert the drive to either NTFS or FAT.

Now that NT knows where and how to install the files, it wants to check and make sure the hard drive is physically capable of handling the installation. It will run CHKDSK to check the drive.

When CHKDSK has been completed, NT begins copying files to the directory specified (default: C:\WINNT.) Once the file copy has been completed, NT is ready to come up on its own, so you are told to remove the floppy and the CD (if present) and restart the computer.

Graphic Mode

If you have installed Windows 95, the graphic portion of the setup will look very familiar.

The graphics portion of the installation gathers information about how the computer will be identified. It wants things like a user name and company, the name of the computer, and where it will be located.

Location is important, because this is how NT knows how to format date, time, and currency information.

If you chose to use a Custom setup, this is the section that deals with all the "extras" you may want to install—accessories, NT messaging, games—the really important stuff. You can also choose whether or not you want network support, setup printers, and setup system applications on the hard drive.

Virtual Memory Configuration

While all the installation is going on, one of the things happening in the background is the determination of how much Virtual Memory the system will be provided. By default, NT creates a page file that is RAM plus 12MB. If your system has 64MB of RAM, the recommended size for the page file would be 76MB.

TIP Be sure to know the recommended size of page files. The formula is RAM plus 12MB.

NOTE To change the size or location of a page file after installation, click Start ➤ Settings ➤ Control Panel. Double-click System, then select the Performance tab, and click Change.

Network Configuration

At this stage of the process, NT is ready to configure the system to talk to the outside world.

If you are using Custom mode, NT will now begin to look for any installed network interface cards (NICs). If you know what kind of NIC is installed in the system and if you have the appropriate drivers, you can choose to do a manual installation. If you are using a Typical installation, NT will automatically start the search for the network card.

Once the card has been discovered, you will be presented with a dialog box showing the input/output port address (I/O) and the interrupt request (IRQ) settings.

After you approve the settings, NT will install the files necessary to drive the NIC, and the Network Control Panel applet will start. If you click OK, the installation utility will bind the appropriate protocols to the card. The system will start the network services, and you will be given the opportunity to have the workstation join a workgroup or a domain.

Final Stages of Setup

Setup will create the Emergency Repair disk. Setup prompts for a blank disk, or one that can be reformatted, and then checks to be sure that it has not been given the Boot Floppy, by checking for TXT-SETUP.INF. Setup will then format the disk and then save the default configuration information (necessary to restore Windows NT) on the Emergency Repair disk. Finally, Setup will ask for the system's time zone setting. Unless the system happens to be in the Greenwich mean time zone, the correct time zone must be selected.

The system reboots again and the process is completed by having you choose the video display type and the time zone the workstation will reside in.

That is the overview of the installation process. For the complete step-by-step process, we move into the Necessary Procedures section of the objective.

Necessary Procedures

The NT installation program works fastest from an NT environment. This presents an interesting dilemma: how do you install from an NT environment without having NT installed? Microsoft has provided a simple solution. There are three 3 1/2" disks in the box. These disks are used to boot the target computer and start the installation. As part of the boot process, the system hardware is analyzed and the CD-ROM is recognized, providing the medium for the installation program.

NOTE There are several methods for installing NT Workstation, including attaching to a share and doing an unattended install (see Chapter 1). This section will assume you are installing for the Windows Workstation CD-ROM.

You may be installing NT for the second, third, or fourth time, and you have the licenses, you have the CD, but the disks seem to have been misplaced. No sweat. These disks, which can make the installation process run much smoother, can be recreated. To re-create the disks:

1. Put the NT Installation CD in a CD-ROM drive and open a command prompt. The operating system of the computer you are using for this procedure does not matter. You need only to have a computer that has a working CD-ROM and a working 3 1/2-inch drive.

2. Change to whatever drive contains the CD. For example, D:.

3. Change into the i386 directory. You will see a file called WINNT.EXE.

4. Type **WINNT /?** at the command prompt. Press Enter.

When you press Enter, you will be presented with a list of all the command lines switches for the NT installation program. The proper syntax for utilizing these switches is:

```
Drive:\i386\WINNT.EXE [/S[:]sourcepath] [/
T[:]tempdrive] [/I[:]inffile] [/X | [/F] [/C] [/
D[:]winntpath]]
```

Table 2.2 provides a list of the functionality the command line switches provide.

TABLE 2.2:   Command-Line Switches and Their Functionality

Switch	Functionality
/S[:] source path	Specifies where the NT files are located
/T[:] temp drive	Specifies where NT stores temp files during the install
/I[:]inf file	Tells NT where the information files are located
/OX	Create boot floppies for CD ROM installation.
/X	Don't create the boot floppies, you already have them.
/F	You will create the boot floppies, but you will not verify the files that are being copied to those floppies.
/C	Skip the free space check on those floppies; you know they are empty and formatted.
/B	Floppyless operation, requires the /S parameter
/U:script file	Unattended operation, requires the /S parameter
/R:directory	Specifies optional directory to be installed
/RX:directory	Specifies optional directory to be copied
/E:command	Specifies command to run at the end of the GUI setup

---

TIP To create a set of installation disks, your command line syntax would be WINNT /OX.

If you have created the disks or have the originals from Microsoft, put the first disk in the A: drive of the target computer. Turn the machine on, and the system will boot making use of at least two of the disks you just created. The Installation Wizard will also load the drivers to access the target system's CD-ROM drive. You must have the NT Workstation CD in that drive. You are on your way!

Here is the step-by-step process:

1. Put the first disk in the floppy drive. Make sure the NT Workstation CD is in the CD-ROM drive. Turn the target computer on. The boot process loads the Windows NT Executive. After the NT Executive has been loaded, the system will load the Hardware Abstraction Layer (HAL).

2. You will be prompted to put the disk labeled Setup Disk #2 into drive A: and press Enter. The computer now loads the NT Setup Wizard from the floppy. The Setup Wizard will load PCMCIA support and video support. Once video support has been loaded, the system loads floppy drive support.

3. With disk #2 still in the floppy driver, you will see the "Welcome to Setup" screen. You have three options: continue the installation (press Enter), repair a damaged installation (press R), or quit (press F3). Press Enter to continue.

4. The Setup Wizard now starts to search for drive controllers. You can press Enter to have the system do it, or press S to have the system skip the search. Press Enter to have the Installation Wizard search the system.

5. You are prompted to insert disk #3. Disk #3 loads CD-ROM support, SCSI Disk Driver support, and any other drivers that NT finds necessary. You are given a Workstation Setup screen that asks if you need to find any additional devices or drivers. If there is nothing else to find, press Enter to continue.

6. Once you have provide the source path, the lawyers get involved: You will see the license agreement. Page down and press F8 to agree.

7. You will now see the Workstation setup screen. Check it to make sure that everything agrees with your system, and press Enter to continue.

8. You will be asked which partition and drive you want to install the system files on. Make your choice and press Enter. From this screen you can also format the partition using either of the default file systems (NTFS or FAT). If a partition does not already exist, you can also create a partition from this menu.

9. Make your choice and choose to format the partition with FAT, format with NTFS, convert it to NTFS, or leave it alone. The selections you see may vary, depending if you are upgrading the computer or doing a new installation to an unformatted partition.

10. Choose which partition you will install NT onto and also which folder will be the root. To install NT into the default folder, choose C:\WINNT.

11. Setup now examines your hard disk for corruption. You are given a choice: Press Enter for an exhaustive search, or press Esc to skip the exhaustive search all together.

12. Since you pressed Enter, the setup wizard examines the target disk and starts copying files. This is one section that may take some time.

13. After the file copying is completed, NT is ready to move on to the next phase of the installation process. You will be told to remove the CD from the CD-ROM drive and remove the floppy disk. Once this has been done, you can press Enter to restart the computer.

14. As the computer reboots, setup initializes and begins asking questions. It will also prompt you to re-insert the installation CD-ROM. Press Enter to continue the process.

15. The Setup Wizard will now set about gathering information about the computer, and this leads to the Preparing to Install screen. This screen has that little blue bar that moves slowly across the screen. Click Next.

16. Now you can choose which setup option you want to use. The choices are Typical, Portable, Compact, or Custom. For the purposes of this exercise, Choose Typical. Click Next.

17. You will be prompted to enter your name and your organization.

18. On the next screen, enter the CD key found on the back of the CD case. Click Next to continue.

19. Enter a unique computer name. Click Next to continue.

20. The next screen has you enter a password for the administrator. You will also have to confirm the password before clicking Next to continue.

21. The Wizard now wants to know if you would like to create an emergency repair disk. If you choose yes, you will be asked for the diskette at the end of the installation process.

22. The next step asks which Windows NT components you would like to install. You can choose to install the most common options or you can see a list of things to install. The list has accessibility options, accessories, communications, games, multimedia, and windows messaging. Make your selections and click Next to continue. This will take you to the Windows NT Setup progress screen.

23. To install Windows networking, from the NT Setup screen, click Next.

24. Since you chose to install networking on the computer, you need to tell NT which kind of networking you want to install. You are presented with options to not connect the computer to a network, to connect to a network via an ISDN line, via a LAN line, or via remote access to network through dial in. Make your selection and click Next.

NOTE If you have parts of networking that you want to install, but you do not want to install the network adapter at this time, you can choose to install the Microsoft LoopBack Adapter. This will give you the opportunity to install network components without having a physical adapter installed.

---

25. The Wizard now starts its search for network adapters. Click Start Search to begin the search, or select from a list. We will install another network driver later, so make your choice and click Next to continue. This will let you choose the protocols to install. Choose carefully. You don't want your workstation flooding the network with unwanted packets!

TIP   One of the tweaks you may want to make after the installation is the binding order of the protocols. The client determines which protocol will be used and the decision is made through binding order. The most used protocol should be at the top of this list. If you are unsure how to change binding order, see the section on installing a network adapter driver.

---

26. When you have selected the protocols to install, click Next. That will return you to an informational screen that lets you know NT is about to install all the stuff you told it to install. Click Next to get rid of the informational screen.

27. If you selected TCP/IP as a protocol, you will be prompted to use DHCP. If your system has a DHCP server on it, this is a great way to minimize addressing headings. Choose Yes or No and the Installation system is off to the races. Once it has finished, click next to start the network.

28. Once the network is started, you will be presented with a screen to make your computer part of a Workgroup or part of a Domain. Add the appropriate information. If you choose to make the computer a member of the domain, you can have your workstation create a computer account in the domain by filling the checkbox and giving the system the Administrator's user name and password.

29. Click Finish and setup will configure your computer.

30. To finish the installation, chose the time zone the workstation will be used in, and check the Date and Time tab before clicking Close.

31. The system will now find the video display type. Choose OK for the adapter type, usually some form of VGA. You need to test the

selection before leaving this screen; click OK to start the test. You will be asked if you saw the test screen. Select Yes or No, and then save settings if the bitmap displayed properly. To continue with setup, click OK.

32. Click OK to close Display Properties.

33. NT now starts the configuration process.

34. If you chose to create an emergency repair disk, now is the time. Place a blank, formatted diskette in drive A:. You will be told that everything on the disk will be erased; press OK to continue.

35. Install copies more files, sets security, deletes all those unnecessary temporary installation files, and then prompts you to restart the computer.

When the system restarts, you will have a computer running NT Workstation.

Exam Essentials

Know how to upgrade an HPFS partition during Windows NT 4.0 installation. If the system to be upgraded is a Windows 3.51 system, convert the partition to NTFS before installation of NT 4.0 Workstation.

Know how binding order affects workstation performance. The client chooses the protocol that is used for communication. The protocol binding order determines which protocol on the client is used. Place the most-often-used protocol at the top of the binding order.

Know how to change the size of the paging file. To change the size or location of a paging file after installation, click Start ➤ Settings ➤ Control Panel. Double-click System, then click the tab marked Performance and click Change.

Know the default size of the paging file. The default size of the paging file is RAM plus 12MB.

Know how to install networking components without installing a network adapter. Choose to install the Microsoft LoopBack Adapter.

Know file system conversions.   FAT can be converted to NTFS; NTFS cannot be converted to FAT. NT 4.0 does not support HPFS.

Know which file system supports which operating systems.
FAT is supported by Windows NT, Windows 95, and Windows 3.1. NTFS is only recognized by Windows NT. FAT32 is only recognized by Windows 95 OSR2.

Know how to recreate setup diskettes if they are lost or misplaced.   From the installation CD in the i386 directory, the syntax is:

```
WINNT /OX
```

Know the minimum hardware requirements for Windows NT.
Windows NT requires a 486/25 with a minimum of 12MB of RAM and 90MB of free disk space. Windows NT cannot be installed on a 386 computer.

Key Terms and Concepts

\WINNT: Default root folder for the installation of Windows NT 4.0.

EIDE: Enhanced Integrated Device Electronics. Allows for drives of higher capacity. An EIDE paddleboard can handle a maximum of four devices.

Emergency Repair Diskette: A set of utilities to help boot an NT server and repair system files in the event of a catastrophe.

FAT: File allocation table. DOS-compatible method of accessing files. In an NT server, drives under 400MB should be formatted as FAT.

HCL: Windows NT Hardware Compatibility List.

IDE: A hard disk technology in which the controller hardware is placed on the disk itself. IDE devices can be disk drives or CD-ROM drives. These devices can be configured as a single device or in pairs.

NIC: Network Interface Card.

NTFS: NT File System. NTFS is most efficient in drives greater than 400MB. In addition to other capabilities, NTFS will allow for local file system security.

Paging File: A special file on a PC hard disk. With virtual memory under Windows NT, some of the program code and other information is kept in RAM while other information is temporarily swapped into virtual memory. When that information is required again, Windows NT pulls it back into RAM and, if necessary, swaps other information to virtual memory. Also called a swap file.

Translation Mode: Software utility that will allow an Integrated Device Electronics (IDE) hard drive that is greater than 504MB in size to work with an older system board.

Sample Questions

1. Workstation performance and network access seem to be slow. What is one way of improving performance?

   A. Change the protocol binding order on the client machine. Move the most widely used protocols to the bottom.

   B. Change the protocol binding order on the server. Move the most widely used protocols to the bottom.

   C. Change the protocol binding order on the workstation. Move the most widely used protocols to the top.

   D. Change the protocol binding order on the server. Move the most widely used protocols to the top.

   Answer: C. The client controls the protocol selection. Moving the most widely used protocol to the top ensures that it is the first used.

2. You are installing NT Workstation on a computer that is currently configured to run NT 3.51. The workstation makes use of the High Performance File System (HPFS). How can you complete the installation?

   A. NT 4.0 supports HPFS, so there will be no problem.

B. Convert the HPFS file system to NTFS before the upgrade.

C. Back up all the data, reformat the hard drive, install NT, reinstall the applications, and then restore the data.

D. NT 4.0 will convert HPFS to NTFS as part of the normal installation process.

Answer: B. NT 4.0 does not support HPFS. You would have to convert HPFS to NTFS before the upgrade.

3. You have just added more memory to a computer. How do you adjust the size of the paging file?

A. From the Performance tab of System Properties in Control Panel

B. You don't have to worry about it. NT supports Plug and Play and will recognize the change in memory and change the size of the paging file automatically.

C. The size of the paging file cannot be adjusted.

D. Memory has nothing to do with the size of the paging file.

Answer: A. The size of the paging file can be adjusted by selecting Start ➢ Settings ➢ Control Panel, double-clicking System, then clicking the tab marked Performance and clicking Change.

Set up a dual-boot system in a given situation.

There will be times where you will want to configure one computer for multiple operating systems—maybe you'll be faced with a critical application that cannot run under NT, or maybe you will need a test bed computer to serve multiple functions. In any event, this objective is concerned with the steps involved in this type of configuration.

Critical Information

As discussed in Chapter 1, there are only two pieces of critical information in this objective:

- While dual-booting is possible, it is not a supported configuration.

- The only file system that will support a dual-boot configuration is the FAT file system.

Non-Supported Configuration

The bottom line here is that Microsoft does not expect you to rely upon a dual-boot configuration as a long-term solution. If you have legacy software that demands either DOS/Windows 3.*x* or Windows 95, you should be in the process of upgrading it to NT compatibility. This may sometimes an unreasonable expectation, but that's the way it is.

FAT Considerations

The FAT file system is required on a dual-boot system. Be aware that this means that there will be no local file or directory level security. Another consideration is that files on a FAT partition are accessible—even without any login authentication—if the machine is booted to a DOS disk. Fat partitions are also vulnerable to DOS utilities that can read deleted files from the disk.

Do not store confidential or critical data on a FAT partition. This might mean that you have to create a NTFS partition that will be inaccessible when the computer is booted to DOS or Windows 95.

WARNING Windows 95 includes the option to use FAT32—a new and improved version of the Fat file system. Windows NT cannot access a FAT32 partition. Do not use the FAT32 file system when installing Windows 95 on a dual-boot computer.

Necessary Procedures

Since this is not a supported configuration, the information is not heavily tested—but the information might come in handy when you are setting up your home lab for studying.

Rather than give two different procedures—one for DOS/NT and another for WINDOW95/NT—this section will detail the process for creating a multi-boot computer (DOS, Windows 95, and NT). If you don't need all three operating systems, just skip the appropriate steps. The most important thing is to install them in the order listed.

NOTE The only dual-boot configuration that Microsoft discusses is that of Windows 95 and Windows NT. If you need to dual boot NT with some other operating system (OS/2 for instance), you will need to research the process.

Setting Up a Multi-Boot Computer

1. Install DOS. Use the setup program for whichever version you have available. Make sure that DOS is working correctly with any programs that will require it before continuing.

2. Install Windows 95. Windows 95 will automatically include the option to boot back to your original version of DOS, if desired. (Press the F8 key during the boot to bring up a menu.)

3. Install Windows NT. NT will automatically include your old operating system in its boot menu choices.

When the computer boots, you will be presented with the NT boot menu. If you want either Windows 95 or DOS, make the appropriate selection. If you want DOS, press the F8 key when you see the "Loading Windows 95" message on the screen.

WARNING Remember, Windows 95 and NT have different structures to their registry files. You must install each application that will be used while booted to each operating system it will be used under. In other words, if you are going to use Excel while booted to both NT and 95, you must install two copies of Excel in different directories.

Exam Essentials

This is a short objective, and not one that is heavily tested. Concentrate on the following points:

Know what file system will support a dual-boot configuration. Since only the FAT file system can be read by DOS, Windows 95, and NT, it is the only file system that will support a dual-boot configuration.

Know the danger of using FAT32. Microsoft Windows 95 includes a new version of the FAT file system called FAT32. Windows NT can not read from a FAT32 partition. Do not use this file system when installing Windows 95 on a dual-boot computer. If you do, you will be unable to install NT without destroying the partition—which defeats the purpose of a dual-boot configuration.

Understand the procedure for setting up a dual-boot computer. See the Necessary Procedures section for details.

Key Terms and Concepts

Dual-boot system: A computer that is configured to boot into multiple operating systems.

FAT (File Allocation Table): The file system used by DOS and Windows 95.

FAT32 (File Allocation Table): A new an improved version of the FAT file system. For our purposes, you should remember that Windows NT cannot read FAT32 partitions.

NTFS (**New Technology File System**): A file system specifically designed for Windows NT.

Sample Questions

1. A user installs Windows NT on his Windows 95 computer in a dual-boot configuration. After the installation, Excel will run when the computer is booted to Windows 95 but not when it is booted to Windows NT. What is the probable cause?

   A. The user has forgotten to migrate the Windows 95 registry to the NT installation.

   B. The user has the Windows 95 version of Excel.

   C. Excel needs to be installed twice—once for each operating system.

   D. Excel needs to be copied into the WINNT directory.

   Answer: C. The registry structure is different for Windows 95 and NT. Each application must be installed while booted to the operating systems under which it will be used.

2. You have decided to move to Windows NT 4.0 and are planning to install over the top of your existing Windows 95 operating system. During the installation you receive a message indicating that there are no usable partitions. What is the most likely cause?

   A. You are out of disk space.

   B. Your disk is not NT-compatible.

   C. Your Windows 95 installation probably used the FAT32 file system.

   D. You need to install a new disk and use it as your Windows NT hard drive.

   Answer: C. Windows 95 can use the FAT32 files system. Partitions using this file system cannot be read by Windows NT.

Remove Windows NT Workstation in a given situation.

This objective is ironic; you spend hours teaching students how to install, configure, and manage an NT computer, and then have to deal with removing the operating system if necessary.

Critical Information

In most cases you will find NT to be so stable, reliable, and easily managed that you would never go want to remove it from a computer. (Okay, thus ends the Microsoft sales pitch.) There are occasions, however, when it will be necessary to remove it. Knowing the proper procedure will prevent unnecessary work.

You might remove NT because you have installed a demo copy whose time has expired or because you want to change the role a server plays in your network. Whatever the reason, the process will depend upon the file system you have chosen for the boot partition. The steps are described in the Necessary Procedures section.

In most business environments, however, you would not install a demo copy of NT on a production computer. If you have to remove NT from a workstation, it is usually easier to delete the partition and start from scratch.

You might want to change the role of a server though. This is why many administrators will create a small FAT partition from which to boot, and will store all data and applications on another volume. This allows you to kill the boot partition without affecting your data. You can then reinstall NT and can use the existing volumes without having to restore your data from tape.

Necessary Procedures

This objective concerns the process of removing NT from a computer. This area is not a heavily tested objective, but you will want to be familiar with the choices available.

Removing NT from a System That Boots from a FAT Partition

1. First, boot the computer from a DOS or Windows 95 floppy that contains a copy of SYS.COM.

2. From your A: drive, type **SYS C:**. This will transfer the appropriate system files to your hard drive.

3. Restart your system, booting from the hard drive.

4. Other than deleting a few NT files to save disk space, you are finished.

5. The following files can be deleted:

   - All paging files—PAGEFILE.SYS (Remember that you might have created more than one in an effort to optimize your computer.)

   - C:\BOOT.INI

   - C:\NT*.*

   - C:\BOOTSECT.DOS

   - The <*Winnt_root*> directory

   - Program files\Windows NT

NOTE The BOOT.INI, NT*.*, and BOOTSECT.DOS files are marked as System, hidden, read-only files; you will have to change these attributes before you can delete them.

Removing NT from a Computer That Boots from an NTFS Partition

Unfortunately, the only operating system that can read and write to an NTFS partition is Windows NT. This means that if your system boots to an HTFS partition you will have to delete it. There are a couple of ways to accomplish this:

- Use FDISK.COM from DOS 6.0 or later.

- Use the OS/2 installation disk to remove all partitions from the first physical disk.

- Boot to the first floppy of the NT setup disks. When prompted for a partition upon which to install NT, select the NTFS partition and press D to delete. Then press F3 to exit the setup program.

Exam Essentials

There are only two essential topics for this objective: the two procedures for removing Microsoft Windows NT from a computer, as discussed above. Be familiar with the steps involved.

Know the three ways to remove an NTFS partition. These methods are:

- Use FDISK.COM from DOS version 6.0 or later.

- Use the OS/2 installation disk.

- Use the NT setup floppies.

Key Terms and Concepts

FDISK.COM: A DOS/Windows 95 command line utility used to manage disk partitions.

PAGEFILE.SYS: A file on a hard disk used as virtual memory by the NT operating system.

SYS.COM: A DOS/Windows 95 command line utility used to make a disk bootable.

Sample Questions

1. Which of the following methods can be used to delete an NTFS system partition?

   A. FDISK

   B. The OS/2 boot disks

   C. The NT boot disks

   D. The disk administration utility

   Answer: A, B, C. The disk administration tool can remove any partition except the system/boot partitions.

2. Which of the following actions would require you to remove NT from your computer?

   A. You have installed a demo-copy and licensed time has expired.

   B. You are going to install a new tape drive in your computer.

   C. You need to change the role of your server form that of a member server to a domain controller.

   D. You have decided that NT is not the operating system for your needs.

   Answer: A, C, D. You do not have to reinstall NT to add a new tape drive, so answer B is not correct. The other three options all describe situations where you would have to remove the Windows NT operating system.

Install, configure, and remove hardware components for a given situation. Hardware components include:

- Network Adapter Drivers
- SCSI Device Drivers
- Tape Device Drivers
- UPS
- Multimedia devices
- Display Drivers
- Keyboard Drivers
- Mouse Drivers

Once the workstation operating system has been installed, it is up to you to customize it to match your individual preferences or, more importantly, hardware configuration. In this section, the assumption will be made that the hardware is already installed on the workstation, and it is up to you to configure or install new drivers.

Critical Information

Installing hardware components isn't as complicated as it sounds, if you know some of the basics. Generally, you locate resources you have available in the computer. You read the documentation that comes with the hardware to find out how to configure the component to take advantage of the available resources. You physically install the component, configure the driver to use the new device, reboot the workstation, and the new component will be available.

Removing resources is even easier, since there is no search for resources. Usually, you remove the driver or service, shut down the PC and physically remove the device. Reboot the PC and things should work. (He says with an all-knowing grin.)

This is a great section to read, especially when you are trying to install something that isn't installing just right. You may learn some tips or tricks. It is also a good section to read before testing, because this material is covered extensively on the exam.

Network Adapter Drivers

At first blush, you might look at this and decide, "Hey, wait a minute, we did this in the installation section." You would be right, but there are lots of reasons why you might be messing around with the configuration of a network adapter.

Windows NT Workstation has the ability to handle multiple network adapters in the same computer. While NT *can* do that, the question is why would it? A workstation rarely would need a second network card. A more likely scenario would be that a network card currently installed in a workstation has had its network adapter driver updated and you would like to remove the old driver and install a new driver. This is done from the Network icon in the Control Panel.

NOTE   One of the fundamental laws of computing states that there is ALWAYS more than one way to do something; you should use the method you prefer. An example is the network adapter driver settings. These can be accessed through the Network icon in Control Panel, or by highlighting Network Neighborhood, and right-clicking and then selecting Properties.

Configuring the network adapter driver is something you will probably do on each workstation. Depending on the driver, the choices you have available to tweak may differ.

To access this window, open Control Panel, double-click Network, click the Adapters tab, and select Properties. Notice that you can use this screen to determine the hardware configuration of the card, the physical address of the card, the cable type, and the line speed. Which of these might have to be configured after installation? Possibly cable detect and line speed. Cable detect determines if you are using (in this case) a 10-Base T connection or Coax connection. Line Speed will vary between 10MB per second and 100MB per second.

NOTE The Network Settings page for each Network Adapter will be different, depending on the driver installed.

If you click OK on the Properties page, you will return to the Network Window. Earlier in this chapter, we discussed the binding order of protocols. The workstation controls which protocol the workstation and the server will use to communicate. Clicking the Bindings tab will open the bindings window. You can make your choices by opening the workstation NetBios Interface, the Server Interface, and the Workstation interface. You can change the binding order so the most frequently used protocol is the first listed.

TIP Don't bind (or install) more protocols than you actually need. Each protocol will generate traffic on your network. If there is nothing to answer, you are generating unnecessary traffic.

SCSI Device Drivers

Small Computer System Interface (SCSI) devices are becoming more and more prevalent in today's computing environment. If you decide that your workstation needs external storage, you may decide to install a JAZ drive. That can be a SCSI device. If you use your NT workstation for building or maintaining Web sites, the scanner you use may be SCSI. In the next section, we will discuss installing a tape device driver. These can also be SCSI devices.

NOTE   The steps involved in installing, configuring, or removing the SCSI device driver are covered in the Necessary Procedures section of this objective.

Once the SCSI device and driver have been installed, there really isn't much that can be done to configure it. The only "configurable" setting for a SCSI Device Driver is the hardware resources Input/Output range and Interrupt. You can remove the driver and reinstall a newer version to keep the driver up to date.

Tape Device Drivers

Tape devices are used for the archiving of data on a removable media. This is referred to as a backup. Backing up data is always considered a good thing. Providing a workstation with a tape backup gives you a better chance at protecting yourself from data loss.

The actual device driver is used to communicate between the computer and the tape backup unit. The driver is installed when the device is installed. It can be removed if you decide to change devices or a new driver becomes available.

Configuration options depend on the tape device that you have installed.

NOTE   The actual installation, configuration, and removal of the tape device driver will be covered in the Necessary Procedures section.

UPS Devices and UPS Service

No, this has nothing to do with the person who stops in every day driving a big brown truck. This is about an Uninterruptable Power Supply, or UPS. If you live and work in an area where the power can go out, a UPS can be the difference between a nice, clean shutdown and a long night trying to recover data from a tape backup unit.

UPSs come in a variety of shapes, sizes, and configurations; the $3.95 power strip from the local hardware store is *not* a UPS. Some UPSs will just keep the server up for 10 to 15 minutes after the power goes out and then shut it down. Some can keep it up for hours. Some will not only ensure that the system will not crash due to a power outage, but will condition the power that comes into your place of business. This provides a constant flow of even current, without the spikes and valleys that can ruin even the best of servers.

How important is buying a good UPS? How important is the data on your server? Next to a tape backup unit, this can be all that separates you from the unemployment line. UPS technology varies, and more features equal more money. Some UPSs will shut the system down. Others will send out broadcast messages saying the system is coming down, others will page you before the system goes down. To configure your new UPS, use the UPS screen in Control Panel.

Multimedia Devices

To paraphrase Moore's Law, the power of the processor that runs your computer will double every 18 months to 2 years. We all know the computer you buy today will be outdated (and much cheaper) in a month. As the technology improves, we demand more and more out of our computers. It wasn't too long ago that having a color monitor set you apart from the crowd. Now, even the least expensive systems come configured to be able to view video clips and listen to music CDs.

Multimedia devices include such things as:

- An audio driver for playback and for recording of voice or music

- A video setting that allows you to choose how you want to view your movie—full screen or in a window

- The Musical Instrument Digital Interface (MIDI), that lets you control several devices, instruments, or computers that can send and receive messages and create music, sound, or control lighting

- A CD music setting (on some machines) that lets you listen to a CD through headphones while the computer is shut off

- Miscellaneous drivers like mixer devices that control the volume of various input channels, video capturing devices, and even a joystick

Display Drivers

Display drivers do just that. They drive your video display. Depending on the type of video card in your computer and the amount of memory it has, you can configure your monitor to display millions of different colors, in clarity that will rival the best home television set on the market.

The selection of a display driver gives you all sorts of options to personalize your computer, from wallpapers to screen savers that deliver a message for the day.

Keyboard Drivers

Keyboard drivers are used to customize the keyboard to meet the individual user's preferences. Some users are very fast (or slow) typists and need to alter the length of time between the repeat rate for keys. The keyboard driver also customizes the keyboard layout for languages other than English.

For systems with multiple users working in multiple languages, keyboards can be configured for several different languages, with one as the default.

Mouse Drivers

While most people view the mouse attached to their computer as a useful device and tool, many don't realize that it is configurable. The Mouse selection in Control Panel gives you the opportunity to configure the mouse to meet your specifications. Lefties can swap the buttons on the mouse. You can even choose how much time there is between clicks to constitute a double click.

Necessary Procedures

Each of the drivers that will be discussed are accessed through the Control Panel folder. To access Control Panel, click Start ➤ Control Panel.

Installing a Network Adapter Driver

If you are installing multiple cards as part of the installation process, once NT finds the first card, there is a button that tells it to go out and look for more. NT will continue looking for cards until it doesn't find any more, or until you run out of manufacturer's diskettes. If you are installing a new PCI card into an available slot:

1. Install the card per manufacturers directions. When you reboot the computer, open the Network window in the Control Panel.

2. Click the Adapters tab.

3. Click Add.

4. From the Select Network Adapter window, select the appropriate network card and click OK or click Have Disk. If you chose Have Disk, insert the disk in drive A:\ or provide the appropriate path, and click OK.

5. If you chose a network card, you will be prompted for the path to Windows NT system files, either from the CD or from the location that the files have been copied too. After providing the path, click Continue. The files will be copied and a default binding provided.

6. Close the dialog boxes and restart the system when prompted.

If you do not have an open PCI slot, you will have to install an ISA-compatible card. Each card has its own installation routine, so before beginning any installation be sure to RTFM (Read The Fine Manual). For example, if you were installing a plug-and-play compatible LinkSys 16-bit ISA-compatible Ethernet card, you would take the following steps.

NOTE   Since each installation will be a little different, this is just for demonstration purposes only; the steps you follow may be different.

1. Turn the PC off.

2. Remove the cover.

3. Physically install the card.

4. Cable the card to the concentrator.

5. Turn the computer back on and log on as Administrator.

The card is now physically installed. The next step is to configure the card to work in your server. Because the demonstration card went into an ISA slot, you have to run the setup utility. Boot the server to DOS and run setup, which shows the default parameters of an IRQ setting of 3 and a memory address of 300. The final IRQ and memory address will be Plug-and-Play Compatible, meaning that the operating system should handle the actual settings.

To install the new card and driver for NT:

1. From the Network window, click the Adapters tab.

2. Next, click Add, which will bring up the Select Network Adapter dialog box.

3. Choose Have Disk.

4. As part of the Insert Disk window, add the path to the software drivers; in this case, A:\WINNT.

5. Select the card by highlighting the card name, then click OK.

6. Enter in an open I/O port or choose Auto, depending on the capabilities of the card.

7. Enter in an open IRQ number or choose Auto, depending on the capabilities of the card.

8. Enter in a network address, if necessary.

9. Click OK.

This graphic shows that both network cards have been installed. When Close is clicked, the system begins to examine the network subsystem and checks to make sure everything is just the way it is supposed to be.

10. Since IP is loaded by default, the first "glitch" the system found was that the new card did not have a working IP address. The Microsoft TCP/IP Properties box opens, from which you can choose to receive your IP address from a DHCP server or from a static address.

11. Enter in DNS information and WINS information, if necessary. Click OK to close.

12. Restart the computer.

Configuring the Network Adapter Driver

From the Network window with the Adapters tab selected and an adapter highlighted:

1. Click Properties to access the Network Settings window.

2. Depending on the type of network adapter card you have installed, the Network Settings screen will display a variety of configuration options. Some common Ethernet options include:

   I/O Port   The I/O port address is the hexadecimal designation of the address the adapter is using. This must be unique.

   Memory Address   The memory address is the hexadecimal designation of the memory location that the card will use to access information.

   Interrupt   Also known at IRQ. This is the channel that the card will use to gain the CPU's attention.

   Cable type   This option will allow you to choose between twisted-pair cable and coax cable.

   Line Speed   This option will let the card auto-detect the line speed; choose 10MB per second or 100MB per second.

3. Make the appropriate choices and click OK when you are finished.

4. Click Close to close the Network window. Click Yes when prompted to shut down and restart your computer to have the changes take effect.

Removing a Network Adapter Driver

To remove a Network Adapter driver, start from the Network window with the Adapter tab selected.

1. Highlight the network adapter driver that you would like to remove.

2. Click Remove.

3. Click Yes to close the window telling you that you are about to permanently remove the component from the system.

4. Restart the computer to allow the changes to take effect.

Installing and Configuring a SCSI Device Driver

Before the computer can access the wonderful world of SCSI devices, a controller must be installed. The installation varies with manufacturer and type, but there are some common threads that run through the process:

1. Install the SCSI adapter and driver as instructed by the manufacturer.

2. Open the Control Panel and click the SCSI Adapters icon. Each system will look different. The following screen is a sample.

As you look closely at this screen, what do you see that seems out of place? There are two entries for the PCI Dual Channel IDE controller. If you look really carefully at the description, it says that these devices are ATAPI compliant. The ATAPI standard is a subset of SCSI drivers. When the designers of NT needed a place to put them, this is where the designers decided they should go.

The PCI Dual channel IDE Controller was installed as part of the NT installation process. It found the controller, loaded the drivers and everything worked. The other driver showing is the Adaptec AHA294x/AHA394x driver. This card was installed after the workstation was configured. The installation went something like this:

1. Shut down the workstation.

2. Install the controller card and the SCSI device, in this case an external CD-ROM.

3. Restart NT, log in as Administrator.

4. Go to Control Panel.

5. Choose SCSI adapters.

6. Choose the Drivers tab.

7. Select Add.

8. Choose the controller manufacturer and select Have Disk.

9. Put the manufacturer's disk in the A:\ drive.

10. Click OK.

11. Restart the computer when prompted.

Other than the Add/Remove button on the Drivers tab, there really is not much configuration here. If you highlight a driver under the Devices tab and click Properties, you will get an information screen on the card. You will also be able to see an information screen on the driver. If you are curious, you can look at the Resources tab of the Properties screen to see which IRQ and memory settings the card is using. Since the demonstration card is a PCI card, there are no changeable settings on this screen.

Removing a SCSI Device Driver

SCSI adapter drivers are accessed through the SCSI Adapters icon in Control Panel. You can open the SCSI page by double-clicking the SCSI Adapters icon and then clicking the Drivers tab.

1. From the Drivers tab, highlight the driver you would like to remove.

2. Click the Remove button.

3. Click Yes or No when asked if you are sure you want to remove this driver.

4. Restart the computer when prompted by clicking Yes.

Installing and Configuring the Tape Device Driver

Configuring a tape drive is a two-step process: First you configure the driver and then have NT discover the tape device. There are some default drivers for some of the more common tape devices, but you might want to have any software drivers that came with the controller and the tape drive handy, just in case.

To install a tape backup unit:

1. Install the necessary hardware, as described by the hardware vendor.

2. Once the hardware has been installed and the computer has been restarted, log on as an Administrator.

3. Open Control Panel.

4. Next, double-click the Tape Devices icon.

5. Select the Drivers tab, click Add.

6. Choose from the list of manufacturers and tape devices shown, or select Have Disk.

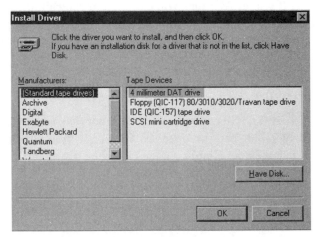

7. Select OK. At this point, the Installation Wizard will copy and install the device drivers. You will be prompted to restart your computer.

8. After the computer restarts, open the Control Panel.

9. Double-click Tape Devices.

10. With the Device tab selected, choose Detect to have NT find and configure the tape device.

Removing a Tape Device Driver

From Control Panel, double-click the Tape Device icon to open the Tape Devices window.

1. Click the Drivers tab.

2. Highlight the driver that you would like to remove and click the Remove button.

3. Answer Yes to the screen that tells you the driver will be removed.

4. Restart the computer after the process has been completed.

Installing and Configuring a UPS

UPS devices usually come with a program that allows for a more robust configuration than the standard NT installation. For the purpose of this book, we are going to use the standard NT installation.

1. Install the hardware according to the vendor's specifications.

2. Make sure you attach a serial cable (usually 9-pin) from the UPS to an available COM port on the workstation. Make a note of which port you use.

3. Open Control Panel.

4. Double-click UPS.

5. Check the checkbox next to "Uninterruptible Power Supply is installed on:" and add the appropriate COM port.

6. You can now configure your UPS to recognize the loss of power. The configuration is accomplished by selecting one or more checkboxes.

NOTE When power is lost, an event is logged and no new connections can be made to the server. Existing connections can continue to work. Warning messages will be broadcast according to the parameters you specify.

---

7. When the Power failure signal box is checked, you can choose how you want NT to react to a loss of power. By selecting Execute Command File, you can write a series of commands for the system to carry out before shutdown:

   - If you opt not to write a command file, you can manually configure the UPS characteristics. Service characteristics include a setting for the time between power failure and the initial warning message. The default is set to five seconds. If you live in an area with frequent storms that cause frequent power hiccups, you may want to change that setting. You can also specify how often you want the message rebroadcast. The default is every two minutes.

   - The other manually configured options revolve around what happens when the power comes back on. The first is the Expected Battery Life. This tells NT how long the UPS is rated to keep the computer up and working before shutting things down. Finally, you can provide an informational selection, showing how long the battery must be recharged for each minute it is run. The default is 100 minutes per minute of down time.

   - NT can also be configured to issue a low battery warning at least two minutes before shutdown. After the server runs on batteries for a while, the system will signal when it is two minutes away from shutdown. If the administration decides to select the Low Battery Signal option, the UPS characteristics remain grayed out.

   - The final configuration is Remote UPS shutdown. This signals NT to start shutting itself down.

The administrator can also configure a command file to execute before shut down. This command file could be designed to shut down services or send out notifications to end users of the pending shutdown.

Removing the UPS

To remove the UPS, double-click the UPS icon in Control Panel and clear the "Uninterruptible Power Supply is installed on:" box.

Installing and Configuring a Multimedia Device

1. Install the hardware (for example, a sound card) per manufacturer's instructions. Keep documentation on any hardware settings for the card.

2. To install the driver for the new device, select the Devices tab from the Multimedia Properties window. Click Add.

3. Choose from the list of available drivers to selected Unlisted or Updated driver. Click OK.

4. You will be presented with a window asking for the details of the hardware install. This may include things like the following:

   - **Direct Memory Access (DMA) channel** The DMA channel provides the component direct access to system memory. You may specify the DMA Channel buffer size by selecting Advanced Settings.

   - **I/O Address** The hexadecimal address of the Input/Output port the component will be using

   - **Interrupt (IRQ)** The channel the component will use to get the CPU's attention

5. Once the Driver window has been filled out, click OK to close the dialog box. Windows NT will go out and look for the device and tell you if it found it at the settings you provided.

6. Close the dialog box and restart the system when prompted by the operating system.

Multimedia devices can be configured by selecting the type of the device from the Multimedia Properties window. Again, the exact settings will vary with the card and system, but you may have Audio, Video, and MIDI.

1. Audio devices can be configured by selecting the Audio tab from the Multimedia Properties screen.

    A. Under Playback:

- You can use the slide bar to set the volume for device playback and also for recording.

- You can choose to show the volume control on the Taskbar by filling in the checkbox.

- You can choose your preferred device.

    B. Under Recording:

- You can use the slide bar to set the volume for recording.

- You can select the preferred device.

- You can select the preferred quality, including Radio Quality, CD Quality, or Telephone Quality.

2. Video devices can be configured by selecting the Video tab from the Multimedia Properties window. You can choose to show videos in a window by selecting Full screen.

3. MIDI drivers can be configured by selecting the MIDI tab from the Multimedia Properties window. MIDI output can use either a single instrument or a custom configuration.

Removing a Multimedia Device

From Control Panel, select the Devices tab from the Multimedia Properties window.

1. Highlight the device you wish to remove, and click Remove. Click Yes to tell the system you really know what you are doing.

2. After the device has been removed, restart the computer as prompted by the operating system.

Installing and Configuring a Display Driver

To change or update a display driver:

1. Log on to the computer as an administrator.

2. Open Control Panel.

3. Double-click the Display icon.

4. Select the Settings tab.

5. Click Display Type. If you know the type of adapter you are using and have the disks, select Change. Otherwise, select Detect.

6. Highlight the appropriate manufacturer and model number of your video card.

7. Select OK twice.

8. When you return to the Settings tab, select Test. If the test is completed successfully, click Yes to save the settings and click OK to restart the computer if prompted. You can also tweak the display from the Settings screen. Settings include:

   - **Color Palette**   Shows the number of colors your video subsystem can display

   - **Font Size**   Allows you to choose between small and large screen fonts

   - **Desktop Area**   How big is your desktop? The desktop is measured in pixels.

   - **Refresh Frequency**   How often the screen will redraw. The default is to use the hardware defaults.

After you have made changes to the display settings, you must test the new settings. If you like what you see, you will be asked if you saw the test bitmap correctly. If you did, click Yes and then click OK to close the Display dialog box.

Removing a Display Driver

Since all computers must have some sort of display, there is no way to remove the display driver other than overwriting it with a new driver. To install the new driver, see the section above.

Installing and Configuring Keyboard Drivers

Keyboard drivers are also installed and configured through Control Panel.

1. Log on as Administrator.

2. Open Control Panel.

3. Double-click Keyboard.

4. Select General.

5. Select Change.

6. Choose the appropriate driver or select Have Disk, then select OK.

7. When you return to the Select Device window, choose OK.

8. Click OK at the Keyboard General window and restart the computer when prompted.

Keyboard configuration revolves around three tabs: Speed, Input Locale, and General.

- The Speed tab allows you to select the repeat delay and the cursor blink rate.

- Input locale allows you to select the country codes necessary for your PC. You can use multiple layouts and set the keystrokes necessary to shift between the styles.

- The General tab just lets you choose your keyboard driver.

Removing the Keyboard Driver

Keyboard drivers are like video drivers—every system has to have one. To remove a keyboard driver, you must overwrite it with another driver. See the section above for installation of new keyboard drivers.

Installing and Configuring Mouse Drivers

To change or update a mouse driver:

1. Log on to the computer as Administrator.

2. Open Control Panel.

3. Double-click the Mouse icon.

4. Select the General tab.

5. Click Change.

6. Choose the appropriate driver, or select Have Disk.

7. Click OK after the file copy and installation has been completed.

8. Restart the computer when prompted.

Configuring the mouse is done using the three tabs across the top of the Mouse Properties page:

- **Buttons**   Choose the Buttons tab to select between a right- and a left-handed mouse. This tab will also let you select the double-click speed.

- **Pointers**   Choose from a variety of different mouse pointers to make the arrow easier to see, or just more interesting.

- **Motion**   You can choose how fast the pointer moves and also whether or not the pointer will snap to the default button in dialog boxes.

Removing the Mouse Driver

Mouse drivers are also like video drivers—every system has to have one. To remove a mouse driver, you must overwrite it with another driver. See the section above for installation of new mouse drivers.

Exam Essentials

On the whole, there is a lot of information on this objective, but not many test questions. The questions that do show up are of the off-the-wall variety.

Know how to install and configure SCSI Adapters and Drivers
If you get a question, it will likely revolve around the installation of the drivers, which is accomplished from Control Panel ➤ SCSI Adapters ➤ Drivers ➤ Add.

Know what the NT Backup Utility can back up.   The objectives say to study how to install and configure the drivers, but the test writers took a different approach. As you study, it is important to remember the hardware requirements to perform tape backups. By installing a tape backup unit on your NT server, you can use that TBU to back up the server and remote workstations. The NT Backup Utility will back up both NTFS and FAT file systems.

Know where and how to configure the UPS. The UPS is configured by selecting Control Panel ➤ UPS.

Know that there must be a serial cable between the UPS and the server. The 9-pin cable must be connected to one of the computer COM ports.

Know how to change the mouse driver. Know the tabs that are lurking under the Mouse icon of Control Panel.

Know which menu is used to set the Display Adapter type. It is in Control Panel, under the Display ➤ Settings tab ➤ Display types.

Know what the Keyboard icon on the Control Panel has to offer and what changes can be made from it. This is more for your personal information than for the exam.

Key Terms and Concepts

ATAPI: AT Application Programming Interface, a subset of the SCSI standard drivers.

NT Backup Utility: Utility provided with NT 4.0 that can back up local and remote computers. Backup will back up NTFS and FAT volumes.

SCSI: Small Computer System Interface. This is an interface providing a connecting point for a wide variety of peripherals, including storage devices and scanners.

TBU: Tape Backup Unit. A device used to archive data currently stored on a hard disk to a tape. The tape can then be stored away from the computer. This is called off-site storage.

UPS: Uninterruptable Power Supply. Supplies power during a power failure. May also condition power when the power is on.

Sample Questions

1. James needs to install a new driver for a SCSI adapter in his workstation. Where will he go to install the new driver?

   A. Workstation Manager

   B. Server Manager

   C. Control Panel

   D. Windows NT Diagnostics

Answer: C. SCSI devices are controlled by the SCSI Adapters icon in Control Panel.

2. Laura needs to provide backup support for an NT server and an NT workstation configured on the same network. How many Tape Backup Units will she need to buy?

   A. 1

   B. 2

   C. 3

   D. 4

Answer: A. Laura could purchase one tape backup unit, install it at the file server, and have it back up the workstation as well.

3. You have finished installing a UPS to your NT workstation. You have plugged it in and have plugged the workstation into the new unit. What is left to do?

   A. Configure the software using Administrative Tools

   B. Configure the software using User Manager

   C. Configure the software using Backup

   D. Configure the software using the UPS utility in Control Panel

Answer: D. The UPS is installed and configured using the UPS utility in Control Panel.

4. Which of the following items can be configured through Control Panel? (Select all that apply.)

   A. A disk array

   B. The mouse

   C. The display drivers

   D. The keyboard drivers

   Answer: B, C, D. Control Panel will provide support for display drivers, mouse drivers, and keyboard drivers.

Use Control Panel applications to configure a Windows NT Workstation computer in a given situation.

In the proceeding objective we discussed many of the tools used to configure the hardware components of your NT computer. This objective is concerned with the process of configuring the NT operating system itself.

Critical Information

Within Control Panel, you will find the System applet. This applet has three main functions:

- Startup and Shutdown properties

- Virtual memory configuration

- Set environmental variables

You can also use the Add/Remove Programs applet to change installation software or change the options you chose when installing the NT operating system.

Startup and Shutdown Properties

This is really two different sets of parameters: Startup and Shutdown. The system startup options allow you to configure which operating system the computer should boot to by default and how long the boot menu should stay on the screen before accepting that default.

The shutdown parameters are much more interesting. These parameters allow you to decide what actions NT should take in the event of a critical error, otherwise known as a *stop screen*. While critical errors are rare, they do bring your server to a crashing halt (hence the name stop screen). You have various choices concerning the actions to be taken by NT when it encounters a critical error, as listed in Table 2.3.

T A B L E 2.3: Recovery Options

Option	Explanation
Write an event to the system log	The system will write an event message to the system event log. These messages can be used to troubleshoot the cause of the error
Send an administrative alert	The system will send an alert to any members of the administrators group who are currently logged in.
Write debugging information to: \<path>	The operating system will attempt to write the contents of memory into a file for later analysis.
Overwrite any existing file	If you have chosen to write debugging information to a file, this option lets you decide whether or not to overwrite the last debugging information. Be aware that there is no compression—if you have 128MB of memory, this file will be 128MB.
Automatically reboot	If this option is chosen, the operating system will reboot itself if it encounters a stop screen.

Virtual Memory Configuration

Microsoft Windows NT has a mechanism that allows it to use hard disk space as if it were RAM. This allows the operating system to give applications more memory than is physically available on the computer—up to the limits of empty disk space. This is called *virtual memory*. The process of exchanging data between RAM and the hard disk is called *demand paging*. Whenever a process needs more memory, it is the responsibility of the operating system to allocate it. NT will look through the memory to see if any is available. If not, it will copy a section of memory into this virtual memory space on a hard disk. The system creates a file named PAGEFILE.SYS to act as repository for this virtual memory (by default, this file is placed on the disk with the most free space).

Moving the paging file to a less busy disk or splitting it into pieces scattered across multiple disks are some of the more common optimization techniques used in NT. They are also topics that are tested upon in multiple MCSE exams. Moving the paging file can have a great impact on performance. Microsoft suggests that the paging file not be on the same physical disk as the operating system files, since that disk will be busy handling other processes.

While the paging file will grow as needed, there is a delay built in to prevent wasted space (the file will never decrease in size on its own). Setting the initial size to the optimum can also increase performance.

You will need to know the procedure for configuring the Virtual Memory system (this process will be discussed in the Necessary Procedures section).

Set Environmental Variables

Variables are just strings of data that can be used by a process for configuration information. Some variables are used by multiple applications, while others are specific to an application or process. Many applications, for instance, know to look for a TEMP variable for the path to the directory where they should place their temporary files.

There are two basic types of variables in an NT environment: system and user. The administrator usually sets system variables and they apply to all users of the system. User variables, on the other hand, are specific to a particular user, and are usually set by that user. Both of these types of variables can be set in the Environment tab of the System Properties dialog box, as we'll see later. NT variables can also be set in an AUTOEXEC.BAT file. As an NT computer boots, it looks for an AUTOEXEC.BAT file and sets any variables it describes.

The value of a variable is not protected by the operating system. That is, the value can be dynamically changed while the system is running. NT sets the values of variables in the following order:

1. Those found in the AUTOEXEC.BAT file

2. System variables

3. User variables

Since the value of a variable is not protected, you could create a system variable that would pertain to all users, and then reset it on a user by user basis for exceptions. A good example would be the default location of files. For most users, you might want documents stored locally, so you would set a system variable to point to a local directory. For a few users, you might want documents to be placed on a server so that you could create a user variable for those users. Since NT reads the values in the order listed above, the user variable value would overwrite the system value.

You can prevent NT from looking for an AUTOEXEC.BAT file by editing the Registry. Add the registry parameter `ParseAutoexec:` `REG_SZ = 0` to the `\HKEY_CURRENT_USER\SOFTWARE\Microsoft\` `WindowsNT\CurrentVersion\Winlogon` key.

SEE ALSO   For more information on editing the Registry, see Chapter 6.

Customizing the NT Installation

If you need to change any of the choices you made (add or remove options) during the NT installation process, you can do so within the Add/Remove Programs window.

You can also add or remove any programs that use a SETUP.EXE or INSTALL.EXE program for installation. Just run the EXE to install or highlight the software in the list, and choose Remove.

Necessary Procedures

Now that we've discussed the options available, we can look at the procedures involved in configuring your Windows NT workstation.

Setting Startup/Shutdown Parameters

1. From within Control Panel, open the System Properties window.

2. Chose the Startup/Shutdown tab.

From here you can set which operating system will be chosen by default and how long the boot menu will remain on the screen. You can also decide what actions NT should take to recover from a critical error.

Configuring Virtual Memory

1. Once again, within the System Properties window, choose the Performance tab.

2. Click the Change button to configure virtual memory.

Here you can determine which drive or drives should hold the paging file and the initial and maximum sizes of that file.

Setting System and User Variables

Within the System Properties window, choose the Environment tab.

Here you can change, add, or delete system and user variables.

Changing the Options Installed on Your NT Workstation

1. Within Control Panel, open the Add/Remove Programs Properties window.

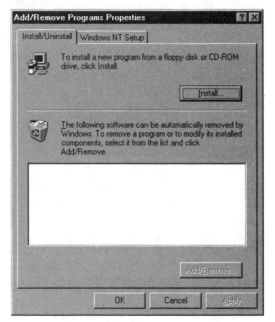

2. To install a new program, click the Install button.

3. To remove an installed application, highlight it in the list and click the Add/Remove button.

Changing the NT Options Installed

1. Within the Add/Remove Programs Properties window, choose the Windows NT Setup tab.

2. Check those items that you wish to install or uncheck those you wish to remove.

3. If you wish to be more specific, highlight a component and click Details. You will then be shown all of the specific components of that choice. Within the Details dialog box, check those items you want to install or uncheck those you wish to remove.

Exam Essentials

Microsoft is pretty proud of the fact that a user can control their own NT Workstation environment (even though there are tons of ways to lock down the configuration). It is important that you understand the basics of system configuration if you are going to support an NT environment.

Know the tools necessary to accomplish all of the listed procedures regarding Control Panel applications. While there are a few topics to remember for the test, most of this objective concerns the actual procedures involved in making changes. Review the steps involved carefully. You will probably see a question that asks Where would you do *xxx*?

Know the recovery options available in the Startup/Shutdown tab of the System Properties window. See Table 2.3 for details.

Know what steps are suggested for optimizing the virtual memory environment. Do not place the paging file on the same disk as the <WINNT_ROOT> directory. Split the paging file into multiple parts and spread them across multiple hard drives. Set the initial size to the necessary value to avoid delays in adjustment.

Know the two types of variables and which users they will affect. *System variables* affect all users on the system. *User variables* affect only a particular user.

Know the order in which NT gathers and sets the values of variables. (1) AUTOEXEC.BAT; (2) System; (3) User.

Key Terms and Concepts

Demand Paging: The process of moving data from RAM to virtual memory.

Stop Screen: A term used to refer the data NT displays when it encounters a critical error.

Variable: A string of data set to a value. This data can be used as a configuration parameter for a process.

Virtual memory: Hard disk space used as an extension to RAM in the computer.

Sample Questions

1. In what order will variables be set?

   A. User variables

   B. Those found in the AUTOEXEC.BAT file

   C. System variables

   Answer: B, C, A. System variables are set in the following order: AUTOEXEC.BAT; system; user.

2. Which of the following are recommendations for optimizing the virtual memory system?

   A. Place your paging file on the same disk as your operating system files.

   B. Do not place your paging file on the same disk as your operating system files.

   C. Split the paging file across multiple hard drives.

   D. Make one big paging file and place it on a key disk.

   Answer: B, C. Remember: You should split the workload across disks to optimize performance.

Configure server-based installation for wide-scale deployment in a given situation.

A server-based installation is simply providing a central point for the storage of the NT Installation files. The files are placed on a server's hard drive or mounted as a shared CD. You then boot the workstation so it can find the network and access the installation files from the share. For IS teams that do tons of installations all over the company, this is a great deal. For the system administrator who does four or five client installs a year, this may fall into the more trouble than it is worth category.

The test writers seemed to like this category. There are some questions on the ways in which to configure and access the server.

Critical Information

The concept is simple. To do an over-the-network installation, you access files normally stored on the NT 4.0 CD from the potential NT Workstation and start the installation. Before you can access files stored on the distribution server, there is some work to be done.

There are two ways to provide access to the files from the NT 4.0 CD. First, you can put the NT Installation CD into a CD Tower or a shared CD-ROM and share various folders. An optional method, if you have the available hard disk space, is to XCOPY the NT Installation CD to a drive and share the various folders. If you opt for this method, be sure to use the /S parameter to the XCOPY command to get all the subfolders copied. In reality, you don't even have to copy over the whole CD, just the \i386 folder and probably the \DRVLIB folder.

TIP You can also use NT Explorer to copy the folders to the disk. Be sure the default settings are changed to allow files with extensions like .DLL, .SYS, and .VXD to be displayed and copied. Default settings for Explorer are changed by selecting View ➤ Options, and then, in the Hidden files list, clicking Show all files.

Why would you go to the trouble of copying all the folders down to a drive when just sharing the CD works just as well? In a word, speed. The shared CD method is much slower than accessing the files from a server's hard disk, but you are not taking up as much disk space.

TIP If you are using a RISC-based computer, the over-the-network method can only be used for upgrades or reinstalls. Original installs must be done from the CD.

Necessary Procedures

How does the installation process discussed in the first objective of this chapter vary if the files are being accessed from a share point rather than from a CD-ROM? In reality, there are not many differences. You configure the new workstation to access the network. Once you have accessed the network, you can authenticate and access the share where the WINNT.EXE is located. Run WINNT.EXE from the share, and it will install the OS to the new computer. In effect, you are using a share point on another server as the NT Workstation Installation Server.

While this seems to be a very easy way of installing NT, the basics must apply. Your potential workstation must be able to access the network to get to the share point. To communicate with the server, the potential workstation (and all workstations, for that matter), must be running a network client.

Creating Network Client Disks

Once your original NT server is installed, you can create a set of network client disks. This will provide the basic communications to the network. In order to create this set of disks, you can access the client administration tools from the Administrative Tools menu, located on the NT server.

Entering into the Administrative Tools menu, you will see the Network Client Administrator utility. Selecting this brings up the menu shown below.

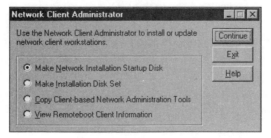

If you check Make Network Installation Startup Disk, you will create a DOS disk that can be used to connect to a network share and install the Windows 95 or Microsoft Network client for DOS and Windows.

To create the disk:

1. Select the Make Network Installations Startup Disk radio button, and click Continue. This brings up the Share Network Client Installation Files dialog box.

2. Enter the path to the client files. If you are using the CD, the path will point to the \CLIENTS directory. This is where the system will copy files *from*.

3. Now you have to make a decision. Are you going to leave the CD on the server and share the CD, are you going to copy the client files to a folder on the server hard drive and then create a share pointing to the folder, or do you already have a folder set up? As you can see in the example above, the client folder on the target server will be located at c:\clients. There is going to be a share name created called clients, and it will take up to 64MB of disk space to accomplish this task. After you have made your decision, select OK.

4. Now the server is configured to work with the clients, but you need a disk to carry around and use on the all workstations. After all the information is copied to your servers folder in step 3, you will get a message that tells you 254 directories were just added and 1141 files had been copied. Memorize this piece of minutia to use at your next cocktail party, and click OK to continue.

5. The Target Workstation Configuration dialog box comes up. Here, choose the size of the disk (Does anyone really still use 5.25-inch disks anymore?) and the network client to install—either Network client 3.0 for DOS/Windows or the Windows 95 client. The final section asks about the NIC that is installed in your workstations. There is a drop-down menu with a large selection. Once you have made your choices, select OK to continue.

NOTE A quick perusal of the list of NICs failed to turn up any selection for PCMCIA cards for laptops. Also, there is no Browse feature to supply your own driver.

---

6. Next, a dialog box appears with the Network Startup Disk Configuration selections. This allows you to enter a computer name, along with the User's Name, the Domain, and the Network Protocol. You can specify whether this computer will be using DHCP to acquire an IP address or if it will have a static IP address. You also select where the destination for the new disk is located. After filling in the appropriate selections, again, click OK.

7. The confirmation screen comes up, reiterating all the information you have just entered. Before clicking OK, make sure the disk in the A:\ drive has been formatted with the appropriate version of DOS and is a system disk. If all the above criteria are met, click OK to continue. This will create the Startup Disk.

Now, it might just be easier to create a set of disks to carry around with you, especially if you only have need of one or two clients. In that case, you can select Make Installation Disk Set from the Network

Client Administrator screen. You will be prompted for the client or service and the drive to create the disks in. Once that information has been provided, you will be told how many disks you really need. Click OK to continue.

Exam Essentials

Know how to start the over-the-network installation.   Before an over-the-network installation can be attempted, the distribution server must be configured. The \i386 directory and the \DRVLIB directory must be shared. Connect to a \i386 share point and execute either WINNT.EXE or WINNT32.EXE (if upgrading from NT 3.51).

Key Terms and Concepts

\DRVLIB folder: A folder on the NT Installation CD-ROM where drivers are located. This is an optional folder that can be XCOPIED to the distribution server.

\i386 folder: A folder on the NT Installation CD-ROM where WINNT.EXE can be found. Should be XCOPIED to the distribution server.

Distribution Server: An NT server configured to provide network access to the files normally found on the NT Installation CD-ROM.

Network Client: Software services run at the client workstation to provide communication with a server.

NT Explorer: Operating system graphical utility that can be used to copy files and subdirectories. If you are using NT Explorer to copy folders and subfolders to a distribution server, the default settings must be changed to allow the utility to show hidden files.

Unattended Installation: Allows a generic automated installation of NT Server. Answers are provided from a file called UNATTEND.TXT. There is a sample UNATTEND.TXT file on the NT Server

Resource Kit, or the file can be generated using the Setup Manager Utility on the NT Server Installation CD-ROM.

WINNT.EXE: The executable that starts the Windows NT Installation Wizard.

XCOPY: Operating system command line utility that can be used to copy files and subdirectories. Used with the /S parameter (copy subdirectories) to copy directories from the NT Installation CD-ROM to the distribution server.

Sample Questions

1. Which folders need to be copied to the distribution server from the NT Workstation Installation CD?

   A. \WINNT

   B. \i386

   C. \DRVLIB

   D. \ADMIN

   E. \TOOLS

   Answer: B and C. The \DRVLIB directory and \i386 folders need to be copied to the distribution server.

2. Which GUI-based utility can you use to copy the \i386 and the \DRVLIB folders to the distribution server? (Select all that apply.)

   A. Administration Manager

   B. User Manager for Domains

   C. User Manager

   D. Microsoft NT Explorer

   E. XCOPY

   Answer: D. Microsoft NT Explorer. XCOPY is not a GUI-based utility.

Upgrade to Windows NT Workstation 4.0 in a given situation.

One of the most demanding tasks that an administrator will face is that of keeping up-to-date. Hardware changes on an almost daily rate—what you ordered yesterday is out of date today (and usually 50 percent cheaper to boot!) Upgrades are a major source of income for software companies, so we face new versions every time we turn around.

Critical Information

There are numerous variables to keep in mind when upgrading to Windows NT 4. This objective concerns each of the possible scenarios that you might encounter.

Upgrading Windows 95 to Windows NT 4

Because the registries of the two operating systems are completely different, there is no upgrade path from Windows 95 to Windows NT. If you are faced with the task of moving an environment from Windows 95 to Windows NT, you will have to completely install NT and then reinstall any applications so that they can register themselves with the NT registry. You should also be aware that NT cannot read from a FAT32 partition—if you have taken advantage of the benefits of FAT32 in your environment, you will have to completely back up your data, destroy the partition, and start from scratch.

Upgrading from Windows NT 3.51

There are a lot of variables involved with this upgrade:

- Was the original computer an NT Workstation or Server?
- Will the new operating system be Workstation or Server?

- If Server, will it be a domain controller?

We'll look at each of these possibilities in this section. Microsoft has written a utility specifically designed to upgrade from earlier versions of NT: WINNT32.EXE. This program was specifically written to run under the NT operating system, taking full advantage of the 32-bit architecture. It is fast and runs as a background process. This means that it could conceivably upgrade a production server with very little impact on the users attached at the time.

WARNING While Microsoft implies that WINNT32.EXE could be run on a server while it was in production, it could be dangerous. While it *should* be safe, you are making some major changes to the operating system. Upgrade your servers during non-business hours to ensure minimum impact on your users.

When a Windows NT computer is upgraded, the process preserves the following:

- User and group accounts
- Network configuration
- Desktop
- Preferences set for administrative tools

Upgrading from NT Workstation 3.51

Table 2.4 lists the options available when upgrading from version 3.51 to 4.0.

T A B L E 2.4: NT Workstation 3.51 Upgrade

Upgrade To	Can Be Done?	Bottom Line
Windows NT Workstation 4.0	Yes	Easy, simple process—basically moving to same type of environment

T A B L E 2.4: NT Workstation 3.51 Upgrade *(continued)*

Upgrade To	Can Be Done?	Bottom Line
Windows NT Server Member Server	Yes	Changing someone's desktop to a server is not done very often, but it can be accomplished.
Windows NT Server Domain Controller	No	If it wasn't a domain controller to begin with, it can't be one when you are done.

Upgrading from NT Server 3.51 Member Server

Table 2.5 lists the options available when upgrading an NT 3.51 Member Server to NT 4.0.

T A B L E 2.5: NT Server 3.51 Member Server Upgrade

Upgrade To	Can Be Done?	Bottom Line
Windows NT Workstation 4.0	No	If it wasn't a workstation before the upgrade, it can't be one after.
Windows NT Server Member Server	Yes	Basically upgrading to the same type of server
Windows NT Server Domain Controller	No	If it wasn't a domain controller to begin with, it can't be one when you are done.

Upgrading from NT Server 3.51 Domain Controller

Table 2.6 lists the options available when upgrading an NT 3.51 Domain Controller.

TABLE 2.6: NT Server 3.51 Domain Controller Upgrade

Upgrade To	Can Be Done?	Bottom Line
Windows NT Workstation 4.0	No	If it wasn't a workstation before the upgrade, it can't be one after.
Windows NT Server Member Server	No	If it wasn't a member server before the upgrade, it can't be one after.
Windows NT Server Domain Controller	Yes	Basically upgrading to the same type of server

Necessary Procedures

The same procedure is performed to accomplish all of the different types of upgrades described in the Critical Information section.

On the Windows NT 4.0 CD-ROM, in the directory appropriate for your hardware (i386 for Intel-based computers), run the WINNT32 .EXE application. It will automatically sense that there is an earlier version of NT on the computer and ask if you would like to upgrade. Answer Yes, and follow the instructions.

Exam Essentials

The exam essentials for this objective concern what can be upgraded and what can they be upgraded to.

Know that there is no upgrade path from Windows 95 to Windows NT. Because the registries are different, there is no upgrade path. You must install NT and then reinstall your applications. Also remember that Windows NT cannot read a FAT 32 partition—if you have used FAT32 on your Windows 95 computer, you will have to back up all of your data and delete the partition.

Know what tool should be used to upgrade from earlier versions of NT. WINNT32.EXE is the utility specifically designed to upgrade from earlier versions of NT.

Know the list of things that are preserved during an upgrade. User and group accounts, network configuration, desktop settings, and preferences set in the administrative tools.

Know what type of NT computer an existing NT 3.51 Workstation can be upgraded to—and which types it cannot become. An NT 3.51 Workstation can be upgraded to an NT 4.0 Workstation or Member Server, but it cannot become a NT 4.0 Domain Controller.

Know what type of NT computer an existing NT 3.51 Member Server can be upgraded to—and which types it cannot become. An existing NT 3.51 member server can only be upgraded to the same role; it cannot become either a workstation or domain controller.

Know what type of NT computer an existing NT 3.51 Domain Controller can be upgraded to—and which types it cannot become. An existing NT 3.51 Domain Controller can be upgraded to the same role; it cannot be downgraded to the status of member server or workstation.

Key Terms and Concepts

Backup Domain Controller (BDC): A domain controller that receives a copy of the domain accounts database from the PDC.

Domain Controller: An NT Server that holds a copy of the domain accounts database. Because it holds the user account database, a domain controller can be used to authenticate users as they log on to the network.

Member Server: An NT Server computer that does not hold a copy of the domain accounts database.

Primary Domain Controller (PDC): A domain controller that holds the master copy of the domain accounts database. This computer is responsible for updating the copy held by each BDC.

Sample Questions

1. Which of the following tools is used to upgrade from Windows 95 to Windows NT 4.0?

   A. UPGRADE.EXE

   B. The Upgrade applet in Control Panel.

   C. WINNT /U:95

   D. There is no upgrade path from Windows 95 to Windows NT.

   Answer: D. Because the registries are different, there is no upgrade path.

2. Which of the following tools should be used to upgrade from Windows NT 3.51 to Windows NT 4.0?

   A. WINNT.EXE

   B. WINNT32.EXE

   C. UPGRADE.EXE

   D. There is no upgrade option.

   Answer: B. WINN32.EXE is the tool used to upgrade from NT 3.51 to NT 4.0.

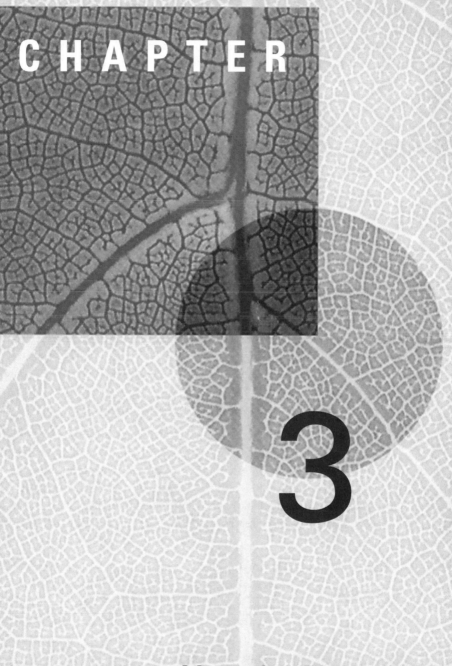

CHAPTER

3

Managing Resources

Microsoft Exam Objectives Covered in This Chapter:

Create and manage local user accounts and local group accounts to meet given requirements. *(pages 107 – 117)*

Set up and modify user profiles. *(pages 117 – 131)*

Set up shared folders and permissions. *(pages 131 – 143)*

Set permissions on NTFS partitions, folders, and files. *(pages 143 – 154)*

Install and configure printers in a given environment. *(pages 154 – 161)*

One of the things that sets Windows NT Workstation apart from all the other operating systems out there is sharing. More than one person can share a workstation and the data on that workstation can be shared or secured, depending on the owner's preference. There are other desktop operating systems that provide some sort of security, but NT is the most robust.

That very broad overview is great for discussions over your favorite cold beverage, but it tends to get complicated really quickly when the amount of people with something to share on a single workstation grows to 5 or 10, or more. It is especially complicated when *you* have to provide others with the opportunity to share files and peripherals on individual desktops throughout the entire company. It can be a daunting task. However, it doesn't have to be that way. As you study this chapter, you will find ways to cut that task down to size.

What exactly does managing resources mean? In Chapter 2, hardware resources were discussed. You learned how to get the most out of your disk drive subsystem, your communication devices, SCSI devices, and tape backup units. Those resources are all *things*. How do you manage the resources that are living, breathing parts of your network—your end users?

Create and manage local user accounts and local group accounts to meet given requirements.

Why do users need accounts? Why can't someone just sit down and use a computer the way they did with DOS or Windows or even Windows 95? Windows 95 did have some desktop security built in, but realistically it was all but non-existent.

With Windows NT Workstation, every user that logs on to the computer must have a user name and a password to access the account. Giving the user a user name gives NT the opportunity to store certain information about the user for retrieval at a later time. In addition, assignments can be made for the user—they can have things like their own user home directory and profile path.

Critical Information

Security of the system starts with the user. A user account is created and a password is assigned for the user using the User Manager utility. The information on the user account is stored in the Security Account Manager database, or SAM.

SEE ALSO For the purposes of this book, a user account is one created on a particular computer. For the user to attach to a domain, they will also need to have a user account created for that domain. For more information on user accounts in a networked environment, see *MCSE: NT Server 4 Study Guide, Second Edition* by Matthew Strebe and Charles Perkins, with James Chellis (Sybex, 1998).

In addition to user accounts, you can also use the User Manager utility to create Local Group accounts. A local group is simply a group of users brought together for a specific purpose. For example, the NT Workstation has the company accounting software stored on it. Over the course of a week, five different people may access the computer, but only three of these will need to access the accounting software. In this case, the local administrator can create an accounting group, and give the accounting group permission to use the accounting software and see information stored in the accounting data directory. The computer can be configured so that others using the computer can be excluded from even knowing that the accounting software or data is stored on this computer. If you are a network administrator, think of this workstation as a mini-server.

To ease the burden of trying to figure out when and how to create users and groups, NT has provided you with some defaults. These are shown in Table 3.1.

T A B L E 3.1: Default Account Types

	Type	Description
Administrator	User	Built-in account for administering the computer
Guest	User	Built in account for guest access to the computer
Administrators	Group	Members of this local group can administer the computer
Backup Operators	Group	Members can bypass file security to backup files
Guests	Group	Users granted guest access to the computer or domain
Power Users	Group	Members can share directories or printers
Replicator	Group	Supports file replication in a domain
Users	Group	Ordinary Users

In addition to setting security preferences for each user, you can make some global settings using System Policies.

Necessary Procedures

To complete this objective, it is necessary to know how to create a user or group and how to add users to the group. Each of these tasks is completed from the User Manager utility. The User Manager utility is accessed through Programs ➤ Administrative Tools (Common) ➤ User Manager.

Creating a New User

To create a new user, start User Manager while you are logged on as an administrative user.

1. From the User Manager screen, select the top menu option of User ➤ New User. This will bring up the New User screen shown below.

2. There are text boxes for providing the Username and Full Name, a description of the user, and assigning and confirming a password.

3. The box User Must Change Password at Next Logon is checked by default. This forces the user to come up with a different password.

4. If you are creating a "system" user—a user than will be used by a program or service—you may not want the user to be able to change the password. The same may be true of a generic user you are creating. In either case, check the box and the user cannot change the password.

5. Checking the box Password Never Expires gives the user the right to keep the same password forever. This would be a wise idea for the "system" user discussed in step 4.

WARNING Checking the Password Never Expires box for an individual user will override any system-wide settings an administrator may attempt to enforce.

---

6. Checking the box Account Disabled temporarily disables an account. You may want to disable an account if the person is leaving for an extended time. You want the account to be available when they get back, but you do not want anyone using it while they are gone.

7. Clicking the Groups button brings up the Group Memberships screen shown below. You will notice that you can add or remove this user from the groups created on the computer.

NOTE   The user may not be removed from membership in the
Users default group.

8. Clicking the Profile button brings up the User Environment Profile screen shown below. Here you can specify where the user
   profile is stored, where the logon script can be found, and where
   the user's home directory is located. You can also connect a drive
   letter to the home directory.

9. Clicking the Dialin button from the New User dialog box brings up
   the Dialin Information window shown below. This screen will let
   you grant this user dial-in privileges to a Remote Access Service
   Server (RAS) and specify how much security is needed. If No Call
   Back is selected, the user can connect without any verification.
   Selecting the Set By Caller radio button will prompt the user for a
   phone number where they can be called back, and the Preset To
   radio button means the user will be called back at that preset
   number.

```
┌─────────────────────────────────────────────────┐
│ Dialin Information                            [X] │
├─────────────────────────────────────────────────┤
│  User:                              ┌──────────┐  │
│                                     │    OK    │  │
│                                     └──────────┘  │
│                                     ┌──────────┐  │
│                                     │  Cancel  │  │
│  ☐ Grant dialin permission to user  └──────────┘  │
│  ┌─ Call Back ──────────────────┐   ┌──────────┐  │
│  │                              │   │   Help   │  │
│  │  ◉ No Call Back              │   └──────────┘  │
│  │                              │                 │
│  │  ○ Set By Caller             │                 │
│  │                              │                 │
│  │  ○ Preset To:  ┌───────────┐ │                 │
│  │                └───────────┘ │                 │
│  └──────────────────────────────┘                 │
└─────────────────────────────────────────────────┘
```

Creating a New Group

To create a new group:

1. Start User Manager while you are logged on as an administrative user.

2. From the User Manager screen, select the top menu option of User ➤ New Local Group. This will bring up the New Local Group dialog box shown below. From here, you can create a new group, give it a name and a description, and add users to the group.

```
┌─────────────────────────────────────────────────┐
│ New Local Group                               [X] │
├─────────────────────────────────────────────────┤
│  Group Name:  ┌────────────────────┐ ┌─────────┐ │
│               └────────────────────┘ │   OK    │ │
│  Description: ┌────────────────────┐ └─────────┘ │
│               └────────────────────┘ ┌─────────┐ │
│                      ┌──────────────┐ │ Cancel  │ │
│                      │Show Full Names│ └─────────┘ │
│  Members:            └──────────────┘ ┌─────────┐ │
│  ┌──────────────────────────────────┐ │  Help   │ │
│  │ 🧑 Administrator                  │ └─────────┘ │
│  │                                  │             │
│  │                                  │ ┌─────────┐ │
│  │                                  │ │  Add... │ │
│  │                                  │ └─────────┘ │
│  │                                  │ ┌─────────┐ │
│  │                                  │ │ Remove  │ │
│  └──────────────────────────────────┘ └─────────┘ │
└─────────────────────────────────────────────────┘
```

Copying a User

While not specifically covered in the objectives, you may get a test question on what it takes to copy a user or when you would do it. Copying a user is effective if you have a new person coming into the organization replacing or working with another person. The new person would need exactly the same rights and permissions as the current user, so rather than reinventing the wheel, you can just copy the current user, change the user name and password, and the account is finished.

To copy a user:

1. Log on to the computer as a user with administrative rights.

2. Start User Manager.

3. Highlight the user to be copied.

4. From the User menu on the top of the screen, choose copy or press F8.

5. You are now presented with the Copy of UserX screen. Fill out the Username, Full Name, Password, and Confirm Password, make any changes to Groups, Profile, or Dialin and click OK. The user will be created with the same attributes as the template user.

Editing a Current User

Again, this is not addressed specifically in the objective, but there may be questions on it.

1. While logged on to the computer as an administrative user, open User Manager.

2. Double-click the user you would like to edit.

3. Make what ever changes are necessary.

4. Click OK to close the window.

Editing a Current Group

You will frequently have to add or remove users to/from an existing group.

1. While logged on to the computer as an administrative user, open User Manager.

2. Double-click the Group you would like to edit.

3. Make whatever changes are necessary.

4. Click OK to close the window.

WARNING   If you add or remove a user to a group, the change will not take place until the user logs off and logs back on again.

Exam Essentials

The entire section on Managing Resources is the source of lots of questions on the exam. This objective gets its share of those questions and some of the questions are rather esoteric.

Know what it means to create a user account on a computer.
When you create a user account on a computer, that account is just for that computer. If you want to access a network, the user must have another account created on the network server, either an NT server or another network operating system.

Know how to create a user account.   User accounts are created using the User Manager utility. If the guest account is disabled for security purposes, each user should have their own individual account.

Know the system-created user accounts.   The system creates two accounts. The Administrator account can be used to administer the system and the guest account. The Guest account is given limited access to the system and is banned from seeing any files or folder that are private. For security purposes, the Guest account may be disabled.

Key Terms and Concepts

Account Disabled: Temporarily closing a user account.

Administrator: A default user created on an NT Workstation who has full rights to the workstation, the file system, and the resources.

Administrators: A default group created on an NT Workstation. Members of the Administrators group have full rights to the workstation, the file system, and resources.

Backup Operators: A default group created on an NT Work-station. Members of the Backup Operators group have file system rights suspended so they can archive the files.

Dialin Information: A user property that sets guidelines for the way the user will be treated when logging on to a Remote Access Service (RAS) Server.

Guest: A default user created on an NT Workstation. The Guest account has no rights to any secured files, folders, or resources. For security purposes, the Guest account may be disabled.

Guests: A default group created on an NT Workstation. Members of the Guests group have the same rights and permissions as does the Guest user.

Home Directory: A unique folder for each user, where that user may store data.

Local Group: A group of users created by an administrator on an NT Workstation.

Password: Part of the NT security schema to authenticate a user to the Security Account Manager (SAM) database.

Permissions: Permissions are granted to users to allow them access to files and folders.

Power Users: A default group created on an NT Workstation. Members of the Power Users can create shares to folders and printers.

Profile: The profile is information on the way the end-user had the system, especially the desktop, configured.

Profile path: This points to the share where the Profile is stored.

Remote Access Service (RAS):   Service run on an NT Server that allows a dialup connection to the server.

Replicator: Default group created on an NT Workstation that supports file replication in a domain.

Rights: Rights are granted to users to allow them access to resources attached to the computer or network.

Security Account Manager (SAM) Database: Database where security information is stored.

Small Computer System Interface (SCSI):   A type of hardware interface allowing up to 14 devices to be hooked up to a single controller card.

Tape Backup Unit: A hardware device used with specialized software to archive the data on a workstation or server.

User Name: Unique name given to a user to allow them to authenticate to the NT Workstation or to a domain. The User Name may bear little or no resemblance to the user's real name.

Users: A default group created on an NT Workstation that contains all the users assigned to that workstation.

Sample Questions

1. When you set up the NT Workstation, you created a system where passwords were set to expire every 30 days. The user BrandiceC never has to change her password. What may be the cause of this phenomenon?

   A. BrandiceC is a member of the Administrators group.

   B. BrandiceC has Password Never Expires checked on her User Properties screen.

   C. BrandiceC does not have an account created on this computer.

   D. You cannot set a computer-wide parameter like how often the passwords expire.

   Answer: B. Checking Password Never Expires on the user property screen will override any computer-wide setting.

2. Two people must share a computer. The Guest account has been disabled. What is the minimal configuration that you must create to make this happen?

   A. Two user accounts

   B. Two user accounts and a group

C. Two user accounts and two groups

D. Two user accounts, individual passwords, and logon scripts

Answer: A. You must create at least two user accounts. The user accounts do not have to have a password assigned, nor must they belong to any group other than Users.

3. Bobbi has an account created on an NT Workstation that is a part of a network that has two separate domains. When the user account is created on the computer, how many domain user accounts are created?

   A. None

   B. One

   C. Two

   D. Three accounts are created, one for the workstation and one for each domain.

   Answer: A. Creating a user account on a computer does not necessarily mean that a user account has been created for the domain.

Set up and modify user profiles.

Wouldn't it be nice to be able to make some universal settings for all users? Things like making sure they use the corporate logo as wallpaper, or making sure the network hookup is just the way you want it. It would also be nice to be able to control some universal settings, things that deal with all the users of a specific computer. This is the flexibility that you gain when you understand user profiles and system policies. If you understand these two tools you can take control of your user's desktops and configure it the same way for each user in a given situation.

TIP Paying close attention to this section will not only help you take control of the desktop, it will also help you on the exam. This area is one of the exam writers' favorites!

Critical Information

A *user profile* is configuration information that is saved on a user-by-user basis. This includes *all* the user settings of the Windows NT environment, such as the desktop arrangement, personal program groups and the program items in those groups, screen colors, screen savers, network connections, printer connections, mouse settings, window size and position, and more. When a user logs on, the user's profile is loaded and the user's Windows NT environment is configured according to that profile. In addition to each user having a profile, you can create and save a mandatory user profile, so an individual user or all users have to have certain things on their desktop, just the way you want it.

User profiles contain those settings and configuration options specific to the individual user—such as installed applications, desktop icons, color options, and so forth. This profile is built in part from System Policy information (for example, those things that a user has access to and those things that the user can and cannot change) and in part from permitted, saved changes that a user makes to customize his or her desktop.

User *profiles* deal with a specific user. User *policies* deal with all users of a computer. User policies are set to configure the following settings:

- **Maximum Password Age** If you work in an environment where security is not an issue, you may choose to have system passwords never expire. If security is an issue, there is a setting that forces passwords to be changed every so many days. Keep in mind that the default is set to 42 days. While decreasing the amount of the time a password is active may make great sense from a security point of view, the chances of your users understanding why they have to change their passwords so often is slim to none.

- **Minimum Password Age**   This forces a user to keep a password at least a certain period of time. By default, users can change their passwords immediately.

- **Minimum Password Length**   How long must a password be? If no changes are made, blank passwords are permitted. If you increase the minimum password length, your users will have to start thinking before typing.

- **Password Uniqueness**   We have all heard the stories of the user who kept the same password for years and years. By the time the user left the company, everyone knew his/her password. This is almost as bad as no password at all. Password Uniqueness, which is turned off by default, will remember a number of passwords, forcing the user to come up with something new every so often. You get to choose the history list.

- **Account Lockout**   This is an attempt to prevent hackers from attempting to access your network over and over again. If Account Lockout is enabled and someone tries to log on unsuccessfully so many times, the account will be locked and the user will not be able to log on to the system. You can set the number of bad logon attempts, reset the count after so many minutes, and set the lockout duration. Once the account is locked, the hacker doesn't know if it is locked for 10 minutes or an hour and 10 minutes. At that point, there are probably easier networks to attack.

- **Forcibly disconnect remote users from server when logon hours expire**   Selecting this button will cause users who are working when the allowed time expires to be kicked off the system. If this is not selected, the remote server user can continue to use the system, but just cannot open any new sessions.

- **Users must log on in order to change password**   This selection means that your users must change their password before it expires. If it expires, then the end user will have to contact the Administrator, and the Administrator will have to reset the password.

NOTE   While user policies are not covered in the exam objectives, the topic dovetails so closely with user profiles that it requires at least a brief mention.

Local User Profiles

User profiles come in two flavors: local and roaming. The local user profile is defined for a user or groups of users (i.e., they all log on using the same logon ID, like dataentry) on a single machine. A roaming user profile is used in a networked environment. The profile is stored in a central repository and no matter which NT Workstation the user accesses, the profile will follow.

User profiles store information on how a user has configured his computing environment. This involves everyday information, such as:

- the last few documents accessed
- share and printer connections
- bookmarks in Help

The subdirectory that contains the user profile information is \WINNT\ PROFILES. When NT Workstation is installed, it automatically creates three subfolders under the profiles directory. These are for the Administrator, All Users, and Default Users. When you create a new user, and that user accesses the system, there will be a folder created for them. As you can see in Figure 3.1, BrandiceC has logged on to the computer for the first time. The figure is a shot of her profiles folder.

FIGURE 3.1: Contents of Profiles directory for BrandiceC

Did you notice a file called NTUSER.DAT? This is the file that contains all the registry entries specific to that end user. There are also folders for Application Data, the Desktop, Favorites, Personal, Start Menu, and other information that pertains to a specific user.

How does the User Profile work? When a user logs on to a system for the first time, the system knows there is no local user profile, so it checks for a network to look for a Roaming User Profile. If there is no Roaming User Profile, NT creates a User Profile subdirectory for the user in the \WINNT\PROFILES directory. NT then needs to provide the user with some of the basics, so it gets the information from the \WINNT\PROFILES\DEFAULT user directory.

At this point the User has the default desktop and default settings. Any changes that the user makes will be stored in the User Profile for the new user. NT never forgets a friend! The next time the user logs on to the local machine, the user will be presented with the system just the way it was left.

There are occasions when you do not want a user to be able to change the desktop. Experience has shown that the administrator's worst nightmare is not the end user that is afraid of the mouse: it is usually the tech-weenie-wannabe end user that will keep you up all night. How do you keep this user from changing the screen colors, redoing the wallpaper with the latest scan from the SI swimsuit issue, or otherwise being obnoxious? Easy, just configure the system just the way you want it for the tech-weenie-wannabe and save the settings by logging out. Go back into the system as an administrative user and change the name of the NTUSER.DAT file to NTUSER.MAN. Adding the *.MAN extension changes the file to a mandatory profile. The user can change the desktop in a variety of fashions, but none of the changes will be retained.

WARNING You will probably want to highlight the filename NTUSER.MAN. It will come up again, probably when there are a hundred dollars on the line. Yep, you could consider this a hint.

Roaming User Profiles

With a roaming user profile, a profile is created and centrally stored. When a user logs into a workstation on the network, the workstation checks for a roaming user profile, finds it, and *voila* the desktop looks just the same, no matter where you log on from.

What happens if there is a local user profile and a roaming user profile and the local user is more recent? NT is nothing if not polite; it will ask which profile you want to use. Otherwise, it will just go with the roaming user profile. When the user logs off, the new profile is saved (if it is not mandatory or if the user has not logged on as guest) and any changes that have been made are saved for posterity.

Now that you know how to standardize your desktop, be sure to share the wealth. There are others on the network that roam too, so you may want to give them the flexibility of a roaming profile.

TIP The path to the roaming user profile is specified using User Manager.

System Policies

Here is another one of those topics that doesn't show up in the objectives, but does show up on the test. Actually, this topic is covered as part of the NT Server exam. If you haven't studied for the NT Server exam, you would have no clue you needed to know this stuff. That is why you bought the book, right?

System Policies allow you to create and share registry settings with everyone who logs on to the network. If this is a standalone workstation, do you care about System Policies? Probably not, because you can't really create them. For the exam writers at Microsoft, however, every NT Workstation is connected to an NT Server, so you had better know this stuff.

System policies are created with the System Policy Editor. The System Policy Editor is an NT Server–based utility. Using system policies, you will be able to maintain machine configurations and user policies from one machine.

The System Policy Editor operates in either Registry mode or System Policy mode. The exam writers think system policies are more significant.

Registry mode allows you to edit all sorts of interesting things. Take a look at Figure 3.2.

FIGURE 3.2: Default computer properties

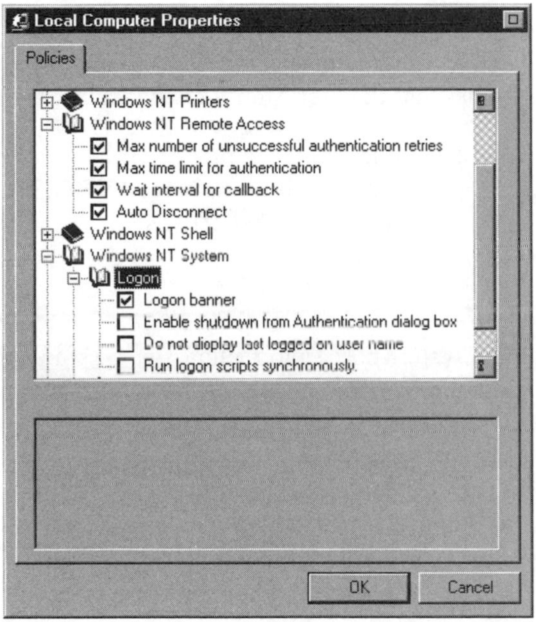

Several things jump out at you while looking at this screen:

- You can specify which applications to run at startup.

- You can create hidden drive shares for workstations or servers.

- From the Windows NT Remote Access section, you can set the maximum number of unsuccessful authentication attempts and for the system to automatically disconnect.

- From the Windows NT System Logon section, you can specify a specific logon banner or make sure the name of the last user who logged on is not displayed.

System Policy vs. Registry Mode

How does System Policy mode differ from Registry mode? System Policy mode is like Registry mode, but with an attitude. If there is a setting in the registry and a system policy conflicts with the registry, the system policy takes precedence.

You can find the system policy file. For NT systems, the file is named NTCONFIG.POL. Suppose you want to impose a set of restrictions on machines that the user cannot change. How is that accomplished?

Use the System Policy Editor to make the changes you want replicated across the network. Save the file as NTCONFIG.POL in the \WINNT\ SYSTEM32\REPL\IMPORT\SCRIPTS folder on the boot partition of the domain controllers.

NOTE If system policy information is being stored for Windows 95 machines, the filename should be CONFIG.POL instead of NTCONFIG.POL.

When a computer attempts to log on to the network, it will check for the system policy. When the computer finds the NTCONFIG.POL file that affects the user or the computer, it brings this information into the registry and configures the workstation accordingly. Put the system policy file in the \NETLOGON directory of the PDC and all Windows NT Workstation users on the domain can access it. This sounds like a good thing, but if the individual computer has a policy that conflicts with the system policy, the individual computer policy takes precedence.

TIP If the changes are made in System Policy mode rather than Registry mode, the changes will overwrite the local registry. What a great topic for an exam question!

Necessary Procedures

Since creating a local user profile is done by the user that logs on, the only profiles the administrator may have to worry about is a mandatory user profile or a roaming user profile.

Creating a User Profile and a Mandatory User Profile

Local User Profiles are created when the user logs on and makes changes to the computer. When the user logs off, these changes are saved in the file \WINNT\PROFILES*USERNAME*\NTUSER.DAT. To change this profile to a mandatory profile, change the extension from DAT to MAN. This has the effect of changing the file to read-only.

WARNING   While Mandatory User Profiles are not mentioned in the objectives, don't be surprised if you see a test question on this subject.

Modifying a User Profile

If a user is not subject to a mandatory user profile, any time the user logs on and makes any changes to the desktop and logs out, the user profile will be modified.

Creating a Roaming User Profile

Roaming user profiles are created from User Manager for Domains. For demonstration purposes, this will create a roaming user profile for the Administrator.

1. Start User Manager for Domains from the Administrative Tools menu of Programs. This program can be accessed from an NT Server or from a workstation that has been configured to use remote administration tools.

2. Double-click Administrator.

3. Select Profile.

4. In the User Profile path, enter a Universal Naming Convention (UNC) path to the \WINNT\PROFILES directory on a central repository like a server. The syntax for a UNC path is *COMPUTERNAME\ FOLDERNAME\SUBFOLDERNAME*; for example, \\SERVER-1\ WINNT\PROFILES.

5. Close the user's Profiles box by clicking OK.

6. Close the user window by clicking OK.

7. Close User Manager for Domains by clicking User|Exit.

You may think nothing has changed. Go to a different machine and log in as Administrator. Your new profile will follow you.

That is great for your account, but how do you do this for another user?

Copying a User Profile to Make It a Remote User Profile

You start by creating a central repository for user profiles on a server attached to the network, something like *SERVERNAME* PROFILES*USERNAME*. Share the directory. Once this has been accomplished, follow these steps:

1. Start Control Panel.

2. Double-click System.

3. Choose the Users Profile tab.

4. Select the profile for the user you want to copy and click Copy To. You will be prompted to enter a path to the location of the share *SERVERNAME*\PROFILES*USERNAME*.

5. Under Permitted to Use, make sure the appropriate user name is selected.

Exam Essentials

As mentioned earlier, the exam writers are fascinated with the topic of profiles and policies, so pay close attention to the material covered here.

Know where user profiles are stored. User profiles are stored in the \WINNT\PROFILES*USERNAME* folder.

Know the name of the user profile file. The name of the file is NTUSER.DAT.

Know how to make a local user profile a mandatory profile. Change the name of NTUSER.DAT to NTUSER.MAN.

Know what happens when the domain controller that contains the mandatory user profile is down, and the user logs on to the network. The user's locally cached profile will be used.

Know where shortcuts are stored on a local machine. Shortcuts are stored as part of the user local profile. The information will be stored in the \WINNT\PROFILES*USERNAME*\DESKTOP directory.

Know how profiles are accessed. During logon, NT looks for a local user profile. If it does not find a local user profile, it will look for a roaming user profile. If it cannot find a roaming user profile, it will create a local user profile using the default user settings.

Know how to create a roaming user profile. Copy the user's workstation local profile to a shared network path. Enter the UNC network path in the User Profile path box from User Manager for Domains.

Know what happens when a local user profile and a roaming user profile both exist. If a local user profile is older than a roaming user profile, the roaming user profile is used. If the local user profile is newer than the roaming user profile, NT will ask which profile the user wants to use.

Know how to copy user profiles to make them roaming user profiles. After you have created and shared the repository directory structure on an server, start Control Panel and choose System. Once System is opened, select the User Profile tab and select the user to copy. Click Copy To and enter the appropriate path. Check to make sure the appropriate users name is covered in the Permitted to Use Window.

Know the name of the system policy file for NT and where it is stored for replication. The system policy file is called NTCONFIG.POL. It is saved to the \WINNT\SYSTEM32\ REPL\IMPORT\SCRIPTS directory on the primary domain controller.

Know where the default system policy file is stored for access by all NT workstation computers. The default system policy file can be stored in the NETLOGON folder of the PDC.

Know the name of the system policy file for Windows 95. The name of the policy file for Windows 95 workstations is CONFIG.POL.

Know what happens when the computer system policy conflicts with the default system policy stored in the \NETLOGON folder. The local policy takes precedence.

Key Terms and Concepts

CONFIG.POL: The name of the file that stores system policies for Windows 95 client workstations.

Local Profile: Information stored on a local computer that reflects how the end user has configured the system.

Mandatory Profile: The process of setting a local profile that the end user cannot change.

NETCONFIG.POL: The name of the file that stores system policies for Windows NT Workstations and servers.

NTUSER.DAT: The name of the file stored in the \WINNT\ PROFILES\ *USERNAME* directory that contains all the settings in the local profile.

NTUSER.MAN: The name of the file stored in the \WINNT\ PROFILES\ *USERNAME* directory that contains all the settings in the mandatory user profile. Changing the extension for .DAT to .MAN turns the profile file into a read-only file.

PDC: Primary Domain Controller. The PDC is the central administration point of the domain.

Profile: Settings that refer to how a user has configured a local computer.

Roaming Profile: Profile created for a user who accesses more than one computer. The user's look and feel will remain the same, no matter which computer is being accessed.

System Policy Editor: The NT Server-based utility used to create system policies. Available through Programs ➤ Administrative Tools ➤ System Policy Editor.

System Policy mode: The mode in which the System Policy Editor can be used to mandate registry settings throughout the domain. Settings changed in the system policy files will override local registry settings.

Sample Questions

1. Your boss is a control freak. She wants to make sure that each NT Workstation has exactly the same system policies. Each workstation is attached to the network and the users must always log on to the domain before starting work. How can you keep your boss happy?

   A. Create a system policy file and export it to each workstation the first time it logs on.

   B. Create a system policy file for each end user and copy it to the users profiles directory on the domain controller.

C. Create a system policy file and copy it to each workstation's \WINNT folder.

D. Create a system policy file that will affect all end users and copy it to the NETLOGON folder of the PDC.

Answer: D. Create a system policy file that will affect all end users and copy it to the NETLOGON folder of the Primary Domain Controller.

2. After you went to all the trouble of creating a system policy and storing it in the NETLOGON directory so people can access it, you find that the policy was virtually ignored by several systems on your network. What is a possible cause?

A. The computers may have a local policy that conflicts with the system policy.

B. The user on the computer is logging on to the domain as Administrator, nullifying any policy changes.

C. The user on the computer is logging on to the domain as Guest, nullifying any policy changes.

D. You screwed up.

Answer: A. If there is a conflict between a local policy and the system policy, the local policy takes precedence. Answer D is never an option, is it?

3. How do you change a user profile to a mandatory user profile?

A. Change the extension on the NTUSER.MAN file to NTUSER.DAT.

B. Change the extension on the NTUSER.DAT file to NTUSER.MAN.

C. That is covered in the rights and permissions section, and we haven't gotten that far yet.

D. Store the profile in the \NETLOGON directory of the PDC with a file name of NETUSER.DAT.

Answer: B. Changing the extension on the NETUSER.DAT file to NETUSER.MAN makes the user profile a mandatory user profile.

4. What happens if a system policy and a roaming user profile have conflicting settings?

    A. The roaming user profile takes precedence.

    B. The system policy takes precedence.

    C. The local user policy takes precedence.

    D. The cached user policy takes precedence.

Answer: B. In this case, the system policy takes precedence.

Set up shared folders and permissions.

One of the reasons many companies select Windows NT Workstation as their desktop operating system is that it offers users the ability to share information stored on their local hard drives. This is done by the users creating shared folders. If the user creates a shared folder, the user will be able to select how many users can access the data at what time, and assign some permissions to the users coming in to share the information. If the data is stored on a partition that is formatted with NTFS, the user will have the ability to move the security to a more granular level.

Critical Information

Folders are shared so that other people on the network can use the information or applications in the folder. You create a share so remote users (users who do not log on to your computer) can put their files on your computer in the *SERVERNAME*\USERS*USERNAME* subfolder. You also put shares on the network so users can access the network version of Excel from *SERVERNAME*\APPS\EXCEL. Another share might point to the *SERVERNAME*\SHARED\ DATA\BUDGETS area.

Shared Folders

Just because you have created a folder called Data with a subfolder called Budgets, it does not mean that anyone else can see the folders: nothing is visible by default. For users to see a directory, the administrator must create the shares and make them available under a readable share name.

The administrator can share any directory on the computer if the administrator has been given the LIST permission. Contrast that to a user who has network administration responsibilities. That user can share any directory on the network, as long as the Administrator account has LIST permissions. If a user on a remote computer has blocked the administrator from having the LIST permission, chances are the user does not want the information spread across the network, so the administrator cannot create a share.

NOTE If you are not sure what the LIST permission is or what it is good for, don't worry. A discussion of all permissions comes up next.

Shares can be created using NT Explorer, My Computer, the command prompt, or Server Manager.

Look closely at Figure 3.3. To access this dialog box, open My Computer from the desktop, browse to a folder, highlight it, right-click it, and choose Sharing. Once the Sharing tab is displayed, choose Shared As and enter the share name—in this case, Applications. You can also add a comment so users will know what the share is for. You will notice that you can set a limit of users who can hack away on this share. You can allow the Maximum Allowed for the server or set a number of users with which you feel comfortable.

Using NT Explorer or My Computer to create a share is not the only way of doing it—it is just one of the most convenient. You can also create a share using File Manager (if you still use File Manager). If you happen to work in Server Manager, you can also create a share while doing normal management tasks. For the GUI-challenged or those of us who still feel most comfortable at a command prompt,

FIGURE 3.3: Sharing a drive using My Computer

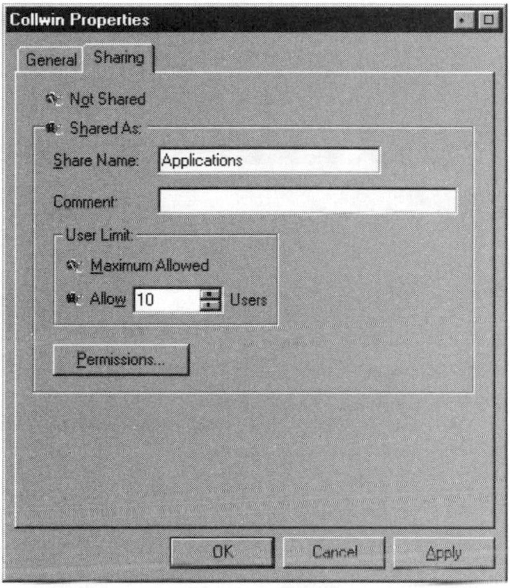

you can use the Net Share utility. Each of these methods will be discussed in the Necessary Procedures section.

In addition to the shares that the administrator creates, if you are using an NT-based system that has a hard-coded access control list (ACL), you will find that there are at least two hidden shares. These hidden shares are the C$ share, which shares the root computer's C: drive, and the ADMIN$ share, which shares the root of the NT installation. These shares give administrators a path to the \WINNT directory or the operating system directory. Remember that a share name ending in $ results in a hidden or nonvisible share.

Permissions

Now that the share has been set up, you need to make sure that those people that need to access it actually can. If you look at Figure 3.4, you will see a list of permissions that you can grant users or groups at a share point.

FIGURE 3.4: Access through share permissions

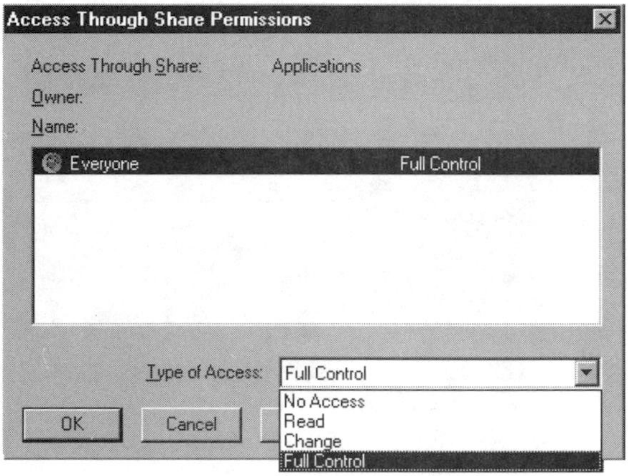

NOTE It is important to remember that we are talking about share-level permissions, not folder or file-level permissions. Share-level permissions can be granted at any share point, even if the share points to a FAT-formatted device. Folder-level and file-level permissions can only be added to storage devices formatted with NTFS.

Table 3.2 summarizes the four share permissions.

TABLE 3.2: Explanation of Share Permissions

Access Through Share Permissions	Permissions Granted
Full Control	The user can read or see a folder, subfolder or file, execute an application, write to a closed file, and delete a folder or file. If the Share resides on an NTFS partition, the user can also take ownership of the resource and change permissions.

T A B L E 3.2:   Explanation of Share Permissions *(continued)*

Access Through Share Permissions	Permissions Granted
Change	The user can read or see a folder, subfolder, or file, execute an application, write to a closed file, and delete a folder or file.
Read	The user can read and execute permissions to the share, folders, subfolders, and files
No Access	Users can connect to the share, but will not be able to access any resources.

As you look at the table, there are two levels to study closely: Full Control and No Access. Full Control gives the user or the group full control over the share. The members of the group or the user can do whatever they want to in the share. If you refer back to Figure 3.4, you will see that by default, the Everyone group gets full control of a share. No Access will allow a user to connect to the share, but the user will not be able to access any resources associated with the share.

In the Microsoft scheme of security, a good rule of thumb to follow is that the most restrictive permission applies, if you are accessing the data from a share. Thus, if Dawn were a member of two groups, one with Full Control of a share and one with No Access to the same share, Dawn would have No Access to the share.

However, if Dawn were accessing the data by logging on the computer locally, the opposite is the case: the LEAST restrictive permissions apply. There is a way to keep this straight. Remember: Share/ Most and Locally/Least. Just when you have that down, there is another step to take into consideration. No matter how the user is accessing the data, through a share or locally, if you see No Access, that means No Access.

Necessary Procedures

Sharing information is what networking is all about. With NT, sharing a folder is done in several ways.

Creating a Share

There are several ways to create a share—by using NT Explorer, My Computer, Server Manager, or the Net Share utility.

To create a share using NT Explorer:

1. Open NT Explorer.

2. Open directories until you locate the folder that you want to share.

3. Highlight the directory name and right-click it.

4. Select Sharing from the drop-down menu. This will open the Sharing tab of the Properties dialog box.

NOTE You can also reach the Properties dialog box by highlighting the directory name, right-clicking, and choosing Properties. From the Properties menu, select Sharing.

---

5. When you reach the Sharing tab, you will notice that the default share name is the name of the directory. Some users are not excited about having a share name such as APPS_EXCEL. You can enter a more user-friendly name for the share. When you change the name of the share, it does not change the name of the directory— it just presents users with a name that makes sense to real people rather than computer people.

6. You can also change the path, but if you have to do that, why did you choose this folder in the first place?

You will notice there is also a spot for comments. Comments are optional—be careful, because what you enter will show up next to the share in NT Explorer. It is really not a good idea to create a share called POLICY, and add the comment that it is a share for some more Dilbert-esque policies created by the management types. While you and the rest of the IT team may see the humor in this comment, other people within the company may fail to see the levity in the situation.

To create a share using My Computer:

1. Open My Computer.

2. Click the drive letter on which the target folder resides.

3. Open directories until you locate the folder that you want to share.

4. Highlight the directory name and right-click.

5. Select Sharing from the drop-down menu. This will open the Sharing tab of the Properties dialog box.

6. When you reach the Sharing tab, you will notice that the default for the directory is Not Shared. Click the Shared As radio button. The usual share name is the name of the directory. You can enter a new name for the share. When you change the name of the share, it does not change the name of the directory—it just presents users with a more user-friendly name.

Net Share is a command-line utility. As such, you start the process by opening a command prompt. To create a share using Net Share, choose Start ➤ Programs ➤ Command Prompt. The syntax for the Net Share utility is shown below.

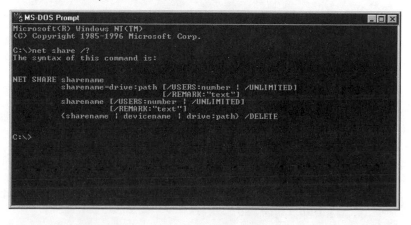

As an example, suppose you need a temporary share to point to D:\APPLICATIONS\EXCEL. You want to call the share Excel and allow 10 users to access the share.

From the command prompt, the syntax would be as follows:

```
Net Share Excel=d:\applications\excel /users:10
```

To delete the share, the syntax would be as follows:

```
Net Share Excel /delete
```

Setting Share Permissions

You can set share permissions only on network shares. Share permissions are usually assigned to a group, rather than an individual.

NOTE As you have already seen from the discussion of creating shares, there are several ways of accessing the Properties page for a share, folder, or file. In the examples that follow, NT Explorer is the utility of choice.

To set share permissions:

1. Log on to the network as administrator or a user with Full Control over the share.

2. Start NT Explorer by selecting Start ➤ Programs ➤ Windows NT Explorer.

3. Browse to the share where the permissions will be applied. Highlight the share and right-click.

4. Click Sharing.

5. Click Permissions.

6. With the Access Through Share Permissions screen showing, click Add, which brings up the Add Users and Groups window.

7. Select the group that will receive the permissions, highlight the group, and click Add.

8. In the lower half of the Add Users and Groups window, use the Type of Access drop-down menu to choose No Access, Read, Change, or Full Access.

9. Click the appropriate choice. This will bring you back to the Add Users and Groups Window.

10. Click OK to return to the ATS Permissions screen.

11. Click OK to return to the share's Properties window.

12. Click OK to return to NT Explorer.

Share permissions can also be granted using My Computer.

1. Double-click My Computer and browse the drives and folder structure until you find the appropriate share.

2. Highlight the share, right-click, and chose Sharing.

3. Click Permissions.

4. Complete the task by adding or removing a group and assigning the group the appropriate permissions.

Exam Essentials

Since this is such an integral part of computer networking, the exam writers spent an appropriate amount of time on this objective. Know the material well, because some of the questions will not be straightforward.

Know the various methods of creating a share.   You can create a share by using NT Explorer, My Computer, or the Net Share command-line utility.

Know how to create a hidden share.   You can create a hidden share by adding $ to the end of the share name—for example, C$ or ADMIN$.

Know how to set ATS permissions. You can assign ATS permissions through the Properties page of the share. From the Properties page, select Permissions.

Know the effect when a user or group has the No Access permission to a share. If a user has been given the No Access permission to a share or folder, either by an individual assignment or through a group assignment, the user will not be able to access that share. Assignments granted through other means cannot override the No Access assignment.

Key Terms and Concepts

Access control list (ACL):   Hard-coded list of users and groups with permissions to various hidden shares. Also, a list of users and groups that have been provided permissions or rights to a resource.

Access Through Shares Permissions (ATS permissions):   Permissions granted at the share point, at the folder level.

Change Permissions: An action that allows the user to change permissions to the file for others.

Delete: An action of deleting a file.

Execute: An action of running or executing a file.

FAT (File Allocation Table):   DOS-based file system.

Full Control: Permission that gives the user full rights to the share, including the permission to determine ownership.

Macintosh-accessible volume: Server-based share that is available to users of Apple's Macintosh.

No Access: Users can connect to a share, but will not be able to access any resources.

NTFS (New Technology File System):   NT file system designed for drives or partitions greater than 400MB.

Permission: Windows NT settings you set on a shared resource that determines which users can use the resource and how they can use it.

Read: Assigns Read and Execute permissions to the share, folders, subfolders, and files. Also an action of reading a file.

Share: Makes resources, such as directories and printers, available to others.

Share name: A name that refers to a shared resource on a server. Each shared directory on a server has a share name, used by PC users to refer to the directory. Users of Macintoshes use the name of the Macintosh-accessible volume that corresponds to a directory, which may be the same as the share name. See also Macintosh-accessible volume.

Share Permissions: Used to restrict the availability over the network of a shared resource to only certain users.

Shared directory: A directory to which network users can connect.

Shared network directory: See shared directory.

Shared resource: Any device, data, or program that is used by more than one other device or program. For Windows NT, shared resources refer to any resource that is made available to network users, such as directories, files, printers, and named pipes. Also refers to a resource on a server that is available to network users.

Take Ownership: An action that allows the user to take ownership of a file.

User rights: Define a user's access to a computer or domain and the actions that a user can perform on the computer or domain. User rights permit actions such as logging onto a computer or network, adding or deleting users in a workstation or domain, and so forth.

Write: The action of writing information to a file.

Sample Questions

1. Given the default permissions assigned to groups, which groups would you need to belong to in order to create a share?

   A. Administrators

   B. Backup Users

   C. Guests

   D. Power Users

   E. Users

   Answer: A and D. Administrators and Power Users can create shares.

2. Denise is member of three groups: Administrators, MIS, and Apps_Acctg. There is a share created called ACCOUNTING. The Administrators group has full control permissions to the Accounting share. The MIS group has been assigned No Access permissions and the Apps_Acctg Group has been given the Change permission. What can Denise do with the share?

   A. Denise has full rights to the share, granted her through the membership in the Administrators group.

   B. Denise can read or see a folder, subfolder, or file, execute an application, write to a closed file, and delete a folder or file. These are inherent in the Change permission Denise received through her membership in Apps_Acctg.

   C. Denise can attach to the share but cannot see or do anything. This is a result of the No Access permission given to the MIS group.

   D. Denise cannot see the share.

   Answer: C. In the Microsoft security model, all bets are off when the No Access permission is granted. If you are given No Access permission from membership in any group, or by an explicit assignment to your user account, you have no access to the share.

3. CJ has been given Change permission to the H_R share. The share points to a folder that resides on a FAT partition. The Human Resources director comes to you and asks that CJ retain Change permissions to the share, but she would like more restrictive permissions placed on the Salary_99 file. Can you help the Human Resources director out?

   A. Yes, NT will allow you to add file-level permissions to the Salary_99 file. Because the file is on a FAT partition, file-level security is allowed.

   B. No, NT will not allow you to add file permissions to the Salary_99 file. Because the file is on a FAT partition, file-level security is not allowed.

   C. Yes, because CJ is accessing the file through a share, that implies he is a remote user. As a remote user, the format of the drive the share resides on has no impact.

   D. We haven't learned about this yet, why are you asking the question?

   Answer: B. Because the share points to a folder on a FAT partition, only share level permissions will apply. Yes, this was discussed!

Set permissions on NTFS partitions, folders, and files.

Shares and permissions assigned to share affect only remote users—those folks who are attaching to your computer, rather than logging on to your computer. Any permission granted at the share point is just that, permission to the share point. A user with Change permissions at the share can potentially have an impact on any folder, subfolder, or file that makes up that share.

Security often needs to be more "granular" than that. Regularly, you need to assign a user more rights at the folder level than perhaps they should have at the file level. That is where folder and file-level permissions enter the picture.

Folder and file-level permissions are only available if the storage device that hosts them has been formatted using NTFS. If the device is a FAT storage device, there can be no file or folder-level permissions applied.

WARNING   Read over that last paragraph VERY carefully. It will come up again!

This objective will have a big impact on your daily life. This is one of those subjects that can make or break a career. Just ask the administrator who had to explain why a key file suddenly was erased.

TIP   When you come up against exam questions on this material, and you will, be sure to read the questions *very* carefully. Sometimes the questions are long, rambling, and very involved. Read them two or three times and make sure you understand exactly what the question is asking before answering.

Critical Information

Some of the permissions that were discussed as part of share points will carry over to this discussion. There is only so much you can do to a folder or a file. Microsoft has a set of tasks called system actions.

To do anything, you need permission. Each permission is made up of one or more system actions. There are six basic actions, four of which apply for both share and NTFS permissions (see Table 3.3).

T A B L E 3.3:   System Actions

Permission	Actions
Read (R)	Users can read or see a file. Usually used in conjunction with Execute.
Write (W)	Users can add data to a file.
Execute (X)	Users can execute a file. Usually used in conjunction with Read.
Delete (D)	Users can delete a file.
Change Permissions (P)	NTFS permission—users can change the access level of other users on this file or folder. This is granted as part of Full Control if the share is on an NTFS partition.
Take Ownership (O)	NTFS partition—users can claim ownership of a file. This is granted as part of Full Control if the share is on an NTFS partition.

Given this information, let's re-examine the ATS share permissions, because this is something you already understand. Full Control is self-explanatory. By default, when you create a share, the Everyone group has Full Control over the share and its folders, subfolders, and files. The newest user on your network can delete anything on the share. If security is an issue on your network, this could pose a problem.

Change gives the user or group the ability to perform the following actions: Read (R), Execute (X), Write (W), and Delete (D). So, the user or member of the group can read, execute, write, and delete information in the share.

The share permission Read grants the user or group the ability to read and execute files on the share. It is usually granted to application executable files—files with the extension .EXE or .COM.

No Access lets the user or members of the group attach to the share, but they cannot access any information from the share.

Directory-Level Permissions

What about the NTFS permissions? NTFS permissions are permissions granted to *local* files and directories on a host computer. These permissions can be granted by the owner of the directory or by an administrator. Separate permissions can be granted at the directory and file levels. The directory-level permissions are listed in Table 3.4.

T A B L E 3.4: NTFS Directory-Level Permissions

Directory-Level Permission	Permissions Granted
No Access	Users cannot access the directory at all.
List	Users cannot access the directory, but can see the contents of the directory.
Read	Users can read data files and execute application files.
Add	Users cannot read any information from the directory or even see the files that are stored in the directory, but can add data to the directory.
Add and Read	Users can see information in the directory and add information (new files) to the directory. Users cannot modify existing files in the directory.
Change	Users can see files in the directory, add files to the directory, modify files in the directory, and delete files from the directory (or even delete the whole directory). Users can also change the attributes of the directory.
Full Control	Users can do everything they can do with Change, but can also make changes to resources they do not own.

Permissions given to a directory flow down into the directory. If you have given the group EXCEL_Users the Read permission to the folder D:\APPLICATIONS\EXCEL, a member of that group can execute the file EXCEL.EXE.

File-Level Permissions

There are times when security needs to be taken one step further, down to the individual file level. Suppose you have a folder that contains files with the payroll information for the next fiscal year. During the budget process, the payroll file is open so certain users can make changes. When the payroll process for the year has been finalized, you want users to be able to read the file, but not make changes to it. Meanwhile, in the same folder, there are files that the management team needs to change. In this case, you would simply change the permissions on the payroll file to allow people to only read the file. When you make the change to just one file, all the other files are not affected. See Table 3.5 for an explanation of file-level permissions.

TABLE 3.5:   NTFS File-Level Permissions

File-Level Permission	Permissions Granted
No Access	Users cannot access the file at all.
Read	Users can read a data file or execute it if it is an application file.
Change	Users can read, execute, modify, or delete the file.
Full Control	Users can read, execute, write to, or delete the file, and change permissions or take ownership away from the owner of the file.

To set NTFS permissions for a folder or file, highlight the folder or file, right-click, and select Properties. From the Properties page, select the Security tab and then choose Permissions.

After these folders and files have all these permissions assigned, what happens if the information is moved? In that case, the information will inherit the permissions of its new home. For example, if Dawn created a file on a share and assigned the Everyone group Read access, and the file was copied to a folder where the Everyone group had Full Control, Everyone would now have Full Control over the file.

By the same token, what happens if you are accessing a folder from a share point and the permissions you have been granted to the share point are more generous than the rights you have been assigned to the folder? Remember the basics of Microsoft security: if accessing the data through a share, the most restrictive permissions apply.

Necessary Procedures

Now that you understand what a powerful tool NTFS permissions can be, it would be nice to know how to establish them.

Setting Permissions on NTFS Partitions, Folders, and Files

To set permissions on an NTFS partition, you would follow the steps listed in the last objective for creating a share and assigning share permissions.

To set lower-level (folder or file) permissions, you must use NTFS permissions. NTFS permissions are not available for FAT partitions.

NOTE NTFS permissions are usually assigned to a group, rather than an individual.

To set NTFS permissions:

1. Log on to the network as someone who has ownership over the folder or file.

2. Start NT Explorer by selecting Start ➤ Programs ➤ Windows NT Explorer.

3. Browse to the folder or file where the permissions will be applied. Highlight the folder or file and right-click.

4. Click Sharing.

5. Click Security.

6. Click Permissions. This brings up the Directory Permissions window.

7. With the Directory Permissions window showing, click Add, which brings up the Add Users and Groups window.

8. Select the group or user that will receive the permissions, highlight the group or user, and click Add.

9. In the lower half of the Add Users and Groups window, use the Type of Access drop-down menu to choose No Access, List, Read, Add, Add and Read, Change, or Full Access.

10. Click the appropriate choice. This will bring you back to the Add Users and Groups Window.

11. Click OK to return to the Directory Permissions window.

12. At the top of the Directory Permissions window, there are two radio buttons.

    ▪ If you select Replace Permissions on Subdirectories, it will push the changes down to any subdirectories.

    ▪ If you select Replace Permissions on Existing Files, it will push the changes down to any files.

13. Click OK to return to the folder's Security tab.

14. Click OK to return to NT Explorer.

Exam Essentials

There may not be much in the Exam Essentials portion of this objective, but there can be multiple questions written about the subject. When thinking about security, follow the Boy Scout motto—Be Prepared.

Know how to set NTFS folder- and file-level permissions. You can assign NTFS permissions through the Properties page of the share. Select the Security tab to begin the process.

Know how to apply the Microsoft security model to various situations. The most restrictive permissions given as an individual user or as a member of a group apply if the user is accessing through a share. If the user is logging on to a local machine, the LEAST restrictive permissions apply. Remember: Shar/Most, Local/Least. What happens if No Access shows up? You are right, No Access, no matter what.

Key Terms and Concepts

Access Control List (ACL): Hard-coded list of users and groups with permissions to various hidden shares. Also, a list of users and groups who have been provided permissions or rights to a resource.

Access Through Shares Permissions (ATS permissions): Permissions granted at the share point, at the folder level.

Add: Directory-level permission that allows the user to add information to the directory. With just the Add permission, the user cannot read any information from the directory or even see other files stored in the directory.

Add and Read: Directory-level permission that allows the user to add information to a directory and see information already stored in the directory.

Change: Permission that allows the user to read, execute, write, and delete folders, subfolders, and files at the share level and below.

Change Permissions: An action that allows the user to change permissions to the file for others.

Delete: An action of deleting a file.

Execute: An action of running or executing a file.

FAT (File Allocation Table):   DOS-based file system.

Full Control: Permission that gives the user full rights to the share, including the permission to determine ownership.

List Permission: Directory-level permission that allows the user to see the contents of the directory, even if the user cannot gain access to the directory.

Macintosh-accessible volume: Server-based share that is available to users of Apple's Macintosh.

No Access: Users can connect to a share, but will not be able to access any resources.

NTFS (New Technology File System):   NT file system designed for drives or partitions greater than 400MB.

Permission: Windows NT settings you set on a shared resource that determine which users can use the resource and how they can use it.

Read: Assigns Read and Execute permissions to the share, folders, subfolders, and files. Also an action of reading a file.

Share: To make resources, such as directories and printers, available to others.

Share name: A name that refers to a shared resource on a server. Each shared directory on a server has a share name, used by PC users to refer to the directory. Users of Macintoshes use the name of the Macintosh-accessible volume that corresponds to a directory, which may be the same as the share name. See also Macintosh-accessible volume.

Share Permissions: Used to restrict the availability over the network of a shared resource to only certain users.

Shared directory: A directory to which network users can connect.

Shared network directory: See shared directory.

Shared resource: Any device, data, or program that is used by more than one other device or program. For Windows NT, shared resources refer to any resource that is made available to network users, such as directories, files, printers, and named pipes. Also refers to a resource on a server that is available to network users.

Take Ownership: An action that allows the user to take ownership of a file.

User rights: Define a user's access to a computer or domain and the actions that a user can perform on the computer or domain. User rights permit actions such as logging on to a computer or network, adding or deleting users in a workstation or domain, and so forth.

Write: An action of writing information to a file.

Sample Questions

1. Jack just started to work for your firm today as a temporary programmer. When you set up his account you made him a member of the following groups, each with permissions given to the share \NEWAPPS: Everyone - List, Users - List, Developers - Full Control, and Temps - No Access. What will Jack's rights be to the \NEWAPPS share?

   A. Full Control

   B. List

   C. No Access

   D. Not enough information has been given.

Answer: C. No Access. When No Access has been granted to any group that the user is a member of, the user will have No Access to a resource.

2. The Windows NT Workstation that you are configuring contains a shared folder than resides on an NTFS partition. How is access to the folder determined?

   A. A user accessing the folder remotely has the same or more rights than a user accessing the folder locally.

   B. A user accessing the folder remotely has the same or more restrictive access permissions than if he were a local user.

   C. A user accessing the system remotely has the same rights as the user who accesses the system locally.

   D. The user who accesses the system locally is not bound by NTFS permissions.

   Answer: B. The user accessing the system remotely will have the same or MORE restrictive rights than the user accessing the system locally.

3. David is an engineer with your company. He has an account on an NT Workstation that contains a folder called \JOBSPECS. The following groups have access to this folder and David is a member of all these groups. Everyone - Read, Users - Read, Engineers - Change, and TechStaff - Add and Read. If David logs on to the computer locally, what are his rights to the \JOBSPECS folder?

   A. Read

   B. Change

   C. Add and Read

   D. The user who accesses the system locally is not bound by NTFS permissions.

   Answer: B. When a user logs on locally, the least restrictive permissions apply. In David's case this would be Change.

4. The folder \JOBSPECS is being moved from David's NTFS partition to a hard drive that utilizes the FAT file system. Given the scenario in question 3, what will David's rights be to the folder?

A. Read

B. Change

C. Add and Read

D. The FAT file system does not have permissions.

Answer: D. The FAT file system does not have permissions. Therefore the only restrictions that can be put on the folder will occur for remote users at the Share level.

Install and configure printers in a given environment.

Printed output is the essence of most office work today. Before we can send output to be printed, we need to have a printer configured. Right? Sort of. You see when you enter into the Microsoft realm of testing one of the things that must be learned is *MicroSpeak*. We need to define some terms, so it will be done here, and again under the Key Terms and Concepts portion of the objective.

NOTE Shakespeare said, "What's in a name? That which we call a rose by any other name would smell as sweet." That is true, except when you are testing. When you are testing, you had better know what the question writers mean when they say "rose."

What is the name of the device that actually puts the ink/toner to paper? You go out and buy an XYZ Laser Printer. In MicroSpeak, the object you load paper into is called a *printing device*. Don't let the name change fool you: A printing device is still connected to a computer by way of a parallel cable or a serial cable. Printing devices can also be connected directly to the network, or through an infrared port.

If a printing device is what puts ink to paper, what is a printer? A *printer* is the software interface that takes the information from your application and redirects it to a printing device.

Another term that requires definition is *print driver*. A print driver is the piece of software that translates application information into the printer-specific commands that are passed on to the actual printer.

At this point you are probably wondering why you are spending so much time on syntax and not installation and configuration of printing. Printing is an objective that gets *lots* of attention. Forewarned is forearmed, or something like that. You have been warned, so read carefully.

Critical Information

In the NT print architecture, the application that you are using to generate the output does not care what kind of printer you are using. It just sends the job off to the printer and somehow, magically, the print job appears. The magic is made up many processes working together to give your users the desired results.

There are two ways that you can add a printer to a Windows NT Workstation: You can add a local printer or add a network printer. A local printer is a printer that is hooked directly to your workstation, a network printer is a printer somewhere in the office that someone has graciously decided to share. Connecting to either is a painless process utilizing either My Computer or the Printers icon from Control Panel.

Configuring a printer takes on many faces, depending on the driver that is supplied with the printer. Usually, you will be able to configure paper size, input trays, duplexing, fonts, and paper layout. You can also specify default settings for specialty printers.

Necessary Procedures

In this section, we will address adding a printer and talk about configuring the printer properties.

Installing a Printer

A local printer is defined as a printer that is physically connected to your workstation, either by a parallel cable or serial cable. To begin the process, open My Computer by double-clicking the desktop icon.

1. Once My Computer has opened, choose the Add Printer icon from the Printers folders. This will start the Add Printer Wizard.

2. Once the Add Printer Wizard has started you will be presented with a choice. You can choose to install a printer attached to My Computer or you can choose to connect to a Network print server. Connecting to a network print server means you will be printing to a printer not hooked directly to your computer.

3. If you choose My Computer and click Next, you can designate the port the printer is attached to, usually LPT1. From this screen you can add a port or configure the transmission retry count for an existing port. You can also choose to enable printer pooling, which allows several similar devices to share printing responsibilities. Make your choices and click Next.

   - Choose the printer manufacturer and model if you are using a printer that NT already has drivers for, or select Have Disk if it is a "non-standard" printer. Click Next.

   - Enter a printer name and decide if this will be the default printer. Click Next.

   - Decide if the printer will be shared with others on the network. If the printer will be shared with others, you will need to specify the operating systems the other users have installed on their computers. The workstation that controls the printer also controls the printer drivers. The drivers will be passed to the requesting clients when there is a printing request. Click Next.

- You are prompted to print a test page. Make your choice and click Finish.

- At this point the system will prompt you for the CD-ROM or a location where the files are stored. Provide the information and the drivers will be copied.

4. If you choose to connect to a Network Print Server and click next, you will be presented with the Connect to Printer box. You will be shown a list of shared printers or you can enter in the path to the printer. Click OK. When you choose to print to that printer, a print driver will be downloaded to your computer.

Configuring Printer Properties

There are times in the world of computing when you just have to say, "It depends." This is one of those times. The properties you can configure depend on the printer and depend on the driver that is supplied with the printer. To configure a printer, open the Printers folder, right-click, and select properties. There are six tabs to explore.

General Tab

This tab is mostly informational, allowing you to comment on the printer or show the location. The driver is listed and there is a button marked New Driver to allow you to change or update the present software.

The Separator Page is known in the Novell world as a Banner Page. It comes out before the print job and gives information about who sent the print job. It can also be used to switch printers between the two printer control languages, PCL and PostScript.

The Print Processor button lets you choose how you want the print jobs to be processed. The default is Winprint.

The Print Test Page button allows you to test the printer at your discretion.

Ports

The Ports tab show which ports are utilized for which printers, and lets you add a port, delete a port, or configure a port. This is a repeat screen from the Printer Installation Wizard. You can also define and configure Printer pooling.

Scheduling

Choosing the Scheduling tab allows you to pick when the printer will be available for general use and which priority the printer will have. Lowest is the default priority.

You can also spool documents so the program finishes printing faster, returning control of the desktop to the end user. Printing can either start immediately or after the last page has been spooled. If you decide not to spool, there is a radio button to print directly to the printer. Finally, the system will allow you to hold mismatched documents, print spooled documents first, or keep documents after they have printed. Usually, when a print job has finished printing, the job is deleted. If you opt to keep the job, the job will be saved.

Sharing

Again, a repeat from the Add Printer Wizard. You can choose to keep the printer private or share it. If you share it, you can assign a share name and determine which operating systems will need drivers.

Security

The Permissions tab lets you give users or groups of users the rights to print to the printer.

Auditing allows you to choose which events you want to audit. The event choice is made by user or group. You could decide to audit the success of all print jobs by the group Management. Before you can audit printers you must enable auditing of File and Object auditing in User Manager.

Ownership lets you decide who will "own" the printer.

Device Settings

This is the setting where you get to pick things like how tray assignments will be handled and what the default paper size will be.

Exam Essentials

The writers of the exam are definitely end users who are frustrated by the network printing subsystem. They want to make sure you know everything about printing.

Know how to set print priorities.   Priorities are set on the Scheduling tab of the Printer Properties page. The default priority is low.

Know where print drivers are stored.   Print drivers are stored on the computer that the print device is attached to.

Know how to schedule print jobs.   Scheduling is handled from the Scheduling tab of the printer properties page.

Key Terms and Concepts

Local printer: A printer that sends to disk the print jobs it receives. It then processes the jobs and forwards them to a print device.

LPR Printer Port: A printer port configured to use TCP/IP print properties.

Network-attached print device: A physical device that connects parallel or serial print devices to the network or a print device that has an internal network interface card.

Print device: The physical printer, or the device that produces printed output.

Print Pool: A collection of similar printers attached to the same print server. The printers must use the same printer driver. Ideally, the printers will be in the same physical location.

Print Priorities: Providing the scheduling opportunities for one set of print jobs to print routinely before another.

Print server: A computer that shares its printers with network clients.

Printer: A software device to which applications send print jobs. A Windows NT *printer* matches a name with a printer driver, an output port, and various configuration settings. (Often referred to in other operating systems, like Novell, as a *queue*.)

Queue: A holding area for print jobs received by a print server but not yet sent to the target print device.

Remote printer: A printer that does not save to disk the print jobs it receives. Instead, it redirects its jobs directly to a print server.

SEE ALSO   For more information on Printing, check out the *MCSE: NT Server 4 Study Guide, Second Edition* by Matthew Strebe and Charles Perkins with James Chellis (Sybex, 1998).

Sample Questions

1. You are sick and tired of people printing large jobs to the printer hooked to your workstation in the middle of the day. Sometimes, you can't print for hours. How can you handle this situation?

   A. Create two printers that use the same print device. Call one of the printers MyStuff and the other printer TheirStuff. Both of the printers should be shared. Tell your coworkers only to print to TheirStuff. Set the priority of MyStuff to 1 and TheirStuff to 99.

   B. Create two printers that use the same print device. Call one of the printers MyStuff and the other printer TheirStuff. Both of the printers should be shared. Tell your coworkers only to print to TheirStuff. Set the priority of MyStuff to 99 and TheirStuff to 1.

   C. Create two printers that use the same print device. Call one of the printers MyStuff and the other printer TheirStuff. Both of the printers should be shared. Tell your coworkers only to print to TheirStuff. In the printer properties page of TheirStuff, specify Only From and choose 8 AM to 6 PM.

D. Create two printers that use the same print device. Call one of the printers MyStuff and the other printer TheirStuff. Both of the printers should be shared. Tell your coworkers only to print to TheirStuff. Set the priority of MyStuff to 99 and TheirStuff to 1. In the printer properties page of TheirStuff, specify Only From and choose 6 PM to 6 AM.

Answer: D. Answer D solves your problem in two ways, first of all, if your coworkers comply, their jobs will be printed only between 6 PM and 6 AM. Even if you have a print job during those times, the priorities are set so your job will print first. This solution will also rid you of all those nasty social obligations that others have to deal with. Chances are, none of your coworkers will speak to you anymore.

2. The Chief Executive Officer of your company comes to you and tells you that she has a problem. It seems that she and all the Executive Vice Presidents print to the same printer, and quite frankly she is tired of waiting for their stuff to print. How can you handle this situation?

   A. Create two printers printing to the same print device. Call the first one Boss and the second one NotBoss. Set the priority on Boss to 99 and the priority to NotBoss to 1. Connect the CEO to Boss and everyone else to NotBoss.

   B. Create two printers printing to the same print device. Call the first one Boss and the second one NotBoss. Set the priority on Boss to 1 and the priority to NotBoss to 99. Connect the CEO to Boss and everyone else to NotBoss.

   C. Get her a printer of her own.

   D. Tell her to work and play well with others and deal with the delay.

   Answer: A. With a priority of 99, the Boss printer will take control of the print device.

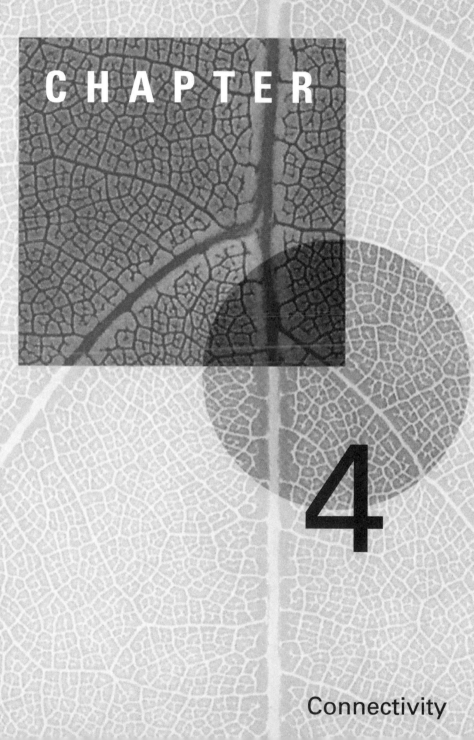

CHAPTER

4

Connectivity

Microsoft Exam Objectives Covered in This Chapter:

▶ Add and configure the network components of Windows NT Workstation. *(pages 164 – 174)*

▶ Use various methods to access network resources. *(pages 174 – 178)*

▶ Implement Windows NT Workstation as a client in a NetWare environment. *(pages 178 – 185)*

▶ Use various configurations to install Windows NT Workstation as a TCP/IP client. *(pages 186 – 193)*

▶ Configure and install Dial-Up Networking in a given situation. *(pages 193 – 200)*

▶ Configure Microsoft Peer Web Services in a given situation. *(pages 200 – 203)*

The objectives in this chapter are concerned with connecting your Windows NT Workstation to a network. These topics are not only important for this exam: they are topics which are touched upon in just about every MCSE test. Microsoft places a lot of emphasis on the networking abilities of the NT operating system.

Add and configure the network components of a Windows NT Workstation.

This entire chapter revolves around the various options available to connect Windows NT to your network. Understanding these options is critical, not only for your MCSE testing, but also for any real-world implementation of an NT network.

Before we can begin to look at the specifics, however, we need to cover the basic NT tools used to configure your workstation as part of a network. The tools discussed in this objective will act as the building blocks for the rest of the chapter. From a testing perspective, it is imperative that you understand these basics before you continue.

Critical Information

This is a *hands-on* objective. That is, there are not many theoretical or design issues. Most of the critical information for this objective will be found in the Necessary Procedures section. You must have a good overall feel for what options are available, and what tools are used, before you can begin to discuss any specific networking scenarios involving an NT Workstation.

There are, however, a few topics that warrant attention before we move to the procedures.

NetBIOS Names

Each computer in an NT network needs a unique identifier called a NetBIOS name. This name is one of the tools used to differentiate computers on the network. When you install an NT Workstation on the network you will be asked to provide this name. You can change the NetBIOS name after the installation by accessing the Network applet in Control Panel.

The NetBIOS name is a 15-character user-friendly name usually assigned during the installation of NT. This is not, however, the end of the story. This name has a sixteenth character that is used to identify each service provided by the computer. Let's say, for instance, that a user had named a computer "Endeavor200." Each time the computer starts, one of the first things it will do is announce itself to the network, using this name combined with a sixteenth character for each service. This is how communication is routed to each of the services on a particular computer.

SEE ALSO For more information on the initialization process of an NT-based computer see *MCSE: NT Server 4 in the Enterprise Study Guide, Second Edition*, by Lisa Donald and James Chellis (Sybex, 1998).

Computer Accounts for Windows NT Workstations

While this exam concerns NT Workstation, you will have to know a little about NT Servers to fully configure any NT Workstation on a network. In an NT domain, certain NT Servers hold a master list of user, computer, and group accounts that are valid on computers in the domain. This list, or database, is called the SAM (Security Accounts Manager database).

When an NT Workstation joins a domain, an account must be created for the workstation in the domain's SAM. This can be done in one of two ways.

One way is for the LAN administrator to create the account, using the Server Manager tool, before attempting to add the workstation to the domain. In Server Manager, the administrator chooses Add to Domain from the Computer menu and specifies the NetBIOS name of the workstation. The other way is to give an administrative user account and password while joining the domain. This will result in the account being created as the workstation joins the domain.

In either event, the domain SAM must have a record for the workstation if it is to join the domain.

Network Redirectors

The NT operating system is made up of various modules, each of which provides a specific function. When an NT computer tries to access a resource on the network, the process of connecting to that resource is handled by a Network Redirector. There are redirectors that know how to communicate to other NT-based computers, to Novell NetWare networks, Banyan Vines networks, and to just about every other type of network found in the business world. Each redirector understands the naming conventions, access rules, and other pertinent communication facets of a particular network operating system.

When an NT Workstation attempts to connect to a network resource it consults a "Network Access Order List" to determine which network it should try first. One of the more common performance optimization techniques is to order this list so that the most commonly used network is tried first.

Protocols Supported

The Microsoft Windows NT operating system can use many different protocols to communicate on the network. We'll discuss each exampertinent protocol later in this book, but for now you should be aware of the more commonly installed protocols. The most commonly used network protocols are NetBEUI, TCP/IP, and NWLink IPX/SPX Compatible Transport. Each protocol represents a different set of rules used to communicate on a network. Each has strengths and weaknesses: these will be discussed later.

Network Interface Card (NIC) Drivers

A NIC is a physical device placed in a computer that connects the PC to the network. There are numerous makes and models of NICs on the market. Before NT can communicate with a NIC installed in your workstation, a driver must be loaded. The NIC driver is software that acts as an interpreter between the operating system and the physical device. NT ships with drivers for most of the more common NICs on the market. If the driver for your NIC is not on the NT CD-ROM, you can install a driver provided by the manufacturer.

Binding Order

In the simplest case, to bind is to join together. In an operating system, to bind is to join together two software components. When you install a NIC in an NT computer, the NIC driver must be bound to the various protocols that it will support. In most cases this will be done for you automatically as part of the installation process for the NIC driver software. There are, however, a few specific cases where you would need to configure this manually.

The order in which the protocols are bound to the driver determines the order in which NT will use those protocols for communication. For instance, if TCP/IP was bound first and NWLink second, NT would always try to use TCP/IP first whenever it was trying to communicate. This would be a great configuration if TCP/IP was the primary protocol used on your network. If, however, your primary (or most used) protocol was NWLink, this would cause a delay for any communication using NWLink. You can change the binding order to optimize for performance.

You might also use the protocol bindings as a sort of firewall. If a protocol is not bound to a NIC, then that NIC cannot use the protocol. One configuration seen fairly often is using protocol bindings to provide security on a server attached to the Internet. The administrator might use only NetBEUI on the company network and TCP/IP for communication to the Internet. In this case, you would unbind TCP/IP from the NIC attached to the company network. This would stop any traffic from the Internet from reaching your company network.

Necessary Procedures

All of the procedures discussed for this section begin with the Network applet found in Control Panel.

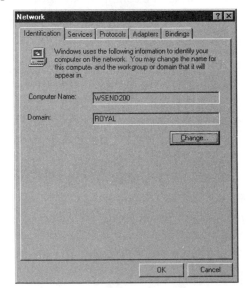

We'll discuss options available within each of the five tabs across the opening window: Identification, Services, Protocols, Adapters, and Bindings.

Identification Tab

The Identification tab allows you to confirm the NetBIOS name or workgroup/domain information for an NT Workstation. Clicking the Change button allows you to change these settings.

Here you can either change the NetBIOS name or workgroup/domain membership. In this case, the NetBIOS name option is grayed out, as the workgroup/domain membership section is active.

If you elect to change the domain membership information, remember that an NT workstation account must be configured in the Domain Security Account Manager database (SAM.) This can either be done before the computer attempts to join the domain using the Server Manager tool or by entering the name of a domain administrator.

Services Tab

Many optional services can be added to an NT Workstation to provide added network functionality. Most of these services will be added by accessing the Services tab and clicking the Add button. We'll discuss each of the exam-pertinent services as necessary for each objective.

If you have multiple network redirectors (software used to connect to various networking environments) installed, you can also change the order in which your NT Workstation attempts to connect to the network. Clicking the Network Access Order button will display a dialog box that lists the various networks that your computer will attempt to attach to; highlight one, and you can move it up or down the list as appropriate.

Protocols Tab

We'll discuss each of the protocols for other objectives, but, for now, we'll concentrate on how protocols are installed and configured on an NT computer. Basically, on the Protocols tab, click Add and choose the protocol off the list. Each protocol will have a different set of parameters that you might have to configure during the installation.

Adapters Tab

The Adapters tab allows you to add, remove, configure, or update the Network Interface Card (NIC) information on your NT Workstation.

Clicking the Add button will bring up a dialog box with a list of the NIC drivers that ship with NT. You will also have the opportunity to click the Have Disk button for drivers not shown on the list.

Each NIC driver will have its own parameters that you may have to configure. Common parameters include the IRQ, port address, and memory address. Before installing an NIC in your computer you should have a firm understanding of your PC and how it is configured.

Bindings Tab

The Bindings tab allows you to disable or enable protocols in use on your workstation and change the order in which they are used to communicate. Changing the binding order so that the most commonly used protocols are used first is a very common performance optimization technique.

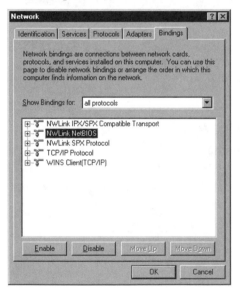

Exam Essentials

In and of itself, this objective is not really heavily tested. It does, however, encompass the basic skills necessary to complete the more complex objectives of this chapter. As such, the information presented is critical to your success on the test. Before continuing, review the information presented in the Necessary Procedures section. If there are any procedures you are unsure of, find an NT Workstation and review the options available.

Understand the concept of a computer account in the domain SAM. For an NT Workstation to join an NT domain, an account for that workstation must be created in the domain accounts database. This account can either be created beforehand by the LAN administrator or created during the process of providing a NetBIOS name for the computer.

Understand how the Binding Order can effect performance. The binding order determines the order in which protocols will be used for communication. For optimal performance, the first protocol in the list should be the protocol most often used on your network.

Key Terms and Concepts

Binding Order: A list that is used to determine the order in which protocols will be used in an attempt to communicate.

NetBIOS Name: A unique identifier for an NT-based computer on the network. This name is used to direct communication to the correct computer *and* the correct service on that computer.

Network Interface Card (NIC) Driver: Software that acts as an interpreter between the operating system and the physical device (NIC).

Network Redirector: Software that is capable of communicating with a specific type of network—NT, NetWare, Banyan Vines, etc. This software understands the process for accessing network resources in a specific type of network.

Security Accounts Manager (SAM): A database of the user, group, and computer accounts defined in an NT domain.

Sample Questions

1. Which of the following describe ways to add a computer account to the domain SAM for an NT Workstation computer?

   A. Use Server Manager before installing the Workstation.

   B. Use the ADDCOMP.EXE command line utility.

   C. It will happen automatically during the installation of the networking portion of NT Workstation.

   D. Choose the option to add the computer to the domain during the installation and provide an account/password for a domain administrator.

   Answer: A, D. On the exam, Microsoft will often give an obscure method of accomplishing a task in the hope that you won't know it. It's best to know a couple of ways to accomplish anything.

2. The binding order controls which of the following?

   A. In what order computers will be listed in the Network Neighborhood

   B. Whether a computer can join a domain

   C. The order that protocols will be used in an attempt to communicate on the network

   D. The order that options were installed to the operating system

   Answer: C. The binding order controls the order in which protocols will be used to communicate on the network.

Use various methods to access network resources.

Once you've added networking to your workstation, the next step is to access network resources. As with most functions in NT, there are numerous ways to accomplish this task. For this objective, we'll discuss the various methods available to access resources on the network.

Critical Information

This is another objective that is mainly concerned with a hands-on process. Most of the critical information will be found in the Necessary Procedures section. There is only one topic that will need further discussion: UNC paths.

Universal Naming Convention (UNC) Paths

The UNC naming standard is a standardized way of naming resources on a network. In a UNC path you must identify both the computer (using its NetBIOS name) and the shared resource on that computer. The format is as follows:

```
\\<server_name>\<share_name>\<directory>
```

Where <server_name> is the NetBIOS name of the device which hosts the resource, <share_name> is the assigned name for that resource, and <directory> is the path to a directory on that resource.

SEE ALSO Since this book is expressly written for experienced administrators or as a supplemental study aid, it is safe to assume that you are comfortable with UNC names. If this is not the case, see *MCSE: NT Workstation 4 Study Guide, Second Edition*, by Charles Perkins, Matthew Strebe, and James Chellis (Sybex, 1998).

Necessary Procedures

As with the proceeding objective, the information presented here is considered part of the basic skill set necessary to work with NT. One of the fundamental reasons to install any kind of network is resource sharing, so it stands to reason that knowing how to access those resources would be a fairly important skill set. The procedures presented here are not heavily tested upon, but they are considered prerequisite knowledge in many of the questions that you will see on your exam.

Using Network Neighborhood to Access Network Resources

There are two ways to use Network Neighborhood to gain access to a shared resource on your network. The first way is to keep opening resources, starting with the "Entire Network" option until you find the computer that the resource resides upon. Then open that computer to see a list of shared resources. Click the resource you wish to access. This method allows you to find the desired resource without knowing its complete UNC path—you just "walk the network" until you find what you are looking for.

Once you've found the appropriate share point, chose Map Network Drive from the file menu. Notice that you are given the opportunity to connect using a different user account in the event that your current account does not have the necessary permissions.

Using the Net Command Line Utility

Microsoft Windows NT's networking components are based upon the LanManager network operating system. Many of the commands that are available in LanManager are available in NT. One such command is the Net command line utility. While this tool can be used to perform many useful administrative functions, we are concerned with only two of its options: VIEW and USE.

The Net command is a command prompt tool. Typing **Net View** *<server_name>* will display the shared resource on a given server.

Typing **Net Use <d>: \\<unc_path_to_resource>** where <d> is a drive letter, will map that drive to the shared resource.

Exam Essentials

You must be comfortable with accessing resources on an NT network for this examination. If possible, spend some time using Network Neighborhood to attach to network resources on an NT network.

Understand the Net View and Net Use command line options. Net view displays a list of shared resources on a server. Net Use is used to map a network drive to a resource.

Key Terms and Concepts

Net command: A utility designed to allow administrative functions to be performed from a command prompt.

UNC Path: An industry standard method of naming and accessing resources on a network.

Sample Questions

1. Which of the following is the correct UNC path to a share point named data on a computer named Endeavor?

   A. \\data

   B. \\Endeavor \data

   C. \\Endeavor\data

   D. \\data\endeavor

   Answer: C. Many of the answers on the exam will include UNC paths—you need to be able to identify them.

2. Which of the following commands will display a list of shared resources on a computer named RoyalTech?

   A. Show \\RoyalTech

   B. Display RoyalTech

   C. Net view \\RoyalTech

   D. View \\RoyalTech

   Answer: C. While the net commands might seem a bit out of date, they are an important skill to master.

3. Which of the following will map drive f: to the resource listed in question 1?

   A. Map f:=Endeavor\data:

   B. Net Use \\Endeavor\data

   C. Net Use f: \\Endeavor\data

   D. Net F: \\Endeavor\data

   Answer: C. The correct syntax for mapping a drive to a shared resource is Net Use <d>:\\unc_path_to_resource.

Implement Windows NT Workstation as a client in a NetWare environment.

No discussion of networking is complete without talking about Novell's NetWare. At one time, not so long ago, Novell owned over 90 percent of the worldwide networking market. Even today, that number is probably still over 50 percent. Given this, the odds are you will have to connect to a NetWare server at some point in your career.

Even if you believe the experts who claim that NetWare is a legacy operating system and that Novell is on a downward spiral to oblivion, common sense tells you that NetWare servers are going to be around for a long time. With Novell's current market share, it would take years for NT to replace the NetWare servers currently installed.

One of the features of Windows NT is its ability to coexist with a Net-Ware environment. This means companies can ease into an NT network, while maintaining the network services that they are currently using.

Critical Information

There are two ways that a Windows NT environment can connect to a Novell NetWare system: one server-based solution and one workstation-based solution. On the server side, NT ships with a tool called Gateway Services for NetWare (GSNW.) This tool allows an NT-based server to connect to a NetWare server and share its resources as if they were part of the NT environment. With this solution, no special configuration is necessary at the client, since they see the NetWare resources as if they were a shared resource at the NT server.

This solution is great in a small network, or in an environment where the NetWare resources are used infrequently. If your users make extensive use of the NetWare resources, however, GSNW can become a bottleneck since all users share one connection to the NetWare server.

For our purposes, that is all you need to know about GSNW. It is covered in more detail in the NT Core Technologies and NT Enterprise Technologies examinations.

This objective is really concerned with configuring an NT Workstation as a NetWare client. This is a two-step process.

1. Configure your NT Workstation with a protocol that NetWare can use to communicate.

2. Add the NetWare client, Client Services for NetWare, to your workstation.

To access resources on a NetWare server, your workstation has to be configured to use the NWLink IPX/SPX Compatible Protocol. This is Microsoft's implementation of the IPX/SPX protocol used in Net Ware environments.

We'll look at the actual installation and configuration process in the Necessary Procedures section. For now, though, you should be aware of the two configuration parameters associated with this protocol—Frame Type and Network Number.

- **Frame Type**   Frame type refers to an industry standard set of rules for organizing packets in an IPX/SPX network. When you send a request to another computer on the network, that request is passed through various layers of software before it is ready to be transmitted. Each layer adds information to the request, building what is known as a *packet* for transmission. The definition of how this management information is organized is known as the Frame Type. If both computers (the originator and the recipient) are configured to use the same frame type, then each computer will know how to interpret the information in the packet. If not, then communication cannot occur.

- **Network Number**   In an IPX/SPX environment, each network segment is given a unique identifier. This identifier is used to deliver the packet to the proper destination. The network number is this unique identifier. To confuse the issue, each network segment has a unique identifier for each frame type. If you are using multiple frame types, you will have multiple network numbers for each segment.

Addressing in an IPX/SPX environment can be a confusing topic. There are three types of addresses used to route information, only two of which we need to discuss here. The two addresses are the node or MAC (Media Access Control) address and the Network Number. The MAC address is the physical address burned into the NIC (Network Interface Card). The Network Number represents a network segment.

In most cases, you will not have to worry about configuring the NWLink protocol. It can automatically sense the frame type and network number in use and will configure itself appropriately. It does this by grabbing one IPX/SPX packet off the network and analyzing its content. If you are configured with multiple frame types, it will not configure all of them and you will have to do this manually.

Once the NWLink IPX/SPX Compatible Protocol is installed and configured, you must add the appropriate client software to your computer. NT ships with NetWare client software known as Client Services for NetWare (CSNW). CSNW is best described as the NetWare *redirector*. A redirector is a software component that passes requests to a particular network operating system—in this case, NetWare.

A computer configured with both the NWLink protocol and CSNW can access a NetWare server using the NetWare Core Protocol (NCP), the internal language of NetWare. CSNW also supports the following:

- Large Internet Protocol (LIP), which determines the optimum packet size to be used for communication

- Long filenames, if the NetWare server is configured to accept them

- NetWare Directory Services (NDS), which is Novell's X.500-compliant directory service used to organize network resources

Necessary Procedures

Microsoft is quite aware of the number of NetWare networks that exist. Windows NT Workstation must be able to connect to these networks or administrators will think twice about implementing the Microsoft solution. You will probably see questions on your exam that concern the implementation of the NetWare client software.

Installing NWLink IPX/SPX Compatible Protocol

This protocol is installed like any other—Use the Network applet in Control Panel. On the Protocols tab, choose Add.

Configuring the Frame Type and Network Number

As mentioned earlier, if you are using only one frame type on your network, you can leave these parameters at the default setting of Auto Detect. If you are using more than one frame type, however, you will have to manually configure this protocol.

1. In Control Panel, open the Network applet.

2. On the Protocols tab, highlight NWLink IPX/SPX Compatible Transport and click the Properties button.

3. To configure the frame type and network number, chose the frame type from the drop-down list and then enter in the network number.

Installing Client Services for NetWare

CSNW is installed like any other service in the NT operating system.

1. From Control Panel, open the Network applet.

2. On the Services tab, choose Add.

3. From the list, highlight Client Service for NetWare and click OK.

4. After the process completes you must restart your computer.

At the first restart of your computer, a dialog box will appear asking for your preferred server or, in a NetWare 4.*x* network, your preferred tree and name context. You can either enter this information at that point or chose the CSNW applet in Control Panel, shown below. The CSNW applet will include a few more options.

Exam Essentials

Since NetWare is firmly entrenched in the business networking market, most administrators will have to connect an NT Workstation to a Novell network at one time or another. Microsoft is very aware of this fact and tests accordingly. You should understand the NetWare client very well before attempting this examination.

Understand Gateway Services for NetWare (GSNW). GSNW is a service that runs on an NT server. It allows the NT server to connect to the NetWare server and share NetWare resources as if they were on the NT system. Clients of the NT network then connect to the Net-Ware resource by accessing a share on the NT server.

Understand Client Services for NetWare (CSNW). CSNW is a software redirector that runs on an NT computer. It allows that computer to connect directly to a NetWare server to access resources.

Understand the differences between GSNW and CSNW. GSNW is a server-based solution. All users share a single-user account in the NetWare environment. It is not a great solution if many users access the NetWare server on a regular basis, since that one connection can become a bottleneck. CSNW allows each NT computer to connect directly to the NetWare server.

Know the two steps involved in configuring CSNW. First install and configure the NWLink protocol, and then install and configure CSNW.

Understand what a Frame Type is. Frame Type refers to the layout of headers within a packet on the network.

Understand what a Network Number is. A network number is a unique identifier for each network segment in an IPX/SPX environment.

Know what services CSNW supports. Services include Access to a NetWare server using NetWare Core Protocol (NCP), Large Internet Protocol, long filenames, and NDS support.

Key Terms and Concepts

Client Services for NetWare (CSNW):   A Microsoft NT Workstation–based solution for connecting an NT client to a Novell NetWare server.

Frame Type: An industry standard definition of how a packet should be organized.

Gateway Services for NetWare (GSNW):   A Microsoft NT Server–based solution to connecting an NT network to a Novell NetWare network.

NetWare Core Protocol (NCP):   The language spoken internally at a NetWare server. Requests made of a NetWare server must be made using this protocol.

NetWare Directory Service (NDS):   Novell's X.500-compliant directory services. Basically, this is a management component of NetWare used to organize network resources.

Network Number: A unique identifier for a network segment in an IPX/SPX network.

NWLink IPX/SPX Compatible Transport: Microsoft's implementation of the IPX/SPX protocol suite used on NetWare networks.

Redirector: A software component on in the NT operating system used to connect to resources on the Network. More specifically for this context, a component of CSNW that allows a client to access resources on a NetWare server.

Sample Questions

1. Frame Type is best described as which of the following?

   A. The protocol in use

   B. A definition of how packets are organized

   C. The hardware configuration of the NIC

   D. Hardware that surrounds a picture

   Answer: B. NWLink and its components are critical to connecting to a Netware system. As such they are important on the test.

2. Client Service for NetWare should be loaded on which of the following computers?

   A. The NetWare servers that any NT client will attach to

   B. Any NT client that will need to connect directly to a NetWare server

   C. Each router between a client and a NetWare server

   D. All computers in your network

   Answer: B. Connecting to a Netware server is a common task and is heavily tested. You need to know how to configure for this connectivity.

Use various configurations to install Windows NT Workstation as a TCP/IP client.

While this is a fairly short objective, it is critical to Microsoft's positioning of Windows NT as an Internet-ready operating system. When you install the networking components of NT Workstation, TCP/IP is chosen as the default protocol.

The information covered for this objective is critical to both the Enterprise exam as well as most of the other tests in the MCSE program. Microsoft places a lot of emphasis on understanding the use of the TCP/IP protocol suite.

SEE ALSO   For a more detailed discussion of TCP/IP, see *MCSE: TCP/IP for NT Server 4 Study Guide*, by Todd Lammle with Monica Lammle and James Chellis (Sybex, 1997).

Critical Information

You cannot finish the MCSE program without at least a rudimentary understanding of the TCP/IP protocol suite. While a full discussion is beyond the realm of this objective, you will need to understand a little bit about why TCP/IP is chosen and how it works.

Why TCP/IP?

TCP/IP was specifically designed to allow dissimilar devices to communicate. This is key to understanding why TCP/IP is so popular in today's networking environments. Most networks are a combination of old and new—legacy systems that would cost too much to replace, and new systems that have been purchased over the years. There are very few networks made up of only one type of hardware running only one operating system.

Many of the early *connected systems* (before the term *network* was coined) were proprietary in nature—that is, they could only communicate with like systems. At the time this was no problem because Wide Area Networks (WAN) did not exist. As companies started to connect their offices together, a need for a common method of communication was perceived. TCP/IP was designed to fulfill that need.

NOTE   There's really more to it than that, but we don't really need the history of TCP/IP—just an understanding of its goals.

This makes TCP/IP the perfect protocol for today's mixed networks. Microsoft has embraced the open nature of TCP/IP in an effort to allow administrators the ability to connect all of their network devices under one umbrella—Windows NT.

How Does TCP/IP Work?

TCP/IP is based upon a common set of rules that define how communication should occur and how each device is located on the network. For our purposes, we will need to understand how each TCP/IP device, or *host*, is configured.

Each host on a TCP/IP network needs to be assigned a unique identifier, known as its IP address. This address must be unique against all other devices on the networks to which this host can connect.

TIP   To put the IP address in perspective, think about the millions of computers attached to the Internet. Each has its own unique IP address that is different from all other computers connected.

This IP address is made up of four octets—each octet is made up of eight bits; an IP address follows this syntax: 206.100.11.179. For this exam you won't really need to understand how those addresses are decided upon—just how they are physically assigned to each workstation.

Of the IP address, a certain number of bits will represent the network to which the device is connected and the rest will represent that device on the network. In other words, the IP address is really made up of two parts—network and host. Unfortunately, it is rarely obvious from the address where the network address ends and the host address begins. To make this distinction, each host must be configured with a subnet mask. The subnet mask is used by the network to determine which part of a computer's IP address is network and which part is host.

Simple, right? Don't be discouraged. TCP/IP is such a complex subject that Microsoft offers a five-day MCSE course on the subject. For now, you just need to be aware that the IP address identifies both the network and the host on that network.

One last important configuration parameter must be set at each host—the Default Gateway. When a computer attempts to communicate with another host, the local networking software must determine if that host is local or remote (on the same network or a different one). If the destination host is remote, the computer must pass its communication to a device that can route the packets to the destination— a router. Each device on a routed network (an environment made up of multiple networks) must be configured with the IP address of the router it should send remote communication to. This is known as the Default Gateway.

To recap—each Windows NT computer on your network will need to be configured with three parameters:

- IP Address

- Subnet Mask

- Default Gateway

The focus of this objective is the procedures used to configure these parameters. There are two methods: manual and dynamic.

NOTE For testing purposes, Microsoft really pushes the use of the dynamic method, so be sure to study it carefully.

Manual Configuration of a TCP/IP Host

When using the manual configuration method, you will have to set parameters at each computer by hand. The procedure is described in the Necessary Procedures section of this objective.

While this method has been used to configure TCP/IP hosts for quite a while, it does have its drawbacks. Since each computer needs to be configured, you will have to travel to each computer, sit down, and manually enter the data. This method is fine in a small environment, but in a large company it can consume hours.

The manual method also invites mistakes. Mistakes in the TCP/IP configuration can mean that no communication will be possible. Overall, the manual method is fine for small environments but is not recommended for larger networks.

Dynamic Configuration of TCP/IP Clients

The TCP/IP protocol suite includes a protocol specifically designed to configure clients automatically as they connect to the network. The Dynamic Host Configuration Protocol (DHCP) is implemented as a service on an NT Server. The administrator configures the parameters that should be configured for clients at that server. When those clients attach to the network, they find the DHCP server and request an IP address and any other configuration parameters that they might need.

DHCP allows the administrator to configure the TCP/IP environment from a central location. This reduces the time, effort, and potential mistakes that the manual method would entail.

Configuring the DHCP service is beyond the scope of this exam, but you will need to know how to configure an NT Workstation to take advantage of dynamic TCP/IP configuration.

Necessary Procedures

The procedures that follow are the main focus of this objective. They are also mentioned in numerous other MCSE examinations. Spend some time getting comfortable with the differences. No matter which method you chose to use to configure your clients, the first step will be installing the TCP/IP protocol.

Installing TCP/IP

1. In Control Panel, open the Network applet.

2. On the Protocols tab, click Add.

3. Highlight TCP/IP Protocol, and click OK. After NT copies in the appropriate files, you will be prompted to restart your computer.

Manually Configuring a TCP/IP Client

1. In Control Panel, open the Network applet.

2. On the Protocols tab, highlight TCP/IP Protocol and click Properties.

3. For our purposes, enter the IP address that the computer has been assigned, the subnet mask, and the IP address of the default gateway. Notice that there are other tabs that contain configuration options. While they are beyond the scope of this exam, in real life you would need to configure numerous other parameters.

Setting up a DHCP Client

There is very little involved in configuring a workstation as a DHCP client. The whole point, after all, is to avoid configuring each client individually.

1. In Control Panel, open the Network applet.

2. On the Protocols tab, highlight the TCP/IP Protocol and click the Properties button.

3. On the opening screen, you will see the option "Obtain an IP address from a DHCP server." Make sure it is selected.

Exam Essentials

This objective concerns the methods of configuring an NT Workstation as a TCP/IP client. Make sure that you have read the Necessary Procedures section and understand the processes described. You should also be comfortable with the following:

Know the three parameters that must be configured at each host on a routed network. These parameters are IP address, subnet mask, and default gateway.

Understand the function of the IP address. The IP address uniquely identifies a device on a TCP/IP network.

Understand the function of the subnet mask. The IP address is actually made up of two parts—the network and host addresses. The subnet mask identifies which parts of the IP address represent network and which parts represent host.

Understand the function of the default gateway. When traffic is destined for a host on another subnet, the traffic will be sent to a router. The router is responsible for routing the traffic to the appropriate network. The default gateway parameter is the IP address that a host should send remote traffic to.

Know the drawbacks to manually configuring TCP/IP clients.
Since configuration information will have to be entered at each computer, configuring a large number of clients can take a lot of time. There is also a large chance of human error that could have an effect on your network.

Know the advantages of using DHCP. Since all IP configuration can take place at a central server, using DHCP reduces the amount of time involved in configuring clients as well as the chance of error.

TIP Notice the wording of the last two items—it would seem to imply that DHCP is the preferred method of configuring clients. This attitude will be evident on your exam as well.

Key Terms and Concepts

Default Gateway: The IP address to which communication with remote hosts should be directed. This is also known as the Default Router address.

Dynamic Host Configuration Protocol: Both a protocol and a service designed to configure TCP/IP clients as they attach to the network.

IP Address: A 32-bit value used to uniquely identify a device on a TCP/IP network. It is made up of two parts—a network address and a host address.

Subnet Mask: A value that defines which portion of the IP address represents the network and which portion represents the host.

TCP/IP: A suite of communication protocols designed to allow dissimilar systems to communicate.

Sample Questions

1. Which of the following parameters must be configured on each TCP/IP client in a routed network?

   A. IP address

   B. DNS server address

   C. Subnet mask

   D. Default Gateway

   Answer: A, C, D. DNS is an add-on service, not a mandatory component of a TCP/IP network.

2. Which service is used to automatically configure TCP/IP clients as they attach to the network?

   A. WINS

   B. Workstation

   C. DHCP

   D. RIP for IP

   Answer: C. Microsoft really pushed DHCP—be sure you understand what it is used for.

Configure and install Dial-Up Networking in a given situation.

Reach out and touch someone has never been more popular than it is with computer people. We are constantly hitting dial-up connections to the Internet, dialing in to the office to pick up e-mail or voice mail, or connecting to bulletin boards to download the latest in patches and drivers. Even now, regular people are getting in the act.

Sales people want to transmit their orders electronically, and management types want to be in contact with the office for more than 24 hours a day. What is a techie to do?

Critical Information

Windows NT Workstation supports two of the most common telephone line protocols: Serial Line Internet Protocol (SLIP) and Point-to-Point Protocol (PPP). Each of these line protocols takes the standard LAN protocols of TCP/IP, NetBEUI, and NWLink and hides them (the actual word is encapsulates, but hides makes more sense) within the telephone protocol. SLIP is the older of the two protocols and is rarely used anymore. PPP is the most popular because it supports things like Dynamic Host Control Protocol (DHCP) as well as static IP addressing.

Windows NT Workstation also supports a procedure called multilink. With multilink, you can have multiple lines calling the same destination at the same time for faster throughput.

In addition to the standard line protocols, NT supports Point-to-Point Tunneling protocol. This protocol allows you to "steal" a part of the Internet to create a Virtual Private Network between your remote location and the office.

Necessary Procedures

Remote Access Service (RAS) and Dial-Up Networking (DUN) can be installed together or separately. They can be installed either at the time of initial NT Workstation installation or later. This section will cover how to install Dial-Up Networking after the initial installation of NT Workstation.

Install Dial-Up Networking

Start the installation of Dial-Up Networking by double-clicking the My Computer icon on the desktop, and then click the Dial Up Networking icon. This will start the Installation Wizard.

1. The first screen you see tells you how you can use either a modem or an ISDN line to use dial-up networking. Microsoft marketing invades the Installation Wizard arena. Click Install to get to work.

2. Once you click Install, NT goes out and starts to copy files. It will locate the Remote Access Service device installed in your computer (your modem or ISDN adapter). If you don't like the modem it found, there are choices to Install a Modem or Install an X.25 pad. Click OK to add the RAS device we installed back in Chapter 1.

3. This brings up the Remote Access Setup screen. The RAS setup screen shows the modem installed and allows you to add or remove components, configure or clone (copy) a component, or click Continue. Click Continue.

4. Windows NT Workstation installs RAS and binds the appropriate protocols. You finally get a message that says DUN has been installed and you need to restart your computer for the changes to take effect. Click Restart.

Configure Dial-Up Networking

The configuration of the Dial-Up Networking client really begins with the configuration of Remote Access Services and the modem. To access the modem configuration options, go into Control Panel, then double-click Modems, highlight the modem, and click Properties.

Depending on the modem, there may not be much to configure. You can configure default line speed, the volume of the modem speaker, and the way the modem connects.

From the modem General page, you can configure your dialing properties. This specifies how your calls are to be dialed.

- You can set your location depending on the area you are calling from.

- You can specify if you need to dial an access code to get an outside line for either local or long distance.

- You can set the system up to use a calling card.

- You can disable call waiting.

- You can tell the system to use tone or pulse dialing.

Once modem configuration has been completed, you can configure RAS. To start the RAS configuration, from Control Panel, double-click the Network icon.

1. Click the Services tab.

2. Click Remote Access Service, then click Properties. This returns us to the Remote Access Setup screen. Click Configure. Configure gives you the opportunity to specify how the port the modem is attached to is used. You can tell the system to use the port for Dial out only,Receive calls only, or Dial out and receive calls. The default is Dial out only. Make your selection and click OK.

3. Click Network. The network selection lets you choose which network protocols will be used on dial out. Your choices are NetBEUI, TCP/IP, and IPX. TCP/IP and IPX are selected by default. Make your selections and click OK. If you made changes to the RAS configuration, you must restart the computer.

At this point, DUN is configured and RAS is configured; we just don't have anyplace to call. Now, we must create a phone book entry. Phone book entries are important, not just because they give us somewhere to call, but because this is where RAS security is configured. Phone book entries, by the way, are part of the configuration information for the user, so the other people who use your NT Workstation won't know where you are calling.

To create a new phone book entry, double-click My Computer on your desktop, double-click Dial-Up networking and click New. This starts the New Phonebook Entry Wizard.

1. You will be asked to name the new phone book entry. Provide a name and click Next.

NOTE If you know all about phone books, you can check the box that says you would rather edit the properties directly.

---

2. You now receive a Server screen, and you can check any or all of the three options:

   ▪ I am calling the Internet.

   ▪ Send a plain text password if that's the only way to connect.

   ▪ The non-Windows NT server I am calling expects me to type login information after connecting or to know TCP/IP addressed before dialing.

   Make any and all choices and click next.

3. Enter in the phone number and choose to use telephony dialing properties. You can add alternate phone numbers, so if your ISP has three local access numbers, NT will try each number. Click Next.

4. Now you can choose your serial line protocol. When in doubt, stay with PPP. It's newer and more widely accepted. Click Next.

5. You are now prompted to enter a login script for after the connection. If in doubt, go with the default of None. Again, click Next.

6. Now you are prompted to enter a static IP address. If you are planning on using a DHCP-assigned address, leave the entry set to all zeros. Click Next. Again, you are asked for some IP addresses, this time for Domain Name Service servers or Windows Internet Name Service servers. When in doubt, leave it at zeros. Click Next.

7. Click Finish.

8. To test the connection, click Dial. This brings up the Connect screen. Here you can add your user name, password, domain (if required), and check the box to save your password. Click OK to dial.

Exam Essentials

This is one of those sections that the exam writers really like, so study carefully!

Know the two dial-up services offered by Windows NT Workstation. The two services are Remote Access Service and Dial-Up Networking (DUN).

Know the differences between SLIP, PPP, and PTPP. SLIP (Serial Line Internet Protocol) is IP over a modem. This is an outdated protocol. PPP (Point-to-Point Protocol) is used with serial or modem communications to provide IP communications, and it can provide additional features such as data compression, DNS, and gateway addressing. PPP has largely replaced SLIP. Windows NT servers can establish SLIP connections only when dialing out or originating a SLIP session. PPTP (Point-to-Point Tunneling Protocol) is PPP with security and is used with the Internet to create an encrypted link to the RAS server. In some areas, this is called creating a virtual private network (VPN).

Key Terms and Concepts

IPX: Internet packet exchange protocol.

ISDN (Integrated Services Digital Network): Provides communications over special phone lines using digital communications.

Modem: From modulate/demodulate. Computer hardware that will turn a computer's digital signal into an analog signal that can be sent over a phone line. The modem at the receiving end will then turn the analog signal into a digital signal that the computer can understand.

Multilink: RAS can combine several serial signals into one, using either ISDN or modems.

NetBEUI: Microsoft networking protocol. Efficient, simple protocol that will not provide routing, but can be used in RAS sessions.

NWLink: Microsoft's implementation of the IPX/SPX protocol. Installed to be compatible with Novell networks. Can be used by RAS servers as a networking protocol.

POTS: Plain old telephone system.

PPP (Point-to-Point Protocol): A data-link-layer transport that performs over point-to-point network connections such as serial or modem lines. PPP can negotiate with any transport protocol used by both systems involved in the link and can realize data-transfer efficiencies such as software compression and automatically assign IP, Domain Name Service (DNS), and gateway addresses when used with transmission control protocol/ Internet protocol (TCP/IP).

PSTN (public switched telephone network):   The phone company.

RAS: Remote access service.

SLIP (Serial Line Internet Protocol):   An implementation of Internet protocol (IP) over a serial line. SLIP has been replaced, by and large, by PPP.

SPX: Sequenced packet exchange protocol.

TCP/IP (Transmission Control Protocol/Internet Protocol):   The standard protocol suite of the Internet.

Sample Questions

1. Which dial-up line protocols does RAS support?

A. PPP

B. TCP

C. SLIP

D. IPX/SPX

E. UDP

Answer: A and C. PPP and SLIP are the only two dial-up line protocols listed.

2. What is multilink?

A. The ability to have two or more modems handling different calls at the same time

B. The ability of two or more modems to call out at the same time

C. The ability to use more than one communication channel for the same connection

D. The ability to have two network interface cards in the same system at the same time

Answer: C. Multilink is the ability to use more than one communication channel for the same connection.

3. What does RAS stand for?

A. Remote Access Service

B. Remote and Secure

C. Remote and Safe

D. Remote Access Server

Answer: A. RAS stands for Remote Access Service.

Configure Microsoft Peer Web Services in a given situation.

This objective is more of a sales pitch for Microsoft's Web server software than a technical discussion. The Peer Web Services component is not heavily tested, but there are a few things you should be aware of.

One of the most important functions of a network is the ability to share information. As networks have developed and grown more and more, companies are finding it difficult to manage the data on their network and ensure that users have the tools necessary to access it. Most companies have numerous servers, each of which has numerous share points. In many companies, this need to disseminate information trickles down to the department level. Each department has information that needs to be accessible to its own employees in a timely, easy-to-understand, and easy-to-manage format.

Critical Information

Peer Web Services (PWS) is basically a Web server designed for departmental-sized environments. While it is not robust enough to handle the amount of traffic an Internet Web server would be subjected to (that's what Internet Information Server is for), it is more than enough for most small networks.

The beauty of using a Web server to disseminate information is in the fact that most business users will already be comfortable with the technology used to access it. Almost everyone will have used a Web browser at some point or another. The interface is fairly intuitive, it is easy to keep the data current, and you can control who has access to the information. All in all, using Internet technologies makes a lot of sense.

Installing PWS

The physical requirements for PWS are fairly straightforward. You will need the following:

- A computer running Windows NT Server 4.0 and TCP/IP

- The NT Workstation CD-ROM and some way to access it (either a local CD-ROM drive or across the network)

- Enough disk space to store the information you wish to publish

PWS is installed through the Network applet in Control Panel—just like any other service you wish to add to your NT Workstation.

PWS Services

PWS performs three services:

- **WWW**   A service that allows you to make data available to Web browsers.

- **Gopher**   A service that allows you to index information, create links to other servers, and create custom menus.

- **FTP**   A service that allows you to set up your NT Workstation as an FTP server. FTP provides the ability to copy files between the client and the server.

During its installation, PWS will add a new group to your Start menu—Microsoft Peer Web Services (Common). Within this group you will find a utility named Internet Service Manager. PWS is managed through this tool.

That's really as deep as you need to get for this exam. In the Exam Essentials section you will find a table that outlines the features of PWS.

Exam Essentials

This objective is more to make sure that you are aware of PWS than it is to make sure you are an expert in its technology. You will need to be aware of the features in the following list as well as the few items that follow it.

- File publication
- Network management
- Security
- Support for common Internet standards (the various tools used to create Web pages)
- Microsoft Internet Explorer
- Scaleability (PWS will run on any platform that NT will run on— including multiprocessor computers.)
- Support for BackOffice applications

Know the physical requirements of PWS.   A computer running Windows NT Workstation and TCP/IP, access to a CD-ROM drive, and enough disk space to store the data you wish to publish.

Know the three services that make up PWS.   WWW, Gopher, and FTP.

Key Terms and Concepts

Peer Web Services (PWS):   Web server software designed for small environments.

Sample Questions

1. PWS provides which of the following services?

   A. WWW

   B. DHCP

   C. FTP

   D. WINS

   E. Gopher

   Answer: A, C, E. WINS is an add-on service related to address resolution, not a function of PWS.

2. The FTP service provides which of the following services?

   A. The Figure Translation Process (FTP) translates graphics from various formats to the HTTP format used on the World Wide Web.

   B. The File Transfer Protocol (FTP) service allows bi-directional copying of files between a server and a client.

   C. FTP is not a service, it is a specific type of hardware used to store Web pages.

   D. The File Transfer Protocol (FTP) service is used by backup programs to transfer data to tape.

   Answer: B. The FTP protocol is a basic component of the TCP/IP protocol suite used to transfer files. The FTP service facilitates these transfers.

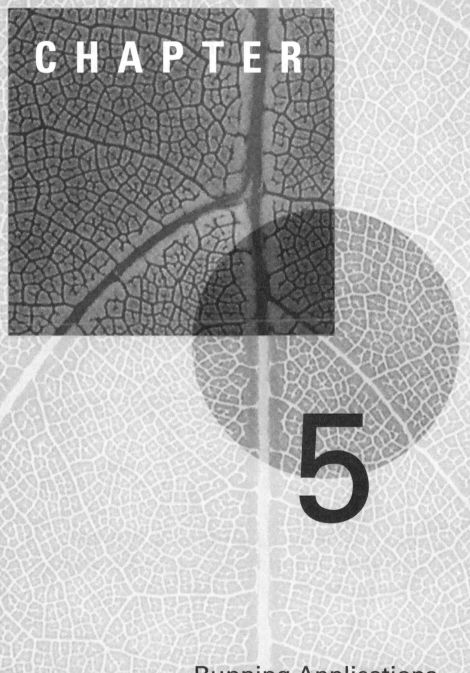

CHAPTER

5

Running Applications

Microsoft Exam Objectives Covered in This Chapter:

▶ **Start applications on Intel and RISC platforms in various operating system environments.** *(pages 206 – 216)*

▶ **Start applications at various priorities.** *(pages 216 – 220)*

Your new Windows NT Workstation 4.0 computer was purchased for one purpose and one purpose only: to run applications. When the new breed of 32-bit operating systems began to appear on desktops, there were few applications written to take advantage of the new features and benefits. Over the years, that has changed significantly, as both Windows 95 and Windows NT have increased in popularity. The fact remains that there are many OS/2 applications, 16-bit Windows, and even DOS-based applications still being run in the workplace. Windows NT Workstation had to be backward-compatible to make allowances for these legacy applications, as well as provide support for POSIX- or RISC-based applications.

NT handles this diversity with something called Executive Services. Executive Services has all the nitty-gritty application support that Windows, OS/2, and POSIX applications require. When an application is started, the API does not have to work with the system hardware, it can work with the Executive Services layer. The Executive Services layer translates requests when a subsystem needs hardware services and passes these requests on to the hardware.

▶ Start applications on Intel and RISC platforms in various operating system environments.

Application problems can always be a challenge to solve. Knowing how the operating system is interfacing with the application will give you a head start in the troubleshooting area. It may even help during testing, too.

Critical Information

Window NT provides support for several different layers of application support. It supports:

- **Win32**   32-bit Windows support for applications written for Windows 95 and Windows NT

- **Virtual DOS Machine (VDM)**   Support for some legacy DOS applications

- **Win16**   16-bit Windows application support for applications from the Windows 3.1 environment

- **OS/2**   Provides support for IBM's OS/2 operating system, in both OS/2 and DOS mode

- **POSIX**   Windows NT does not "run" POSIX programs, it provides easy access to compile the POSIX program so it will run in an NT environment.

To understand how each application works with Windows NT, we need to look at how some of the pieces fit together.

Win32 Subsystem

The Win32 application subsystem is a *big* player in running applications. The Win32 subsystem is the programmer's playground. It lets programmers write 32-bit applications that utilize multiple threads. Each application that uses the Win32 subsystem is given a 2GB address space to work in, and has memory protection built in.

If you are a computer gamer, you just have to love the Win32 subsystem. This is where the 2-D and 3-D graphics operations come from using the industry standard OpenGL interface. This subsystem also supports ActiveX, DirectX, and OLE support.

32-Bit Processor

The Win32 subsystem is written to take advantage of the Intel 32-bit processors, which is everything after the 386. There are other processor manufacturers, and if a 32 bit processor is made, NT supports it. This includes the MIPS, PowerPC, and even the 64-bit–capable

Alpha chip. A 32-bit processor can work with larger numbers, so it handles instruction sets more quickly than the old 16-bit processor.

Multiple Threads

Since the 32-bit subsystem can handle larger numbers, what does it mean to you that the system can handle multiple threads? A thread is the lowest form of work that a processor can do. In older environments, a program was executed a line at a time, and the instruction was completed. With multiple threads, more than one instruction can be carried out at the same time.

2GB Address Space

This is a programmer's tool that allows programs to be written in larger chunks and to take advantage of larger data sets. This provides better performance. The NT Virtual Memory Manager utilizes disk space, and RAM comes up with the address space each application needs.

Memory Protection

Since each application runs in its own memory space, it does not have to worry about infringing on the rights of other applications. Memory issues have plagued computer users since the early days of computing. If your computer simply stops, there is generally a memory issue. Two applications want to access the same memory space. When there is a conflict, your computer does not do conflict resolution. It stops. Memory protection keeps these work stoppages to a minimum.

Application Interface

Each application running on an NT Workstation creates an input queue for instructions. You may have five applications running on the workstation, but when you move the mouse, or enter information from the keyboard, it goes into the queue for just that application. By keeping this information separate, NT is eliminating the problem of conflicting instruction sets.

Virtual DOS Machine

While not all DOS applications will run on a Windows NT computer, many of them will, thanks to something called the VDM or Virtual DOS machine.

Software Components of the VDM

To run a DOS application, the NT system needs to trick the application into thinking it's not as powerful as it really is. The software pieces that make this work include the NTVDM.EXE which runs in protected mode, just like the old 8088 machines. NTVDM translates the DOS application calls into the Win32 calls, and then forwards those calls onto the Win32 subsystem.

NTIO.SYS and NTDOS.SYS replace the IO.SYS and MSDOS.SYS pieces of the DOS environment. NTDOS.SYS runs in real mode, just like a 386 computer.

The last software piece is the VDMREDIR.DLL. This dynamic link library redirects file system calls and input/output calls to the Win32 subsystem.

Virtual Device Drivers

NT uses a group of files called virtual device drivers, or VDDs, to create the hardware environment that the DOS applications require. DOS applications usually talk directly to the hardware. NT has two or three layers between the application and the actual hardware component. The VDDs make the application "think" the hardware is really there.

Configuration Files

DOS applications don't use registry entries or INI files, they use the AUTOEXEC.BAT and CONFIG.SYS files. With the VDM, it reads from the AUTOEXEC.NT file and the CONFIG.NT file to start the application.

Win16-Bit Applications

WOW! No, really, 16-bit applications run because of WOW, or Windows on Windows. 16-bit applications are all those legacy applications that were written to run on earlier versions of Windows, but were never upgraded to Windows 95 or Windows NT. Just like when Windows runs on a DOS machine, the Win16 subsystem makes use of the default VDM.

Windows applications were designed to interact with other Windows applications. In the Win16 subsystem, when you start multiple 16-bit Windows applications they all run in the default VDM. If you run any other Win16 applications, they run in a separate VDM. No matter how many 16-bit applications you have running in the VDM, it just appears as one application to the Win32 subsystem.

NOTE When you start a Windows 16-bit application you have the choice of running it in the Default VDM or in a separate VDM. The only VDM that supports running multiple 16-bit applications is the Default VDM.

Software Components of WOW

WOW makes use of all the components of the Virtual DOS Machine. In addition, WOW uses:

- **KRNL386.EXE**   Windows 3.1 modified to run under NT

- **USER.EXE**   Modified version of Windows 3.1 USER.EXE. This one passes calls on to the Win32 subsystem.

- **GDI.EXE**   Translates graphics calls to the Win32 subsystem

- **WOWEXEC.EXE**   Windows emulation for the VDM

Input Queue

WOW uses the single input queue. All applications running under WOW will use the same instruction queue.

Scheduling

WOW scheduling is handled in the same way as Windows scheduling. Each application gets its shot at the microprocessor in turn. You can have multiple applications open at the same time, but the processor is paying attention to only one application at a time. WOW applications can be started from the command prompt, from the Start menu, or from NT Explorer.

OS/2 Subsystem

At one time IBM and Microsoft were working on a version of OS/2 together. As a result, native NT will not support any application written for OS/2 version 2.0 or greater. In order to provide for OS/2 support for applications greater than 2.0, you need to install an add-on Presentation Manager subsystem.

Software Components of the OS/2 Subsystem

Like most things IBM, OS/2 works in a world all its own. This is not a knock on OS/2, just a statement of fact. After all, who makes personal computers that are not IBM-PC compatible? IBM.

- **OS2SS.EXE and OS2SRV.EXE**   These provide the environment the OS/2 applications expect. If you have multiple copies of OS/2-based applications running, only one version of OS2SRV will be loaded.

- **OS2.EXE**   For each OS/2 application running, there is a separate version of OS2.EXE running. It handles all the program-specific management tasks.

- **NETAPI.DLL and DOSCALLS.DLL**   These contain the NT versions of the application programming interfaces that OS/2 programs are looking for.

POSIX

The Portable Open System Interface or POSIX is a programming specification that is independent of any operating system. NT support for POSIX is not for applications. Rather, it is designed to provide a friendly environment for POSIX applications to be compiled in, so they will run successfully under NT.

POSIX offers several challenges. Like UNIX, it uses case-sensitive naming. That means that RESUME, Resume, and resume are not the same file. POSIX also has hard link support. Hard link support means that one file can have two different names. NT supports this process. Any application written to be POSIX-compliant must be written using a library of C routines that are POSIX.1-compliant.

Software Components of POSIX

- **PSXSS.EXE** Main POSIX component. It is loaded when the first POSIX application is run and remains in memory until the user unloads it. Only one instance will be loaded, no matter how many POSIX applications are running.

- **POSIX.EXE** Handles communication between POSIX and Executive services.

- **PSXDLL.DLL** Contains the library routines that POSIX says must be present.

Necessary Procedures

Applications for each of the supported subsystems are started by using the Start menu, Explorer, or the command line. While there are several ways to start the application, you can view the processes it kicks off by doing the following:

1. Log on to the NT Workstation as Administrator.

2. Run NT Task Manager by right-clicking an empty space in the taskbar and selecting Task Manager.

3. Click the Process tab and view the processes that are currently running to establish a base line.

4. Start an application from one of the supported operating systems.

5. Review Task Manager to see the changes that have taken place.

6. Close Task Manager.

You can start 16-bit Windows applications from the NT command line using the Start command.

The Start command uses the following switches: `["title"]` `[/Dpath]` `[/I]` `[/MIN]` `[/MAX]` `[/LOW | /NORMAL | /HIGH | /REALTIME]` `[/B]` `[command/program]` `[parameters]`.

- **"title"**   The title displayed in the Windows title bar

- **Dpath**   The directory where the application is started from

- **I**   The new environment will be the original environment passed to the command interpreter and not the current environment.

- **MIN**   Start minimized.

- **MAX**   Start in a maximized window.

- **LOW**   Start application in the IDLE priority class.

- **NORMAL**   Start application in the NORMAL priority class.

- **HIGH**   Start application in the HIGH priority class.

- **REALTIME**   Start application in the REALTIME priority class.

- **B**   Start application without creating a new window.

- **parameters**   These are the parameters passed to the command/ program.

NOTE   There will be a discussion of priority classes as part of the next section.

Suppose you wanted to start an application called TESTME.EXE. The program resides in the C:\APPS\TEST folder, and you wanted it maximized in its own memory space, and run at high priority with I PASS as the Windows title. The command would be:

```
start "I Pass" /C:\apps\test /max /HIGH TESTME.EXE
```

Exam Essentials

This is a popular objective with the people writing the exam. Most of the questions will revolve around the standards of DOS and Windows applications. POSIX and OS/2 do not get much attention.

Know all about the Virtual DOS Machine. Because the Virtual DOS Machine is the cornerstone of running both legacy Windows applications and DOS applications, it is an easy target. Things to know include:

- The default VDM is the only one that can run multiple Win16 programs.

- Each VDM operates in its own memory space.

- The default VDM can run Windows on Windows.

- The Win16 VDM can be preemptively multitasked.

- Threads with the VDM cannot be multitasked.

Know how to start an application in its own memory space. This can be done from the command prompt and by using the Run command from the Start menu.

Know the syntax of the Start command. The START command uses the following switches: ["title"] [/Dpath] [/I] [/MIN] [/MAX] [/LOW | /NORMAL | /HIGH | /REALTIME] [/B] [command/ program] [parameters].

Know how running an MS-DOS application differs from running a Win16 application. DOS applications are executed in their own VDM; Win16 applications are executed in the default Win16 VDM. DOS applications cannot share memory; Win16 applications can. DOS applications can be preemptively multitasked and started at different priorities. Win16 applications can not be prioritized.

Know the VDM configuration files AUTOEXEC.NT and CONFIG.NT. AUTOEXEC.NT is like AUTOEXEC.BAT and CONFIG.NT is like CONFIG.SYS.

Key Terms and Concepts

AUTOEXEC.NT: Configuration file in a Virtual DOS Machine that corresponds to the AUTOEXEC.BAT file.

CONFIG.NT: Configuration file in a Virtual DOS Machine that corresponds to the CONFIG.SYS file.

OS/2:   Provides support for IBM's OS/2 operating system, in both OS/2 and DOS mode.

Posix: Portable Open System Interface. Standard programming interface that is independent of any operating system.

Preemptive Multitasking: Several applications can be open at one time, but the processor will only work with one application at a time.

Thread: A thread is the lowest form of work that a processor can do.

Virtual Device Driver (VDD):   Software drivers designed to work with DOS applications in a Virtual DOS Machine.

Virtual DOS Machine (VDM):   Application support for applications from the DOS environment.

Win16:   16-bit Windows application support for applications from the Windows 3.1 environment.

Win32:   32-bit Windows support for applications written for Windows 95 and Windows NT.

WOW (Windows on Windows):   A descriptive term for the way Windows NT runs 16-bit Windows Applications.

Sample Questions

1. What two files correspond to AUTOEXEC.BAT and CONFIG.SYS when running DOS applications on a Windows NT Workstation?

   A. AUTOEXEC.BAT and CONFIG.SYS

   B. AUTOEXEC.WIN and CONFIG.WIN

   C. AUTOEXEC.DOS and CONFIG.DOS

   D. AUTOEXEC.NT and CONFIG.NT

   Answer: D. AUTOEXEC.NT and CONFIG.NT

2. Windows on Windows supports which type of applications?

   A. 16-bit Windows applications

   B. 32-bit Windows applications

   C. OS/2 applications

   D. POSIX applications

Answer: A. Windows on Windows, which runs in the default Virtual DOS Machine, supports Windows 16-bit applications.

3. Windows NT Workstation assigns how much address space to each application?

   A. 2K

   B. 2MB

   C. RAM+2MB

   D. 2GB

   E. 2TB

Answer: D. Each application receives 2GB of address space.

Start applications at various priorities.

Since Windows NT Workstation allows you to run multiple applications simultaneously, it only makes sense that you be allowed to prioritize which applications should get the most processor time.

Suppose your workstation also served as a performance monitor for the network. You would want applications that you were using to do "real" work to get more of the processor time than the background-information gathering tools.

Critical Information

Processors have a finite number of cycles that can be devoted to any application. By using a multitasking operating system like Windows NT, multiple applications can be run simultaneously, each getting a piece of the processor pie.

NT allows you to set the priority to processor time. This can be done when the application starts (from the command line) or can be accomplished from Task Manager after the application is running.

Even if you don't take any action on the priority of an application, NT changes things around for you without any user input. When you start an application, it is given a base priority rating of 8. Base priority ratings go from 1 (basically comatose) to 31 (real time). Base priority ratings from 0 to 15 are to be used for dynamic applications, and ratings from 16 to 31 are reserved for real-time applications that cannot be written to the NT pagefile.

NT will increase the priority of the application if it is running in the foreground. It will also boost the priority for lower-priority applications on a random basis. This prevents the higher priority application from hogging the processor or resource.

TIP Real-time applications are those applications necessary for the performance of the operating system.

One of the switches for the Start command allows you to set one of four priority levels. You can start an application at Low Priority, Normal Priority, High Priority, or Real-Time Priority.

Necessary Procedures

As mentioned above, there are two ways of boosting the priority rating of an application. The priority can be altered as the application starts by using the Start command or by increasing the priority of an application that is already running by using Task Manager.

Start Command

The Start command uses the following switches: ["title"] [/Dpath] [/I] [/MIN] [/MAX] [/LOW | /NORMAL | /HIGH | /REALTIME] [/B] [command/program] [parameters].

- **"title"**   The title displayed in the Windows title bar
- **Dpath**   The directory where the application is started from
- **I**   The new environment will be the original environment passed to the command interpreter and not the current environment.
- **MIN**   Start minimized.
- **MAX**   Start in a maximized window.
- **LOW**   Start application in the IDLE priority class.
- **NORMAL**   Start application in the NORMAL priority class.
- **HIGH**   Start application in the HIGH priority class.
- **REALTIME**   Start application in the REALTIME priority class.
- **B**   Start application without creating a new window.
- **parameters**   These are the parameters passed to the command/ program.

Suppose you wanted to start and application called TESTME.EXE. The program resides in the C:\APPS\TEST folder, and you wanted it maximized in its own memory space, and run at high priority with I PASS as the Windows title. From the command line, the command would be:

```
start "I Pass" /C:\apps\test /max /HIGH TESTME.EXE
```

Task Manager

To access Task Manager after the application is running:

1. Press Ctrl+Alt+Del, and click Task Manager.

2. Click the Processes tab.

3. If the Base Priority column is not showing up, choose View ➤ Select Columns ➤ Check the Base Priority column and click OK.

4. In the Process list, right-click the application you want to change.

5. Highlight Set Priority and click the new priority.

6. Click Yes to the Task Manager warning.

Exam Essentials

There really is not a lot of material in this section, but you will see questions on it.

Know the four priority levels you can use from the Start command. The four priority levels are Low, Normal, High, and Real-Time.

Know how NT addresses priority levels. The lowest priority level is 0, the highest is 31.

Know the two ways you can change the priority level of an application. You can set a priority level from the Task Manager after an application is already running, or you can use the Start command from the Command Prompt.

Key Terms and Concepts

Base Priority: Setting between 0 and 31 to gauge an application's use of processor time.

High: Switch used with the Start command to start an application with a Base Priority of 13.

Low: Switch used with the Start command to start an application with a Base Priority of 4.

Normal: Default priority setting of 8.

Priority: Setting that allows the user to determine how much processor time will be allocated to a running application.

REALTIME: Switch used with Start Command to start an application with a Base Priority of 24.

Sample Questions

1. You are running a Windows 3.1 application that is performing slowly. How can you increase performance?

   A. Go into Control Panel ≻ System ≻ Processor and assign a higher priority.

   B. Right-click the application icon and edit the PIF file.

   C. The next time you start the application, use the Start command with the /HIGH option.

   D. Upgrade to a 32-bit application.

   Answer: C. You can run a Windows 16-bit application from the command line using the Start command and the /HIGH option. This runs the application at High Priority, giving it a larger percentage of the processor time.

2. Which application is getting more processor time, the application with the priority of 8 or the application with the priority of:

   A. 1

   B. 4

   C. 8

   D. 12

   Answer: D. The application with a priority of 12 will receive more processor time. The higher the priority number, the higher the priority.

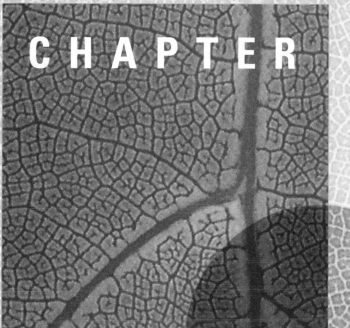

CHAPTER

6

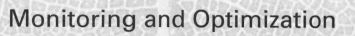

Monitoring and Optimization

Microsoft Exam Objectives Covered in This Chapter:

▶ **Monitor system performance by using various tools.**
(pages 222 – 234)

▶ **Identify and resolve a given performance problem.**
(pages 234 – 245)

▶ **Optimize system performance in various areas.**
(pages 245 – 249)

This chapter will act as an introduction to the tools used to monitor the performance of your workstation, detect and correct problems, and optimize your environment. The NT operating system can be a complicated beast. Knowing the tools available to tame it can be extremely valuable in the workplace. If you stop to think about it, there is a vast array of components in an NT Workstation—everything from the physical computer itself to each subsystem of the operating system. Each piece could potentially be a bottleneck, depending upon how you use your computer. NT includes tools that allow you to monitor and optimize just about every facet of your workstation.

Monitor system performance by using various tools.

Before we can begin our discussion of optimization, you will have to be familiar with the tools available to monitor your computer. This objective is concerned with the tools that are included with Windows NT and how to use them. Be prepared for questions that ask which tool should be used to troubleshoot a particular type of problem.

Critical Information

There are three tools with which you will need to be comfortable for this objective:

- Server Manager
- Windows NT Diagnostics
- Performance Monitor

For the exam you will want to know what each tool monitors, and how each tool is used.

Server Manager

Server Manager is found in the Administrative Tools group. It is basically used to monitor network-related information for an NT computer. It can be used to manage both your local machine and other computers on the network. With Server Manager you can view:

- A list of connected users
- Open resources
- Shared resources

Server Manager also allows you to:

- Send messages to connected users
- Administrate shared resources
- Create a list of users who should receive Windows NT system alerts

Each of these elements will be discussed in the Necessary Procedures section.

Windows NT Diagnostics

Windows NT Diagnostics is used to gather information about the hardware and software settings of an NT computer. It is used to help troubleshoot hardware- and memory-based problems.

Performance Monitor

Of the three tools discussed in this objective, Performance Monitor is covered most extensively on the test. You can use Performance Monitor to gather very specific information about the various components (both hardware and software) of your computer.

Within Performance Monitor you will find *objects* that can be monitored. An object is a major sub-component of you environment—things like the processor, disk subsystem, memory, or network. Each object has specific *Counters* that represent items that can be tracked—memory, for instance, includes counters like % Committed bytes in use, Available bytes, and Cache bytes. As you can see, using Performance Monitor demands a good working knowledge of how NT operates. For this exam we won't go into too much depth—but for later exams in the MCSE program, you will be expected to understand many of the various objects and counters available.

TIP If you are pursuing the MCSE, it would be prudent to take the time to understand the objects and counters in Performance Monitor. Not only will you be tested upon the tool itself, you will be expected to understand the dynamic relationships between the various components of the NT operating system. Performance Monitor allows you to view, in real time, how the various pieces of NT interact. Understanding how to use Performance Monitor early in the certification process can make life a lot easier for you later on! For more information, see *MCSE: NT Server 4 in the Enterprise, Second Edition*, by Lisa Donald and James Chellis (Sybex, 1998).

Necessary Procedures

This objective concerns your ability to use the various tools. For this reason, most of your critical information will be found here.

Using Server Manager

Server Manager can be broken down into two types of functions—
passive and active. The passive functions allow you to view information, while the active functions allow you to make changes to the
configuration of the system.

Passive functions include:

- Viewing a list of connected users

- Viewing a list of shared resources

- Viewing a list of open resources

Active functions include:

- Sending a message to users connected to a server

- Administering shared directories

- Creating a list of users who should receive administrative alerts

Viewing a List of Connected Users

There are many occasions when you will want to view a list of users
who are attached to your computer. Each evening, for instance,
before you shut down the operating system, you will want to ensure
that no one is using one of your shared resources.

To view a list of users attached to your computer, open Server Manager. Double-click the computer you wish to check. The dialog box
shown below will appear, in this case, in reference to a computer
named END200. We'll be referencing this graphic a number of times
as we look at some of the other options available.

Notice the options across the bottom of the dialog box. We'll be looking at each of the choices available. For now, click the Users button and you will see a list of users connected to the chosen computer.

From here you can see who is connected to the computer and which shared resources they are using. You can also disconnect any or all users from this screen.

Viewing a List of Shared Resources

From the Shared Resources dialog box, click the Shares button. From here you can see all of the various shares that have been created. You can also highlight any share and see a list of who is connected to it.

Viewing a List of Open Resources

Click the In Use button and you will see a list of the resources
currently open.

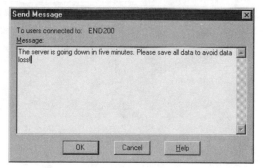

Sending a Message to Users Connected to a Server

It is often necessary to send a message to all users connected to a server
before shutting the server down. Server Manager provides an easy way
to accomplish this task. From the main screen, highlight the server you
are going to shut down and chose Send Message on the Computer
menu. As shown here, you then just type in your message and click OK.

Administering Shared Directories

Server Manager also allows you to create new shares or manage
existing shares on the target computer. Highlight the chosen

computer and chose Shared Directories from the Computer menu.
You will see a list of shared directories and actions that you can take.

Create a List of Users Who Should Receive Administrative Alerts

Administrative alerts are generated by the operating system to warn
of security and access problems, user session problems, power problems (when the UPS service is also running), and printer problems.
Server Manager allows you to create a list of users who should receive
these administrative alerts. From the Properties dialog box, choose
the Alerts button. Add users to the list as shown below.

Using Windows NT Diagnostic

Windows NT Diagnostic is used to view information about a computer's hardware and software configuration. It provides a graphical
interface and the ability to print reports.

TIP Many administrators use Windows NT Diagnostic to document
the computers on their network. They either print the reports and file
them, or "print" them to a file and store them on a server.

The opening screen of Windows NT Diagnostic is shown below. While you won't need to know every detail of the tool, you will need to know the general purpose of each option.

Table 6.1 lists each of the options available and what type of information they provide.

T A B L E 6.1: Using Windows NT Diagnostic

Tab	Usage
Version	Operating system information
System	ROM BIOS and CPU information
Display	Video driver and adapter information
Drives	Information about the drives on your system, including file system and drivers
Memory	Physical and virtual memory information
Services	A list of the services in the CurrentControlSet and their status

T A B L E 6.1: Using Windows NT Diagnostic *(continued)*

Tab	Usage
Resources	Device information including physical configuration (Memory addresses, IRQ, DMA, and port addresses)
Environment	Shows a list of environmental variables
Network	Network related information, including current statistics

Using Performance Monitor

Performance Monitor offers many ways to view the statistics that it gathers. You will need to be familiar with each of them for the exam.

Chart View

The chart view provides a real time graph showing the values of the counters you have chosen. The first step is to add the counters to your view. Highlight the appropriate object and then pick a counter from the list.

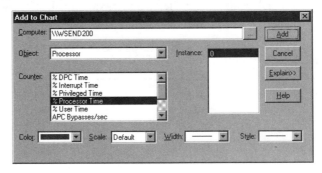

When you have added all of the counters you want to graph, click Done. The graph will show the value of those counters in real time.

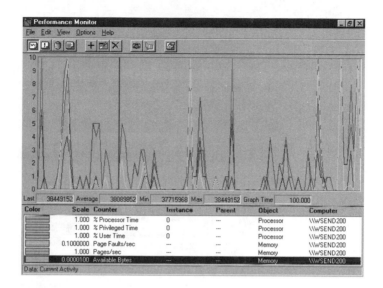

Report View

The report view shows the same information as the chart view. With the report view, the values are shown in the form of a report, rather than as a graph.

Log View

The log view allows you to save the data to a file. In the chart view you do not pick counters—all counters for the objects you choose will be tracked. Choose your objects, and pick a destination directory and filename.

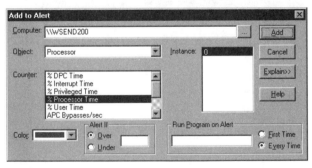

Alert View

The alert view is different from the other three views. With the alert view, you set a threshold for a counter. When this threshold is reached, you can have Performance Monitor run an application.

Exam Essentials

Most of the exam questions for this objective will be of the form "what tools would you use to…". There may, however, be a few which ask for more specific information. Know the three tools listed, their function, and how to use them.

Know what can be done with Server Manager.   With Server Manager, you can see a list of connected users, see a list of open resources, see a list of shared resources, send messages to connected users, administer shared directories, and create a list of users who should receive administrative alerts.

Know what Windows NT Diagnostics is used for.   Windows NT Diagnostics is used to view hardware and software configuration information.

Know how to use Performance Monitor.   Performance Monitor is used to gather statistics about specific components of an NT computer. You choose an object (a main subsystem of your computer) and various counters (specific items that can be monitored) about that object.

Know the four views available in Performance Monitor.   Chart view provides a real-time graph of the counters you have chosen; report view provides the same information as a chart view, only the data is shown as text; log view allows you to save the data to a file for later analysis; and alert view allows you to set a threshold on a counter. When the threshold is reached, you can have Performance Monitor run an application.

Key Terms and Concepts

Administrative alerts: Messages generated by the operating system to warn of security and access problems, user session problems, power problems (if the UPS service is also running), and printer problems.

Counter: Within Performance Monitor, a counter is a specific statistic of an object.

Object: Within Performance Monitor, an object is a major component of the environment.

Sample Questions

1. Windows NT diagnostic performs which of the following tasks?

    A. Displays CPU information

    B. Displays captured information from the network

    C. Lists the configuration of memory on an NT computer

    D. Lists all services currently running on an NT computer

    Answer: A, C, D. Microsoft will often ask questions that relate you to your knowledge of the functions of utilities.

2. Which of the following utilities allows you to view a list of shared resources and who is currently attached to them?

    A. Performance Monitor

    B. Windows NT Diagnostics

    C. Server Manager

    D. User Manager for Domains

    Answer: C. Server Manager allows the management of server-based functionality.

Identify and resolve a given performance problem.

Knowing what questions to ask, and how to interpret the answers, is critical to both problem solving and optimization on your network. In this section, we will discuss the Performance Monitor counters to watch on each of the major subsystems of an NT server.

Critical Information

While any given environment might stress particular areas, there are four main physical components to any NT server—Processor, Memory, Disk, and Network. These four areas are a good indicator of the "health" of your system. When monitoring any NT server, always start with these four components and then add any additional counters that might be appropriate in your environment.

Tracking Processor Counters

To determine if the processor is the bottleneck, monitor the counters listed in Table 6.2:

TABLE 6.2: Processor-Related Counters in Performance Monitor

Counter	Acceptable Value	Description
% Processor time	Under 75 percent	If the processor is consistently busy more than 75 percent of the time, it is likely that the processor is the bottleneck.
% Privileged Time	Under 75 percent	This is the amount of time that the processor is busy performing operating system tasks.
% User Time	Under 75 percent	This is the amount of time the processor is busy performing user tasks, such as running a program.
Interrupts/sec	Varies	This is the number of hardware interrupts generated each second. Each type of processor can handle a different number. On a 486/66 this number should be under 1000, while on a Pentium 90 system, this number could run as high as 3500. If this number is consistently high, the system probably has an IRQ conflict, or a piece of hardware is going bad.

TABLE 6.2: Processor-Related Counters in Performance Monitor *(continued)*

Counter	Acceptable Value	Description
System: Processor Queue Length	Less than 2	This represents the number of threads that are ready to execute, but are waiting for the processor.
Server Work Queues: Queue Length	Less than 2	This is the number of threads in the queue for a given processor.

Tracking Memory Counters

Before we discuss the counters to monitor to determine if memory is your system bottleneck, we need to review how NT uses memory.

Memory in an NT system can be divided into two classifications: Paged and Non-Paged. Paged memory is used by most applications. It can be made up of either physical RAM or virtual memory (hard disk space). Non-Paged memory is used by programs which can not be "paged" to the hard disk. The operating system and its components use Non-Paged memory.

NT uses a virtual memory model. In this model, applications that can use paged RAM are given a full set of memory addresses to work with. The operating system keeps track of actual physical memory. When memory is full, the OS will move "pages" of memory to a file on the hard drive (PAGEFILE.SYS). If that code is needed later, it will be moved back to physical memory. By using a virtual memory model, your applications can use more memory than is physically available (up to the limits of your hard drive).

Whenever the data a program needs is not in RAM, it must be acquired from the hard drive. This process is called a "hard page fault." A consistently high number of hard page faults—over five per second—could indicate that there is not enough memory available on the server. The goal on an NT Server is to have enough memory in the server so that most data requested is found in memory. (Obviously, the first time it is used it will have to come from the disk, but after that, having enough memory for file caching can greatly increase performance.)

TIP To appreciate the importance of file caching, compare the access speeds of your memory and your hard disk. Hard disk access times are measured in milliseconds, or thousandths of a second. Memory is measured in nanoseconds, or millionths of a second.

Monitor the counters listed in Table 6.3 to determine if memory is your bottleneck.

TABLE 6.3: Memory-Related Counters in Performance Monitor

Counter	Acceptable Value	Description
Pages/sec	0–20	Total of the number of pages that were either not in RAM when requested, or needed to be moved to virtual memory to free up space in RAM. This is really a measure of disk activity related to memory management.
Available Bytes	Minimum of 4MB	The amount of available physical RAM at any point in time. This number will usually be fairly low, as NT will utilize memory that is available and free it up as needed.
Committed Bytes	Should be less than the physical amount of RAM in the computer	This indicates the amount of memory in use. If the number is greater than the amount of physical RAM in the machine, it indicates a need for more memory.

T A B L E 6.3: Memory-Related Counters in Performance Monitor *(continued)*

Counter	Acceptable Value	Description
Pool Non-Paged Bytes	Should remain steady	This is the memory used by non-paged processes (i.e. the operating system). If this number fluctuates, it could indicate a process that is not using memory correctly.

Tracking Disk Counters

The disk is usually the slowest component on your computer. NT compensates for this by using file caching and memory management to reduce the number of disk accesses. Often what appears to be a disk problem is really just a lack of memory, so be sure to watch both subsystems.

Before you can track disk counters in Performance Monitor, you must turn on those counters. The disk counters are not activated by default because tracking physical disk access adds measurable overhead to the server.

To activate the disk counters, type **diskperf –y** at a command prompt. If your disks are configured as a RAID set, type **diskperf –ye**.

NOTE The added overhead of tracking disk counters is constant once they are activated—not just when you are monitoring them. It is a good idea to turn them off when you are not actively watching them. To turn them off type **diskperf –n** at a command prompt.

Once activated, monitor the counters listed in Table 6.4.

T A B L E 6.4: Disk-Related Counters in Performance Monitor

Counter	Acceptable Value	Description
%Disk Time	Under 50 percent	This is the amount of time that the disk drive is busy. If this number is consistently high, you should monitor specific processes to find out exactly what is using the disk. If you can, move some of the disk-intensive processes to another server.
Disk Queue Length	0–2	This value represents the number of waiting disk I/O requests. A high number indicates that I/O requests are waiting for access.
Avg. Disk Bytes/Transfer	Depends on use and type of subsystem	The larger this number, the more efficient your disk subsystem is working. This value will depend on the type of access; are your users saving many small files or a few large ones? It is also dependent on the type of disks and controllers.
Disk Bytes/sec	Depends on use and type of subsystem	The larger this number, the more efficient your disk subsystem is working. This value is dependent on the disk and controller type.

Tracking Network Counters

Due to the complexity of today's networks, monitoring the network portion of your environment can be a difficult task. The network doesn't end at your NIC card—it includes the entire infrastructure that makes up your enterprise. Everything attached to your network could be a potential problem. To monitor a network, you have to have a little familiarity with all components on that network, the routers, the wiring, the protocols, the operating systems—this list goes on and on.

The list can be a little intimidating. The first task in troubleshooting is to limit your view. Don't try to fix the entire network—try to find out which component is causing the problem and fix it.

Performance Monitor has a few counters, listed in Table 6.5, that can help you determine where the problem lies. A few analyze the overhead on the server itself, while others give an overview of what is happening on the wire.

TABLE 6.5: Network-Related Counters in Performance Monitor

Counter	Acceptable Value	Description
Server: Bytes Total/sec	Varies	This counter shows the number of bytes sent and received through this server. It is a good indicator of how busy the server is.
Server: Logon/sec	Varies	Use this value to determine the authentication overhead being placed on the server. If this number is high and other services are slow, it might indicate the need for another domain controller.
Server: Login Total	Varies	This is the number of logon attempts the server has serviced since the last time the server was started. Can be used to justify another domain controller.
Network Interface: Bytes sent/sec	Varies	Used to determine if a particular Network Interface Card is being overused.

T A B L E 6.5:   Network-Related Counters in Performance Monitor *(continued)*

Counter	Acceptable Value	Description
Network Interface: Bytes total./sec	Varies	Total number of bytes sent and received through a particular NIC.
Network Segment: %Network Utilization	Usually lower than 30 percent	Shows the percentage of network bandwidth in use. This number should be lower than 30 percent for most networks. Some network technologies can sustain a higher rate.

The Network Segment object is not available until you install the Network Monitor Agent as a service on the server. Once installed, Performance Monitor will put the NICs in promiscuous mode when you are monitoring Network Segment counters. When in promiscuous mode, a NIC processes *all* network traffic, not just those packets destined for the server. This can add a tremendous amount of overhead to the server.

Each protocol that you add to your server will also have its own counters. These counters allow you to determine the overhead being placed on your server by each protocol. Most of these counters have no "acceptable" range of values. The values will be dependent upon the hardware, topology, and other protocols in use on your network.

NetBEUI and NWLink Counters

These two protocols have similar counters, listed in Table 6.6.

T A B L E 6.6: NetBEUI- and NWLink-Related Counters in Performance Monitor

Counter	Acceptable Value	Description
Bytes Total/Sec	N/A	The total number of bytes sent and received using this protocol. This counter is an excellent way to compare network overhead created by various protocols.
Datagrams/sec	N/A	The total number of non-guaranteed datagrams (usually broadcasts) sent and received
Frames sent/sec	N/A	The number of data packets sent and received

TCP/IP Counters

The counters list in Table 6.7 will not be available unless both the TCP/IP protocol and the SNMP service are installed on the server.

T A B L E 6.7: TCP/IP-Related Counters in Performance Monitor

Counter	Acceptable Value	Description
TCP Segments/sec	N/A	The total number of TCP frames sent and received
TCP Segments re-translated/sec	N/A	The total number of segments re-translated on the network
UDP datagrams/sec	N/A	The number of UDP-based datagrams (usually broadcasts) sent and received
Network Interface: Output Queue Length	Less than 2	The number of packets waiting to be transmitted through a particular NIC. A high number can indicate a card that is too busy.

Exam Essentials

Trying to out-smart the test writers at Microsoft is often an exercise in futility. There is, however, one common thread—they want to ensure that you have the skills necessary to provide your environment with an efficient NT network. The following items are critical to that goal.

Understand NT's virtual memory model. NT extends physical RAM by using disk space. When a program needs memory, NT will allocate physical RAM. If there is not enough RAM available, NT will move a "page" of memory to the PAGEFILE.SYS file on the hard drive. To the application that originally placed that information in memory, it appears as if the data is still in RAM. When that application needs the data again, NT will page something else to the disk, and place it in physical RAM for use.

Know the difference between Paged and Non-Paged memory. Paged memory can be "paged" to the PAGEFILE.SYS file. Non-Paged memory contains data that cannot be moved to virtual memory (usually this code will be part of the operating system).

Know how to activate the disk counters in Performance Monitor. From a command prompt, type diskperf –y. In a RAID implementation, type diskperf –ye.

Be familiar with the various counters discussed in this section. Reread this section, paying close attention to the counters listed. These are the counters most likely to be mentioned on the exam.

Key Terms and Concepts

Datagram: A term usually used to describe a non-directed packet on the network (broadcasts, acknowledgments, etc.).

Frame: A term usually used to describe a directed packet of data.

Non-Paged Memory: An area of memory that cannot use virtual RAM. Usually used by the operating system.

Paged Memory: An area of memory that can be extended using virtual memory space.

Virtual Memory model: A memory system that uses hard drive space as if it were RAM.

Sample Questions

1. The Performance Monitor counter %Privileged Time represents which of the following?

   A. How much time a given application has been allowed to stay in memory

   B. The percentage of the processor cycles being used by the operating system

   C. The percentage of the processor cycles that is being used to handle user requests

   D. The amount of time the user has been logged on to the server

   Answer: B. This value should be consistently under 75 percent.

2. Which of the following memory counters represents the number of pages that were not in RAM when requested?

   A. Pages/Sec

   B. Available bytes

   C. Committed Bytes

   D. Pool non-Paged bytes

   Answer: A. Pages/Sec is one of the more useful memory related counters, and is tested heavily.

3. Which of the following reasons is the most likely cause of receiving 0 values for all disk counters in Performance Monitor?

   A. Your disks are not being used.

   B. The counters have not been activated.

C. Performance Monitor has become corrupted.

D. Your disk controller does not support Performance Monitor requests.

Answer: B. Remember that the disk counters must be activated by using the diskperf command.

Optimize system performance in various areas.

Now that we've taken a close look at how to use Performance Monitor to track resources at your computer, we can stop and analyze the results. Based upon this we can then make suggestions with the goal of optimizing system performance.

Critical Information

This is a very short objective, but it is critical to your success on the examination. Microsoft is working very hard to avoid certifying individuals who cannot use the information presented in the MCSE courses in a real-world situation. Many of the questions you will see will describe a scenario and expect you to analyze the data and choose the appropriate action.

In the preceding objective we talked about the various Performance Monitor counters that you might want to track, and gave some suggested values for those counters on a healthy computer. Based upon that information, you should be able to analyze the data and determine which component is the bottleneck on your system.

WARNING The definition of bottleneck is "the slowest component." Every system has a bottleneck—it's up to you to determine if it is affecting the level of service that the computer can provide to users. Bottom line: Don't fix what ain't broke! Before you start making changes, ensure that your environment will benefit enough to warrant the expense or time involved.

We'll look at the four main components of an NT environment and offer suggested actions for optimizing each of them.

Processor

If the bottleneck is your processor you can:

- Add a faster processor.

- Add another processor.

- Move processing to another server.

WARNING These are the Microsoft answers. In reality you very seldom have the option of the first two choices. Upgrading the processor in today's quagmire of choices (Pentium, Pentium Pro, Pentium II) is never as easy as it sounds. As for adding a processor, nobody buys a multiprocessor motherboard and leaves a slot open.

Memory

If memory is the bottleneck on your server, the fix is simple—add more RAM! In the interim you could move users to another server or unload services.

Disk

If you find that the disk subsystem is the bottleneck you can do the following:

- Add a faster controller.

- If you are using RAID, add more disks to the set. This spreads the work across more physical devices.

- Move disk-intensive processes to another server to spread the workload.

WARNING   None of these solutions is really a simple fix. Adding a faster controller will only help if your disks are compliant with the controller type. If they are not, you will have to replace the disks as well to see any benefit. As for the RAID solution, adding a disk is dependent upon you having a slot open and the funding for more hardware. As for moving the process to another server, this depends on you having a server that is not too busy to accept the extra workload. The proper solution to this problem is to have prevented it in the first place. Proper capacity planning (projecting throughput needs, comparing technologies, and implementing the best solution) is the best "fix."

Network

The following are potential fixes if the network is your bottleneck:

- Upgrade the hardware at the server. Add an additional or faster NIC, add RAM, or upgrade the processor.

- Upgrade the physical components of your network, such as routers and bridges.

- Decrease the number of protocols in use on your network.

- Segment your network to split the traffic between segments.

- Add servers to split the workload.

Exam Essentials

The most important thing you can do to prepare for this objective is study the preceding objective on resolving performance problems. Also know the following:

Know the suggested "fixes" for bottlenecks in each of the four major subsystems. See the Critical Information section above for details.

Key Terms and Concepts

Bottleneck: The slowest component in a system. Usually this definition is expanded to mean the slowest piece that is effecting the quality of service.

RAID (Redundant Array of Inexpensive Disks): A disk technology that provides fault tolerance. Fault-tolerant disk systems can withstand the failure of a hard drive without causing a loss of data.

Sample Questions

1. Which of the following would be fixes for a system in which the processor is the bottleneck?

   A. Add another processor.

   B. Move some applications to another server.

   C. Upgrade the processor.

   D. Add a faster NIC card.

   Answer: A, B, C. Adding a faster NIC card would be more appropriate if the network were the bottleneck.

2. Which of the following would be an appropriate fix for a system in which the network is the bottleneck?

    A. Add another NIC card to segment your LAN.

    B. Upgrade the NIC card to a faster type.

    C. Upgrade the bridges, routers, and other network devices involved in communication.

    D. Add another processor to your server.

Answer: A, B, C. Adding a processor probably wouldn't do much in this scenario—the problem (as described) is getting the packets to the processor, not processing them.

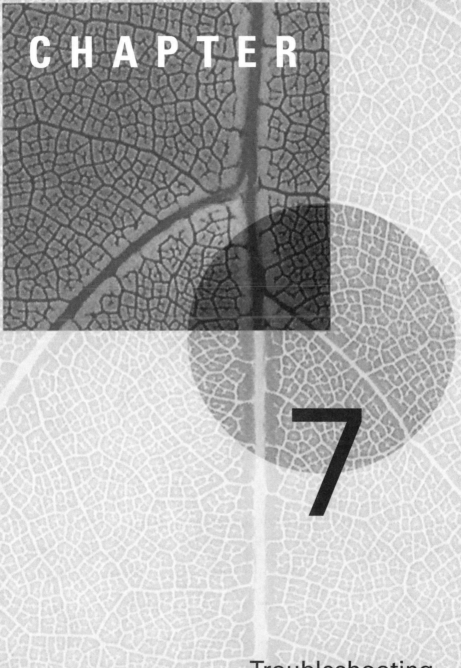

CHAPTER

7

Troubleshooting

Microsoft Exam Objectives Covered in This Chapter:

▶ **Choose the appropriate course of action to take when the boot process fails.** *(pages 253 – 264)*

▶ **Choose the appropriate course of action to take when a print job fails.** *(pages 264 – 272)*

▶ **Choose the appropriate course of action to take when the installation process fails.** *(pages 272 – 275)*

▶ **Choose the appropriate course of action to take when an application fails.** *(pages 276 – 278)*

▶ **Choose the appropriate course of action to take when a user cannot access a resource.** *(pages 279 – 283)*

▶ **Modify the registry using the appropriate tool in a given situation.** *(pages 283 – 291)*

▶ **Implement advanced techniques to resolve various problems.** *(pages 291 – 300)*

T he test objectives for this chapter cover the actions you should take to correct a specific set of problems. Some of these problems are very common in the workplace, while others rarely occur. Whether common or rare, knowing how to correct them is a very big part of being a network administrator.

Learning to troubleshoot technical problems is a life-long process. You can pick up some useful tips by reading books or taking classes, but you can never know all there is to know. Unfortunately, experience plays a big role in developing troubleshooting skills. Almost every company has someone who can walk up to a problem, press a few keys, and walk away confident that the problem has been fixed. The reality is that these individuals have a "troubleshooting database" in their head. They've seen the problem—or a similar one—before, and they can draw upon that experience to quickly analyze a situation. No book, magazine, or class can provide that level of expertise. We can, however, act as a starting place to help you build your own "troubleshooting database."

Each section will have a specific set of steps to take when trouble-shooting the appropriate type of problem. For the exam it is important to know the steps described.

Choose the appropriate course of action to take when the boot process fails.

There is nothing worse than a computer that won't finish the boot process. You are left staring at some obscure error message or worse, at a blue screen filled with what appears to be hieroglyphics. In this section we'll take a look at the most common error messages, their cause, and the appropriate action to take to correct the problem. We'll save the discussion of blue screens for later in this chapter.

Critical Information

NT goes through four distinct phases during the boot process. For the MCSE examination you will need to know what happens in each phase. After we have discussed the stages, we'll look at specific errors that might occur and possible solutions.

NT Boot Phases

The four phases of boot are:

- Initial
- Boot Loader
- Kernel
- Logon

Initial Phase

During the initial phase the computer performs a Power On Self Test (POST), during which it determines how much memory is installed and whether the required hardware is available. During this process, the computer reads the information stored in CMOS to determine what storage devices are available, the date and time, and other parameters specific to the hardware.

In CMOS, the computer will read the type and configuration of possible boot devices. Based upon this information it will determine which device it should examine to find operating system boot information. If your computer is configured to boot from the hard drive, it will read the first sector in an attempt to find the Master Boot Record (MBR). The MBR contains critical information for the boot process, such as a list of partitions defined on the disk, their starting and ending sectors, and which of the partitions is "active." (The active partition is the one that the computer will attempt to boot from.) If there is no MBR on the disk, the computer will be unable to boot to an operating system. This is why many computer viruses attack the MBR.

Once the computer has determined which partition it should look to for boot information, it will access that partition and read the Partition Boot Sector (PBS). The PBS contains operating system–specific information. In the case of Windows NT it directs the computer to load a file called NTLDR found in the partition root folder. If the PBS is missing or corrupted you may see an error message like "No Operating System Was Found" or "Non-System Disk or Disk Error."

Boot Loader Phase

Once NTLDR has been found and starts to load, the Boot Loader Phase begins. During this phase NT uses various programs to gather information about the hardware and drivers needed to boot. The following files will be utilized during this phase:

- **NTLDR**   This is the operating system loader (NTLDR stands for NT loader). It must be in the root directory of the active partition.

- **BOOT.INI**   A text file that controls which operating system will be loaded. The user will see a menu offering various operating system choices. This file must also be in the root directory. We'll discuss the BOOT.INI file in more detail later in this section.

- **BOOTSEC.DOS**   If the computer is configured to dual boot between NT and another operating system, the NT installation program will gather all of the information needed to boot the other OS and place it in this file. When the user chooses to boot to another OS, NT will call this file.

- **NTBOOTDD.SYS**   A device driver used to access a SCSI hard drive whose controller is not using its BIOS.

- **NTDETECT.COM**   A program that attempts to analyze the hardware on the computer. It passes the information it finds to the operating system for inclusion in the registry later in the boot process. NTDETECT.COM can detect the following components: Computer ID, Bus/Adapter type, Video, Keyboard, Communication Ports, Parallel Ports, Floppy Disks, and Mouse/Pointing device. While it is performing its function it displays the following on the screen:

      NTDETECT V1.0 Checking Hardware…

NTLDR controls the initial startup of NT on the hardware. It changes the processor from real-time to 32-bit flat memory mode, starts the appropriate mini-file system (NTLDR has code that enables it to read FAT and NTFS partitions), and reads the BOOT.INI file to display the menu of operating system choices.

Once NT has been selected and NTDETECT.COM has run its course, NTLDR will display the following message:

      OS Loader V4.0
      Press SPACEBAR now to invoke Hardware Profile/Last
      Known Good menu.

If the spacebar is not pressed, and there is only one hardware profile, NTLDR will load the default control set. If the spacebar is pressed, NTLDR will display a screen offering Hardware Profile choices and the option to use the Last Known Good Configuration.

Once the hardware configuration has been chosen, NTLDR will load the NT kernel—NTOSKRNL.EXE. It loads it into memory but does not initialize it at this point. Next, the boot loader loads the registry key HKEY_LOCAL_MACHINE\SYSTEM. It scans all of the subkeys in CurrentControlSet\Services for device drivers with a start value of 0. These are usually low-level hardware drivers, such as hard disk drivers, needed to continue the boot.

Kernel Phase

The boot loader phase ends when NTLDR passes control to NTOSKRNL.EXE. At this point the Kernel Initialization phase begins, and the screen will turn blue.

The kernel then creates the HKEY_LOCAL_MACHINE\HARDWARE registry key using information passed to it by the boot loader (gathered by NTDETECT.COM).

The next step is loading the device drivers. NTOSKRNL.EXE looks in the registry for drivers that need to be loaded, checks through their DependOnService and DependOnGroup values, and determines the order that drivers should be loaded in. It then loads the services, reads and implements the parameters specified, and initializes the various services and drivers needed.

Logon Phase

An NT boot is not considered successful until a user successfully logs on. The Windows subsystem automatically starts WINLOGON.EXE. The Logon Information dialog box now appears on the screen. The user can press Ctrl+Alt+Del to logon even though other services might still be initializing in the background.

The Service Controller does one last sweep through the registry to located any last services that need to be loaded. At this point, NT has just about finished the boot process. It then takes the CurrentControlSet and copies it to create the last known good configuration (for use in the next boot of this computer).

Now that we've looked at the boot process, we can cover some of the specifics required for the examination.

The BOOT.INI File

The BOOT.INI file is a text file located in the root of the boot partition. Below is an example of a BOOT.INI file:

```
[boot loader]
timeout=30
default=multi(0)disk(0)rdisk(0)paritition(1)\WINNT
[operating systems]
multi(0)disk(0)rdisk(0)paritition(1)\WINNT="Windows NT
Server Version 4.0"
multi(0)disk(0)rdisk(0)paritition(1)\WINNT="Windows NT
Server Version 4.0 [VGA mode]" /basevideo /sos
C:\="Windows 95"
```

There are two sections to a BOOT.INI file. In the [boot loader] section you will find settings that control the defaults—how long the menu should be on screen before a default is selected and which operating system should load if the user makes no selection. In the [operating systems] section, you find the various choices that will be presented to the user and the path to the operating system files for each choice.

You might notice that there are some things here that we have not discussed. Note for instance that the lines that represent the choices the user will see begin with some arcane computer jargon. This is called an ARC path. An ARC path describes the physical directions to a device. In our example, the text:

```
multi(0)disk(0)rdisk(0)paritition(1)\WINNT
```

describes the physical device and directory where the NT operating system will be found. For this exam you do not need to understand the syntax involved, only the purpose.

SEE ALSO For more information on ARC paths, check out *MCSE: NT Server 4 in the Enterprise Study Guide, Second Edition*, by Lisa Donald with James Chellis (Sybex, 1998).

If there is no BOOT.INI file, the system will attempt to boot from the location that the NT installation program places boot files by default: the \WINNT directory on the active partition. If you have placed the operating system files in another location, then the BOOT.INI file is critical to the boot process.

BOOT.INI Switches

There are numerous switches that can be used within the BOOT.INI file to help you control the way that NT boots. These switches are placed at the end of the line describing the location of the operating system.

- **/basevideo**   This forces NT to boot using a standard VGA driver. This allows an administrator to recover from installing an incorrect or corrupted video driver that disables video output. The NT installation program creates an operating system choice in the BOOT.INI file that implements this switch. You can thereby fix a video driver problem by rebooting, choosing the VGA option, and replacing the bad driver.

- **/maxmem:n**   This switch allows the administrator to specify how much physical memory NT can use. You can use this switch to troubleshoot various memory problems such as parity errors or bad SIMMs.

- **/noserialmice=[COM x or COM x,y,z]**   NT will occasionally detect a device on a communication port and assume it is a mouse—even if it is some other type of device. When this happens, that device will be unusable in Windows NT because a mouse driver will be loaded that uses that port. This switch disables detection on the communication port(s) specified.

- **/sos**   This switch will cause NT to display the names of drivers as they are loaded rather than the default progress dots.

- **/crashdebug**   This switch enables the Automatic Recovery and Restart capability in the event of a stop screen. This parameter can also be set in the System applet in Control Panel.

There are a number of switches that relate to advanced trouble-shooting techniques that we will cover later in this chapter. These switches configure NT to "dump" its memory contents into a file for analysis. You can configure where this memory dump file will be placed. Often, the problem will be so severe that the computer is inaccessible. On this type of error you will want to configure the system to dump its memory to another computer's hard drive. The following switches control this transfer.

- **/baudrate=nnnn**   This switch is used to configure the communication port if you are going to dump memory to another computer.

- **/debugport=comx**   This switch sets the communication port to be used.

BOOT.INI Error Messages

There are various error messages that are commonly seen when there is a problem with the BOOT.INI file. If the BOOT.INI file is missing, or if the operating system line does not point to the NT operating system files, you will see the following message:

```
Windows NT could not start because the following file
is missing or corrupt:
<winnt root>\system32\NTOSKRNL.EXE
Please reinstall a copy of the above file.
```

If the ARC path points to a nonexistent disk or partition you will see the following error:

```
OS Loader V4.0
Windows NT could not start because of a computer disk
hardware configuration problem. Could not read from the
selected boot disk. Check boot path and disk hardware.
Please check the Windows NT documentation about
hardware disk configuration and your hardware reference
manuals for additional information.
```

In either event, you can either edit the BOOT.INI file to correct the problem or restore the BOOT.INI file off of your emergency repair disk.

Last Known Good Configuration

If your Windows NT server refuses to boot after you have added new hardware or software, you can attempt to boot using the Last Known Good configuration. This is the hardware configuration used during the last successful boot. Remember, though, that if you log on to the computer you will overwrite the Last Known Good configuration with the current control set.

If one of the files used during the boot process has become corrupted, you can attempt to replace it with a good copy. There are a couple of ways to accomplish this task. If you boot to a FAT partition, you can boot to a DOS disk, and copy the new file over the suspect file. The only file that is unique to the server's hardware is the BOOT.INI file. All of the other files are generic, so you can grab a copy from any other NT server. You can also expand a copy from the NT Server CDROM using the Expand –r utility.

Another way to replace suspect boot files is to use your Emergency Repair Disk (ERD). You create the ERD by running the RDISK.EXE utility. This tool creates a disk with the following files on it:

- **SETUP.LOG** An information file that is used for verifying the system files

- **SYSTEM._** A copy of the system registry hive

- **SAM._** A copy of the security accounts manager database

- **SECURITY._** A copy of the security hive

- **SOFTWARE._** A copy of the software hive

- **DEFAULT._** A copy of the default hive

- **CONFIG.NT** The Windows NT version of the CONFIG.SYS file used to configure an NT virtual DOS machine

- **AUTOEXEC.NT** The Windows NT version of the AUTOEXEC.BAT file used to configure an NT virtual DOS machine

- **NTUSER.DA_** A copy of the <SYSTEMROOT>\PROFILES\ DEFAULTUSER\NTUSER.DAT file

Files with an underscore (_) in their extension are in compressed form and can be decompressed using the Expand utility. By default, the repair Disk utility will not backup the default, SAM, or security files. Use the "/s" switch when running this tool to get a complete backup. If you do not use this switch, your repair disk will have a default user accounts database. If you should have a problem with the registry and have to restore from the ERD you will lose all of your user account information.

To restore from the ERD you must boot from the setup disks provided with Windows NT server (or create a set from the CD-ROM). On the screen that asks if you want to install NT or repair files, type **R** to select the repair option. From then on just follow the instructions.

The repair process can:

- Inspect the Registry Files   Replace existing registry files with those on the ERD. Remember that you will lose any changes that have occurred since the last time you updated the ERD.

- Inspect Startup Environment   This option will attempt to repair a BOOT.INI file that does not list NT as an option in the user boot menu.

- Verify Windows NT System Files   This option will verify each file in the installation against the file that was installed originally (this is what the SETUP.LOG file is used for). If it finds a file that does not match the original it will identify the file and ask if it should be replaced.

- Inspect Boot Sector   This option will copy a new boot sector to the disk.

Exam Essentials

When a workstation will not boot correctly, it is imperative that you understand the process so that you can analyze the problem. Microsoft tests fairly heavily on the information covered for this objective.

Know the four phases of the NT boot process and what happens in each. The *Initial Phase* is mostly hardware related. The computer does a POST, reads the CMOS, finds the boot device, and reads the Master Boot Record.

In the *Boot Loader Phase*, NTLDR gathers information about the hardware that is needed to boot. It reads the BOOT.INI file and displays the operating system menu, runs NTDETECT.COM to discover the computer's hardware, and loads NTOSKRNL.EXE.

The NT operating system initializes in the *Kernel Phase*. NTOSKRNL.EXE creates the hardware registry key using the information gathered during the Boot Loader Phase, reads the registry to find out which device drivers need to be loaded, and loads services that are marked as start value 0 in the registry.

The *Logon Phase* is the last phase. The Winlogon service starts and displays the logon box. An NT boot is not considered successful until a user logs onto the machine.

Understand the function of the BOOT.INI file. The BOOT.INI file has two sections: the [boot loader] and [operating system] sections. The [boot loader] section contains information about defaults—how long the menu should stay on screen before a default operating system should be chosen and where that default operating system is located. The [operating systems] section contains the choices that the user will be presented with and the location of the available operating system files.

Know the BOOT.INI command switches and what function they perform. These switches include /basevideo, /maxmem:n, /noserialmice, /sos, /crashdebug, /debugport, and /baudrate.

Understand the Last Known Good Configuration. The Last Known Good configuration is a saved copy of the Current Control Set in use the last time NT was successfully booted. It is overwritten when a user logs on. Since the configuration information within it was sufficient to log a user on, you can always use it to bypass any major errors. You can then log on and correct the problem.

Understand the process involved in creating and using the emergency Repair Disk (ERD). Use the RDISK.EXE utility to create an ERD. Remember to use the /s switch to ensure that your security and account information is backed up. You use the ERD by booting to the NT setup floppies, and typing **r** for repair when asked if you want to install NT or repair files.

Key Terms and Concepts

CMOS: Configuration information used by the computer at boot. For our discussion here, this is how the computer knows which device to boot from.

Emergency Repair Disk (ERD): A floppy that contains replacement copies of critical system files. This disk can be used to recover from boot problems caused by the deletion or corruption of these files.

Master Boot Record (MBR): A section of the boot device that contains a list of the partitions on the disk and which partition is the active partition.

Partition Boot Sector (PBS): A sector of the disk that contains specific boot instructions.

Power On Self Test (POST): A process run by the computer in which it determines the amount of memory installed and confirms the existence of required hardware.

Sample Questions

1. The Current configuration becomes the Last Known Good configuration at which point in the boot process?

   A. After all services have successfully loaded in the kernel phase

   B. After a user successfully logs on

C. After the BOOT.INI file has executed

D. When the user chooses Save Configuration on the Startup/ Shutdown tab of the System Applet

Answer: B. An NT boot is considered successful when a user logs on at that computer. At that point, the current configuration is considered to be valid so it is written to the Last Known Good configuration.

2. The /basevideo option in the BOOT.INI file does which of the following?

A. Instructs the operating system to use the highest resolution of the currently loaded video driver

B. Instructs the operating system to use a generic VGA video driver

C. Forces the boot process to stop and prompt the user for video configuration information

D. Instructs NT that the hardware will handle MPEG files

Answer: B. This allows a system to boot even if an incorrect video driver has been configured.

Choose the appropriate course of action to take when a print job fails.

Oh, the horror stories you could tell. How many times have you had to trek all the way across the building, up four flights of stairs, through a crowded hallway, only to find a gaggle of people standing around a printer getting mad because "The printer doesn't work!" Once you have added paper to the printer, the users are happy and you are now the one mad and frustrated. See how easily anger transfers? Wouldn't it be wonderful if knowledge transferred just that easily?

Critical Information

Printing problems are easy to resolve, if you understand the printing process. Experience has shown that printing problems fall into two basic categories: either it's an end user problem or a system problem. The end user problems can usually be solved by taking the following steps:

- Plugging the printer in
- Turning the printer back on
- Putting paper in the printer
- Clearing the paper jam in the printer
- Putting the printer back online

Troubleshooting printing sub-system problems can be more difficult. A useful method to work in troubleshooting printing problems is to generate a mental flow chart of where the print job goes. If you can figure out which step along the way is causing the problem, you are usually a long way toward solving it.

Printing to a local printer attached to the workstation starts with an application sending output to the Graphical Device Interface or the GDI. The GDI takes the application output and turns it into a print job that has been translated into the print device's native language.

NOTE The Microspeak definition of a Print Device is what you and I would probably call a printer. You know, that thing at the end of the cable that paper comes out of?

Just because the print job is in the native language of the print device does not mean it is there yet. The print job now gets sent to a spooler and the spooler writes the job to a temporary file on the disk. The temp file is created just in case of a temporary failure of some sort.

The spooler process is two sided. It has a client side and a server side. If the printer is attached to the computer, both the client and the server reside on the same machine. If the printer is attached to an NT Workstation peer on the network, the two processes are on different computers. In either case, the client side passes the file off to the server side. The server side writes the file to disk until the actual print device is ready to handle the job. When the print device is ready, it calls for the print job, which goes through a separator page process. The separator page process sends the job to the print monitor and the print monitor finally sends the job to the print device.

If you remember the process, you can check each step along the way. When you find out where the print job stops, you can reset the application that is to handle the next step. If the job comes out garbled, you can make sure the printer driver is up-to-date, or you know to check to see if it's an end user problem.

Necessary Procedures

We are going to break print troubleshooting into the following key areas:

- End user problems
- Application (non-Windows)
- Print Drivers
- Spooling
- Printing Speed

Troubleshooting End-User Problems

End users can be very creative at creating printing problems. If you get a call, check the easy things first. Are the cables plugged in, is the printer turned on, does it have paper in it, and is it online? You would be surprised how many times it is the small things that causes the failure.

If you are a new system administrator, remember that the end user may not be the most reliable source of information. If you ask questions that seem to be simple troubleshooting questions, it may all be technobabble to the end user. There are times when the best solution to the problem is actually going to the printer and troubleshooting from there.

Troubleshooting Non–Windows-Based Applications

Non–Windows-based applications can be tricky, because they bypass the normal print routine. Here are some things to check.

1. Each non–Windows-based application needs to have its own set of printer drivers. Does this application have the right drivers?

2. Each non–Windows-based application needs to be told where to go. Is this application network aware, or do you have to use the NET USE LPT1: command?

Troubleshooting Print Drivers

Print driver problems manifest themselves in strange ways. Print jobs suddenly take on strange appearances. Here are some common print driver problems.

- A print job is submitted for a small document. Instead of your document, you receive page after page of smiley faces or other strange characters. Make sure the user has a PCL print driver selected in the application. This is a classic case of a print job using a PostScript driver to print to a PCL printer.

- A print job is submitted for a document. You can trace the print job all the way to the printer, but nothing comes out. Other than this job, the printer works fine. Check the print driver. The user may be sending a job formatted with a PCL driver to a PostScript printer. PostScript will not act on any job submitted that is not formatted with the appropriate driver.

- A print job comes out with garbage embedded in the document. This may be especially prevalent in graphics. Check to make sure that tabs and form feeds are turned off for the job. This is primarily true of jobs going to PostScript printers. This is a workstation setting.

- When you find a print driver update, the update only needs to made at the print server, the print server will distribute the driver to the clients.

Troubleshooting Spooling

Spooling is simply the act of copying a file from one spot to another. Spoolers must be running at both the print server and at the workstation.

- If print jobs get stuck in a print spooler, stop and restart the spooler. This is done from Start ➤ Settings ➤ Control Panel ➤ Services ➤ Spooler.

- The spooler can also be started and stopped using the NET START SPOOLER and NET STOP SPOOLER commands from the command line.

- By default, print spoolers are stored in the \WINNT\SYSTEM32\ SPOOL\PRINTERS folder. Be sure the disk that contains this folder has plenty of free disk space. Bad things happen when you try to print a 100MB file to a print spooler that resides on a drive with 50MB free. The location of the print spooler may be changed from the Advanced tab of the Server Properties dialog box.

- You can assign a separate spooler for each printer. This is done by entering a path for the new spool directory in the registry. The path will be the data for the value SpoolDirectory . The printer name is also needed. The registry entry is HKEY_LOCAL_MACHINE\ SYSTEM\CURRENTCONTROLSET\CONTROL\PRINT\ PRINTERS\<PRINTER>. Be sure to stop and start the spooler for this to take effect.

- If the computer that houses the print spooler should suffer an unexpected shutdown (read that to mean crash) the jobs that are in the spooler should print when the print spooler is restarted.

TIP Print jobs in the spooler are made up of two files, *.SPL and *.SHD. The file with the extension SPL is the actual spool file and the SHD file is a shadow file. Check the spooler directory occasionally to clean out the old corrupted files. You can tell them by the date and time stamp.

Troubleshooting Printing Speed

A VERY common complaint of end users everywhere is the speed of the network. You can do some things to improve their lot in life.

1. Print spooling is a background process. NT Workstation assigns it a priority of 7. NT Server, on the other hand, has a thing for spooling, so it gives it a higher priority of 9, which means that it is as important as a foreground application. If your NT Workstation is "just" a print server, up the priority. To change the priority, you add a value called PriorityClass of type REG_DWORD to HKEY_LOCAL_MACHINE\SYSTEM\CURRENTCONTROLSET\CONTROL\PRINT and set it with the priority class you desire.

TIP Priority is a funny thing—what you give to one you take away from another. Just a word of caution.

---

2. Many times third-party print servers are faster than NT-based print servers. Printers that have a built-in network card are the fastest providers.

NOTE One common printer manufacturer (Hewlett Packard) requires the Dynamic Link Control (DLC) protocol be installed for a network interface to communicate with the rest of the system.

Exam Essentials

Printing is a great topic for the exam writers. It is something they understand, and it is complicated enough to provide lots of questions!

Know that HP is different. HP requires that the Dynamic Link Control (DLC) protocol is loaded when you have a printer with an integrated network interface card. If during installation you do not see an option to install a port for the printer, DLC is not installed.

Know that HP is different, part deux. Suppose DLC is loaded at the workstation and at the printer and you still cannot print. Using the HP utilities, check and see if another computer is attached to the print device using continuous connection mode. If that is the case, the other user is hogging all your resources.

Know what happens in the event of a printer jam. If a job has been submitted and the printer jams, you can restart the document by going into the Printers folder and choosing Restart from the Documents menu.

Know what happens in the event of a printer jam in a printer pool. If one printer of a printer pool jams, the job that is printing at the time of the jam will be held at that printer until the jam has been cleared. Other jobs will be routed to other printers in the pool.

Key Terms and Concepts

Direct Connected Printer: Printer devices that have onboard network interface cards, connecting the device directly to the network.

Print Device: The actual hardware that puts the ink on the paper.

Print Driver: The software component that interfaces the print devices to the operating system.

Print Server: A computer to which printers are attached and connected to the network.

Print Spooler: Temporary holding areas for print jobs. Print Spoolers are stored in the \WINNT\SYSTEM32\SPOOL\ PRINTERS folder.

Printer: Software applet that runs at the workstation. The printer takes the print job from the applications and begins to prepare it to traverse the system and come out as ink on paper at the print device.

Printing Pool: A number of print devices that are connected to the same printer. The printer directs the print job to an available print device in the pool.

Sample Questions

1. Brandice is troubleshooting a printing problem with a print device that prints using the Printer Control Language(PCL). When a user sends the print job to the printer device, the job comes out with page after page of happy faces. What could be the problem?

   A. The printer is corrupted.

   B. The print spooler has some corrupted file in it.

   C. The print driver needs to replaced.

   D. This device uses both PCL printing and PostScript, therefore is doesn't need a printer port.

   E. The user is sending a job that has been formatted using a Post-Script driver to a PCL-based printer.

   Answer: E. The most common cause of strange characters showing up while printing is the printer driver. Make sure the document is formatted to use the right print device language.

2. Some older HP printers use a protocol that can cause printers to not be recognized or to become unavailable. What is this protocol?

   A. IPX/SPX

   B. NetBEUI

   C. NetBIOS

   D. TCP/IP v6

   E. DLC

   Answer: E. Some older HP print devices use the DLC protocol. The workstation used to configure and work with these printers must also be using DLC.

3. A print spooler could also be referred to as:

A. Print Queue

B. Print Device

C. Print Server

D. Printer

Answer: A. A print spooler can also be referred to as a print queue.

Choose the appropriate course of action to take when the installation process fails.

In the real world, installation failures are fairly common. They are also the best types of problem—a problem that manifests itself before the server has been placed in production. While you are usually under some sort of deadline, there is probably less pressure to get the problem fixed immediately.

Critical Information

There are many reasons that an NT installation might fail. The easiest way to avoid installation problems is to purchase equipment that has been tested to be compatible with Microsoft Windows NT. Microsoft provides a tool called NTHQ that will help you determine if your equipment in on this list. This tool can be found on your NT server CD-ROM or can be downloaded from the Microsoft Web site. NTHQ tests your hardware to determine if any components are not on the list.

WARNING Always download the latest version of NTHQ from the Web site. The version found on your CD-ROM will not contain information about hardware that has been certified since the CD-ROM was created. Before you purchase equipment you can access the compatibility list on the same Web site. You should make it a policy to specify "NT 4.0 certified" when you talk to vendors.

Now let's look at some specific problems that you might encounter.

Media Errors

If you get an error that indicates that a particular file cannot be copied or is corrupt during an installation of NT, this could indicate some sort of media error. Try using another CD-ROM if you have one available. If not, try using another method of installation. Copying the i386 directory to the C: drive (assuming it is a FAT partition) and trying the installation from there is a good option. Another option is to copy the i386 directory to another server, share the directory, and then install from that share point.

Non-Supported SCSI Adapter

If your CD-ROM is attached to a SCSI adapter that is not supported by NT, you can lose the ability to read from it half way through the installation process. Unfortunately, even if the company provides an NT SCSI driver, you don't have the opportunity use it until after NT is installed. If you run into this problem, you will have to try the same techniques as listed above, under "Media Errors." Try installing from a share point on another server, or boot to DOS, copy the i386 directory to the C: drive, and install from there.

Insufficient Disk Space

This is really just poor planning. Know the minimum requirement before you start the install, and make sure your hardware meets or exceeds them. The only fix for this is to provide NT with enough disk space either by deleting an existing partition or adding another drive.

Failure of Dependency Service to Start

This is usually a configuration error. Go back to the Network setup section of the installation and ensure that the correct protocols are configured correctly, you have chosen a unique computer name, and that the network interface card settings are correct.

Inability to connect to the PDC

Ensure that you have typed in the domain name correctly, check the NIC card settings to ensure that they are correct and that you have chosen the correct protocols. This problem comes up quite often—usually when trying to install a BDC on a computer that has a non-supported NIC. If NT doesn't provide a NIC driver, then the card can't initialize, and you can not communicate with the server.

Error in Assigning a Domain Name

When installing a PDC, ensure that the domain name is not already in use on your network. It cannot be the same as any other domain or computer name.

Failure of NT to Install or Start

This usually indicates a piece of hardware that is not compatible with NT. Run NTHQ to determine which component is not on the hardware compatibility list and replace it.

Exam Essentials

Knowing what problems you might encounter can help you to avoid them.

Understand the various reasons that an NT installation might fail. The most common reasons for failure are either human error or incompatible hardware.

Key Terms and Concepts

HCL (Hardware Compatibility List):   A list of hardware that has been tested and approved for use with Microsoft Windows NT.

NTHQ: Software that will check your hardware to ensure that all components are on the hardware compatibility list.

Sample Questions

1. Which of the following actions should you take if you encounter a media error when installing NT?

   A. Try another NT CD-ROM.

   B. Try another method of installation: across the network, copy the i386 to the local drive first, etc.

   C. Give up and try another operating system.

   D. Clean your CD-ROM drive.

   Answer: A, B, D. Although answer C might seem like the easiest method in the short term, it is not a Microsoft-recommended solution.

2. You have purchased a new computer and plan to install NT on it. On your purchase order, you specifically requested that the computer be on the NT Hardware Compatibility List (HCL). The installation on NT fails and when you check the HCL, you find the make and model are not on it. You call the vendor and they insist the computer is on the HCL. Which of the following might explain the discrepancy?

   A. The computer is not on the HCL and your vendor is lying.

   B. You are checking an out-dated version of the HCL and need to download the latest copy.

   C. The salesperson assumed that since their other computers are on the list, this model must be as well.

   D. Trust the vendor—the problem must not be hardware related.

   Answer: B. While all of the answers listed might actually be true, the Microsoft exam answer would be B. If you are buying new equipment you must check for an up-to-date copy of the HCL.

Choose the appropriate course of action to take when an application fails.

There is some good news about applications failures. Usually when an application fails, it does *not* bring down the entire system. This is in direct contrast to earlier versions of Windows and DOS applications. If you look back at the discussion in Chapter 5 on running applications, you can thank the Win32 Subsystem and all those multiprocessing threads.

There is some better news about application failures. With the advent of 32-bit applications written especially for Windows NT, the failure rate is bound to decrease.

Critical Information

Applications fail for a variety of reasons. Sometimes, it might just be that the application is having a bad day: applications tend to act just like petulant people, they simply stop working. When this happens, you have to figure out how to close the application that is not responding to any of your best computer-geek tricks. When in doubt, try Ctrl+Alt+Del. This "three-finger salute" will open a dialog box that will allow you to access Task Manager. From Task Manager, it is a simple process to open the Applications tab, select the application, and choose Close. Problem solved.

What causes applications to fail? Good question. Sometimes, the cause of failure is easy to spot, like you are running a DOS application on an NT machine. Sometimes, the application helps you out, by giving you an error message. Rarely, but sometimes, the application helps you out by giving you an error message that makes sense. This happened once, back in 1987, approximately. Most of the time, these things just happen. You close them out, restart the application, and everything goes along just fine.

Some applications have error logs. If the offending application has a log, check it, and the manual. You might get lucky. Then again, you might not. For consistent errors, refer to the application's Web site and check for patches. When in doubt, call the application's tech support hotline.

Necessary Procedures

Thank goodness for multitasking. Now there is an operating systems that will allow you to simply close an application that has stopped responding.

Closing a Failed Application

To close an application that has stopped functioning:

1. Press Ctrl+Alt+Del to open the Windows NT Security dialog box.

2. Click the Task Manager button.

3. Click the Applications tab.

4. Select the application (it will say Not Responding) and click the End Task button.

5. Close Task Manager.

Exam Essentials

There are several objectives that are really light on content. This is definitely one of them.

Know how to access the Windows NT Security dialog box to close an application. Press Ctrl+Alt+Del. Select the Task Manager tab, and click Applications.

Key Terms and Concepts

Three-Finger Salute: Tongue-in-cheek reference to the Ctrl+Alt+Del key sequence.

Sample Questions

1. Which type of application is least likely to fail in a Windows NT environment?

   A. DOS Application

   B. Windows 16-bit application

   C. Windows 32-bit application

   D. POSIX application

   Answer: C. A 32-bit application is least likely to fail in a Windows NT environment.

2. If an application has frozen, which utility can be used to shut it down?

   A. Application Manager

   B. Task Manager

   C. Disk Manager

   D. Computer Manager

   Answer: B. Task Manager can be used to shut down applications.

3. If an application has failed, how do you access Task Manager?

   A. Start ➤ Control Panel ➤ Task Manager

   B. Ctrl+Alt+Del

   C. Application Manager

   D. Computer Manager

   Answer: B. Ctrl+Alt+Del

Choose the appropriate course of action to take when a user cannot access a resource.

Resource access problems are usually pretty straightforward. It is a yes or no decision, either someone can or cannot do something to something. If a user is supposed to be able to use a printer and can't, you have a resource access problem. If a user is supposed to be able to write to a file and can't, you have a permission problem. The tricky part comes in figuring out where the problem lies.

Critical Information

In previous examples, the difficulty in the process has been locating the problem. Once the problem has been located, the solution was self-evident.

In the case of access problems or permission problems, locating the problem is simple. Finding the solution can be more difficult. The problem may be that people cannot access a resource because they cannot log on. Is that a hardware problem, a software problem, a network problem, or an end user problem?

Access problems will jump out at you. There is never any gray. The user can either do too much or not do enough. Now what do you do about it?

Necessary Procedures

Your pager has gone off. You answer the call and it is a frantic end user or help-desk person. Something isn't working! What do you do now?

Troubleshooting Access and Permission Problems

When someone calls and cannot get access to the system or to a resource, follow these steps:

1. Ask questions. Is it just one person or are there more than one person involved? What resource is it? Is it a hardware problem? Is the printer shut off?

2. If the user cannot log on, make sure the user is attached to the right domain, is using the right logon name, has the caps lock key on or off (PASSWORD is not the same as password), and ensure that the user is supposed to be on during that time.

3. If the user cannot access a resource, can you access the resource using a different account? If you can access the resource using a different account, you have a permissions problem.

4. When you have determined that the access problem is due to permissions rather than a hardware problem, the next step is to determine how the user was supposed to be able to access the account. Were the permissions to be assigned to a group? Can the rest of the group access the resource? If the rest of the group can access the resource, then the problem lies with the individual and the group or user memberships they have been given.

TIP Be wary of the NO ACCESS permission. If a user belongs to a group that is given NO ACCESS to a resource, that user will not get access to the resource, no matter what other group membership they enjoy.

---

5. Make sure the user is spelling the name of the resource correctly. If this is a new occurrence, don't rule out syntax too quickly. You

would be surprised how fat fingered some users can be, and it is amazing how long you can look at \\SERVER-1 before realizing it is not the same as \\SERVER_1.

6. If no one can log on, has the NetLogon Service stopped? Check it by going to Start ➤ Settings ➤ Control Panel ➤ Services. While you are there, check the Server and Workstation service.

7. Rights and permissions will take affect the next time the user logs on. If it is a new assignment, have the user log off and log on again, and see if that solves the problem.

8. One last place to look would be the System Policy editor. Is there a new system policy for the user or for the user's computer? That can also mess up the works!

Exam Essentials

Rights and permissions are areas that are stressed by the exam writers.

Know that the most restrictive rights and permissions are the ones that apply. When you look at the rights and permissions a user has been granted, take into account all groups the user belongs to, as well as the individual user assignments. The most restrictive rights apply.

Know the impact of the NO ACCESS assignment. If a user has been given NO ACCESS permissions to a file, folder, or share, that is the permission that will override all others. So if the user TMENDAL had Full Control through his membership in the ADMIN group, READ access through his membership in the Management Group, and NO ACCESS through his membership in the Accounting group,

TMENDAL would be out of luck. NO ACCESS would be the permission that overrode everything else.

Know when rights and permissions take effect. A user must log off and log on again to generate a new Security Identifier or SID. Once the new SID has been generated, the new rights or permissions will take effect.

Key Terms and Concepts

SID: Security Identifier. Code generated to identify a specific user or group to the NT Security subsystem.

Sample Questions

1. What can a user do who has NO ACCESS permission to a folder?

   A. It depends on what permissions the user has as members of a group.

   B. Permissions are cumulative, so whatever permissions the user has on the files will follow to the folder.

   C. If the folder resides on a FAT partition, the user will not be able to see the folder.

   D. A user with NO ACCESS permissions to a folder will be able to see the folder, and attach to it, but do nothing else.

Answer: D. The user will be able to see the folder and attach to it, but nothing else.

2. A user calls and says that he cannot log on to his workstation. What are two things to check?

   A. Is the network card plugged in?

   B. Is the user using the right logon name?

   C. Is the user typing the correct password, in the correct case?

D. Is the user typing the correct password; case does not matter?

Answer: B and C. Logging on to a workstation does not involve network communication. The logon name and the password must be correct and case does matter with a password.

3. What permissions can be granted to a folder on a FAT partition?

   A. Full Control

   B. No Access

   C. Read, Write, and Supervisor

   D. Folders on FAT permissions cannot receive permissions.

   Answer: D. The FAT file system does not have the ability to accept permissions. Only folders on an NTFS partition can have permissions.

Modify the registry using the appropriate tool in a given situation.

Just about everything you do on an NT-based computer will access the registry. The registry contains information about your hardware settings, the drivers needed to access that hardware, your user profiles, the software you have installed—this list goes on and on. Each time you boot, the registry is read to determine what should happen. When you run a program like Microsoft Word, the registry is read to determine where the program is located. When you log on to the system the registry is read to build your security context. In other words, the registry is critical to the health of your server.

With this in mind, the objectives for this section cover the tools that you can use to back up the registry and edit its contents. Always remember to do these two things in *that* order: back up, then edit. Since the registry is so important, you always want to have a current backup before you make any changes to it.

Critical Information

Before we can discuss the tasks listed in this test objective, we must discuss what the registry is and how it is structured. The registry is a database that contains NT configuration information. This database is organized in a hierarchical structure that consists of subtrees and their keys, hives, and values.

NOTE Don't be intimidated by the term "hierarchical." You are already familiar with a hierarchical structure: the DOS file system. If you understand the directory, subdirectory, and file structure of DOS, you understand the structure of the registry. Hierarchical structures use a series of containers and subcontainers to organize the data that they hold.

The NT registry is made up of five subtrees, each of which holds specific types of configuration information. Each subtree holds "keys" that contain the computer or user databases. Each key can have both specific parameters and additional subkeys. The term *hive* refers to a distinct subset of a key. Hives can be backed up as a single file.

It is important that you know the five main subtrees and understand the type of information that is found in each one.

- **HKEY_LOCAL_MACHINE** Contains hardware and operating system configuration parameters for the local computer, such as bus type, processor, device drivers, and startup information. This is the subtree most commonly used in the troubleshooting process.

- **HKEY_CLASSES_ROOT** Defines file associations and configuration data for COM and DCOM objects.

- **HKEY_CURRENT_USER** Contains the user profile for the user that is currently logged in. You will find parameters for the user's desktop, network connections, printers, and application preferences.

- **HKEY_USERS** Contains all actively loaded user profiles, including a copy of HKEY_CURRENT_USER.

- **HKEY_CURRENT_CONFIG** Contains the current hardware configuration.

Backing up and Restoring the Registry

There are four methods of backing up the registry:

- Use "Save Registry" in the backup utility found in the Administrative Tools (Common) group. This is the preferred method if you have a tape backup unit. This method can back up and restore the registry while Windows NT is running.

- There are two command line tools available that can also backup and restore the registry while NT is running—REGBACK.EXE and REGREST.EXE. These tools are included in the Windows NT Resource Kit.

- Within the Registry editor, on the Registry menu, click Save Key. This process saves a single key, and everything beneath it, to a file. Online restores using this method are not guaranteed, so use the backup utility whenever possible.

- Create or update your Emergency Repair Disk. Remember to use the /s switch to ensure a complete backup.

Editing the Registry

Most of the time you will want to avoid editing the registry directly—you will use various tools to adjust the configuration of your environment, and these tools will write to the registry for you. There are, however, many optimization and troubleshooting techniques that will require you to use the registry-editing tool. There are two things to remember when working with the registry—backup and read-only mode.

Backing up is a simple form of protection against a moment of clumsiness. Everyone makes mistakes; the trick is to be prepared for them. The best protection against yourself is a good backup.

The registry editor has an option that allows you to put it in read-only mode. In this mode, you can look at parameters, do your research, and exist confident in the fact that, at the very least, you didn't inadvertently make the problem worse. After careful consideration of your options, you can then go back into the editor and make changes to the registry (after making a good backup).

Many of the troubleshooting and performance optimization techniques that we have discussed have required you to make changes to the registry. By default, only members of the Administrators group have the ability to change the registry; normal users are limited to read-only access. NT ships with two tools designed for manual editing of the registry database—the Windows NT Registry Editor (REGEDT32.EXE) and the Windows 95 version of the Registry Editor (REGEDIT.EXE.) While both provide the ability to edit the registry, there are certain keys that can only be edited using the NT version.

When editing the registry, certain changes may take effect immediately while others might require some action on your part. In general, when editing values in the CurrentControlSet subtree, the computer must be restarted before changes will take effect. When editing values in HKEY_CURRENT_USER, the user will often be required to log off before changes take effect.

WARNING   The bottom line when using the registry editor is to take your time and be sure before you commit to any changes.

Necessary Procedures

Almost every exam in the MCSE series includes at least one example of a change that you might have to make to the registry. Understanding the process will only make your studying easier.

Using the Registry Editor to Back Up a Key

Both the NT and Windows 95 versions of the Registry Editor allow you to back up the registry. They accomplish this goal in different ways—the NT version, shown below, will save each subkey as a separate file, so you will have to save each of the five main hives individually.

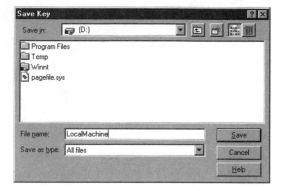

The Windows 95 version will allow you to save the entire registry as a single file.

The Windows 95 version will allow you to save the entire registry as a single file.

Creating or Updating an Emergency Repair Disk

Run RDISK.EXE from a command prompt. The program will ask you for a floppy to copy the information to. Remember to use the /s switch when running RDISK.EXE so that you get a complete backup of the registry.

Using the Registry Editor to Search the Database

Both the NT version and the Windows 95 versions allow you to search the database—there is, however, a difference in functionality.

As the screen above illustrates, REGEDT32.EXE allows you to search for any key by name; for instance, you could search for the CurrentControlSet key. The only problem with this is that you must know the correct name of the key.

As shown in the following screen, REGEDIT.EXE gives you a few more choices as to what you can search for. You can search for the actual value or data within a key. This will come in handy if you are looking for information, but don't know which subkey it should be in. As an example, let's say you had a problem with a device set to interrupt 5. In the NT version, you would have to know the name of the key that this value was stored in; in the Windows 95 version you could do a search for the number 5.

Using the Registry Editor to Add or Edit the Value of a Key

Follow these steps:

1. Open REGEDT32.EXE.

2. Choose Add Value on the Edit menu.

3. You will have to determine what type of data will be entered. There are five types of data:

- REG_BINARY represents data as a string of binary numbers.

- REG_SZ represents data as a string.

- REG_EXPAND_SZ represents data as an expandable string.

- REG_DWORD represents data as a hexadecimal value with a maximum size of 4 bytes.

- REG_MULTI_SZ represents data as multiple strings.

Luckily, unless you are a software developer, you will probably not have to determine the type of data—just the value. You will choose the type based upon information found in a manual or reference.

Using the Registry Editor to Troubleshoot a Remote Computer

The Registry Editor can be used to access the registry of a remote computer. You are allowed to access the HKEY_LOCAL_MACHINE and HKEY_USERS subkeys of the remote machine. Chose "Select Computer" on the Registry menu.

Exam Essentials

For this exam you are not expected to understand every detail of the registry, but you are expected to know what it is used for, how it is organized, and the processes involved in backing it up and editing its content.

Know the five main keys and understand what type of data is contained in each. The five main keys are HKEY_LOCAL_MACHINE, HKEY_CLASSES_ROOT, HKEY_CURRENT_USER, HKEY_USERS, and HKEY_CURRENT_CONFIG.

Know the four methods of backing up the registry. The Backup tool located in the Administrative Tools (Common) group, the two command line utilities REGBACK.EXE and REGREST.EXE, the Registry Editor, and the Emergency Repair Disk.

Know the various functions of the Registry Editor utility. Reread the Necessary Procedures section of this section. Know what you can accomplish using the Registry Editor and how to perform those tasks.

Key Terms and Concepts

Hierarchical: A structure used to store information. The registry is a hierarchical database made up of keys and subkeys that hold values.

Hive: Any subtree and its values, including any subtrees beneath it. Think of it as a branch of the tree.

Key: A subtree that contains per-computer or per-user configuration databases.

Registry: A database that contains the configuration parameters necessary for the NT operating system to function.

Value: Within the registry, a specific parameter's setting.

Sample Questions

1. Which of the following are methods used to back up the registry?

   A. Use any Windows-based backup software.

   B. Use the Save Registry option in the NT backup utility.

   C. Use REGBACK.EXE from a command prompt.

D. Update your Emergency Repair Disk

Answer: B, C, D. Answer A is not complete enough to accept: the software must be Windows NT 4.0–certified.

2. Which of the following command line tools is used to restore a backup copy of the registry?

   A. BINDREST.EXE

   B. REGREST.EXE

   C. RESTORE.EXE

   D. There is not a command line tool to do this: You should boot to DOS, copy the files to the System32 directory, and restart the computer. The files will be automatically restored.

Answer: B. REGREST.EXE is the NT command line utility used to restore the registry.

Implement advanced techniques to resolve various problems.

There is no such thing as a "crash-proof" workstation, only workstations that have yet to meet the set of circumstances necessary to bring them to their knees. When a workstation crashes, it is often a complex set of circumstances that has caused the problem. This objective covers some of the actions you can take to analyze the situation.

Critical Information

While Microsoft doesn't stress this objective, you are expected to know what to do in the event of a problem on an NT computer.

Diagnosing and Interpreting a Blue Screen

When the Microsoft NT operating system encounters a fatal error it will display a stop screen, often called a "blue screen" (more often called the "blue screen of death" but never by Microsoft). The stop screen contains debugging information useful in interpreting exactly what was happening at the time of failure. If the system recovery options are turned on, NT will also generate a file with this debug information.

At first glance, the blue screen can seem intimidating, but there is actually a small amount of data that you will use to determine the cause of the error. With some errors, the cause of the problem is immediately apparent from this information. With others, you might have to rely upon Microsoft Technical Support for assistance.

There are five distinct areas on a stop screen. Each area provides specific information regarding the error or recovery options.

Area 1: Debug Port Status Indicators

Later in the section we will look at a process that allows you to dump the debug information out the serial port to another computer. This connection is seen much like a modem connection. In the upper-right corner of a stop screen, you will see a series of indicators that display the status of this connection. The various indicators are listed in Table 7.1.

T A B L E 7.1: Connection Status Indicators

Status Indicator	Description
MDM	Modem controls are in use
CD	Carrier detected
RI	Ring indicator
DSR	Data set ready
CTS	Clear to send
SND	Byte being sent

TABLE 7.1:   Connection Status Indicators   *(continued)*

Status Indicator	Description
RCV	Byte received
FRM	Framing error
OVL	Overflow
PRT	Parity error

Area 2: BugCheck Information

This area starts with *** Stop, after which is the error code. There are also up to four developer-defined parameters in parentheses, followed by an interpretation of the error. Don't get your hopes up on the interpretation: While there are occasions where it leads you to the solution of your problem, it is more likely to be some obscure message.

Area 3: Driver Information

This area lists information about the drivers loaded at the time of the error. The three columns list the preferred load address, the creation date (also knows as the link time stamp), and the name of the driver. This can be useful because many stop screens list the address of the instruction that caused the problem. You can compare that information with the preferred load address to determine which driver might have caused the problem.

Area 4: Kernel Build Number and Stack Dump

This area shows two things—the build number of the operating system kernel (it will not indicate the presence of any service packs); and a range of addresses that *may* indicate the failed code.

Area 5: Debug Port Information

This area confirms the configuration of the communication port used to dump information to another computer (if configured), and it indicates whether a dump file was created.

Each stop screen will have a unique stop code. For information on a particular stop screen, search the Microsoft TechNet for the code found in area 1.

Configuring a Memory Dump

When an NT server displays a blue screen, you will have to correct the problem as soon as possible to minimize server downtime. Sometimes the solution will be obvious from the data displayed. You might also have a good idea of what caused the problem by looking through the server change log and noting recent changes to its configuration. On those occasions where the solution is not obvious, you might have to take more drastic measures—you might have to have the memory contents at the time of the stop screen analyzed. There are three ways to accomplish this:

- **Local Debugging**   On-site analysis of memory. Two computers are attached using a null modem cable, the target (the server with the problem), and the host. The host runs debugging software designed to analyze problems in NT.

- **Remote Debugging**   Once again, the target and host are connected with a null modem. The difference is that Microsoft Technical Support uses RAS to dial into your system and they analyze the memory contents remotely.

- **CrashDump**   By far, the most common method is to configure NT to dump the contents of memory into a file when the fatal error occurs. You can then send this file to Microsoft Technical Support for analysis.

To set up the target and host computers, you must have two computers each running the same version of NT, including any service packs you have installed. They should be connected by a null modem cable (or you can set up a dial-in connection from the host). The host computer must have the proper symbols files installed. The symbols file contains code used in the debug process. You must have the symbols file that matches the build, including service packs, of the target computer.

Once you have met the prerequisites, you modify the BOOT.INI file on the target server. Add the /debug switch to the appropriate operating system choice line. On the host computer you must configure the communication port by setting some environmental variables.

Next restart the target computer. When the stop screen is generated you will be able to debug the problem from the host computer.

It is unlikely that you will actually debug a stop screen. Most administrators do not have the technical knowledge necessary to accomplish this type of task. It is far more likely that you will generate a memory dump file to be sent to Microsoft Technical Support.

In the Control Panel, System applet, you will find a Startup/Shutdown tab. On this tab you can configure NT to perform certain functions when a fatal error is encountered. You can have NT write a message to the system event log, send an administrative alert, write the contents of memory to a file, and automatically reboot the system.

If you choose to have the contents of memory written to a file, the system dumps the contents of RAM into the PAGEFILE.SYS file. When the system restarts, this information is written to a file named MEMORY.DMP. You can then send this file to Microsoft for analysis. Be aware that there is no compression involved in this process so the dump file will be at least as large as your memory.

NT ships with three tools for processing memory dump files— DUMPFLOP, DUMPCHK, and DUMPEXAM. For the exam we only have to concern ourselves with the latter two.

- **DUMPCHK.EXE**   Verifies the contents of a dump file to ensure that it will be readable by a debugger. Running this program can help to ensure that you don't waste time uploading a corrupt dump file to Microsoft.

- **DUMPEXAM.EXE**   Analyzes the contents of the dump file and extracts any useful information. This information is placed into a text file that can be considerably smaller than the dump file itself.

Using the Event Log Service

The two main skills necessary to troubleshooting are gathering pertinent information and correlating that information into a plan of action to correct the problem. A common mistake is to address the symptoms without understanding the underlying cause. This is true of troubleshooting anything—not just computer systems.

NT ships with a great tool for gathering information about errors on your server—the Event Log. You can use this information to avoid treating the symptoms without fixing the problem.

The Event Log service tracks certain activities on your server and logs information about those events into a series of log files. There are three distinct log files: System, Security, and Application.

Each log file is responsible for tracking different types of events. Many events will not be tracked unless the system is configured to audit those types of events. The application log tracks application-related events, such as the starting and stopping of application related services. The security log tracks NT security events, such as the logons. The system log tracks events that affect the operating system.

There are also different levels of event messages. Some are purely informational; for instance, an application might generate an event message when it is started. Others are generated when an error is encountered. Still others are indicative of the failure of a service. For the purpose of troubleshooting, the fatal error messages can be extremely informative.

Figure 7.1 shows the contents of a typical system event log. The circle icons with an "I" in them indicate informative messages. The stop sign icons indicate failure messages.

Each message will contain the data and time that the event occurred, an Event ID, the service that generated the message, and a short message, as shown in Figure 7.2.

You can often use this information to determine the cause of a problem. Make sure to look through all of the fatal messages though, because many services are dependent upon other services. The last message listed might only be a symptom of the real problem.

Sometimes the information in the event messages will give you enough information to determine the cause of your problem. In these cases you can write down the Event ID, and research that particular error in TechNet. Microsoft Technical Support will often request the Event ID of any errors when you call for support.

FIGURE 7.1: Event Log

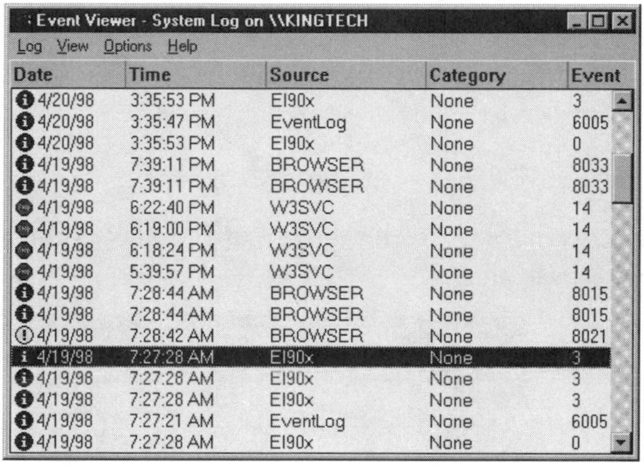

FIGURE 7.2: Event Detail

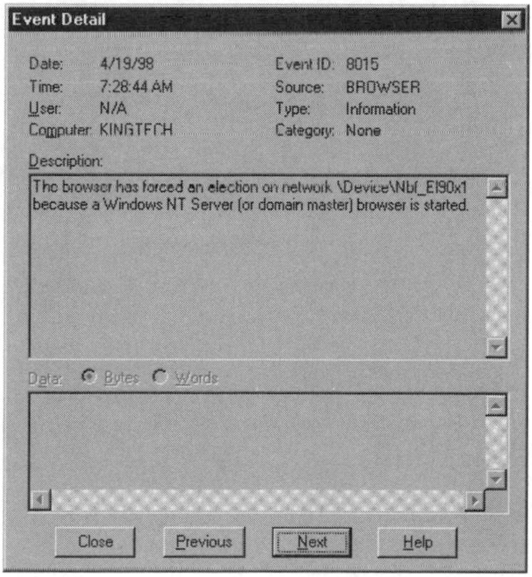

Necessary Procedures

The only real procedure for this objective concerns dumping memory into a file for later analysis (usually by someone at Microsoft Technical Support).

1. In Control Panel, open the System applet.

2. Access the Startup/Shutdown tab and make your choices of the options available.

Exam Essentials

Knowing what to do in the event of a problem is both a career and a examination necessity.

Know the five main areas of a stop screen.   Debug Port Status Indicators, BugCheck Information, Kernel Build Number and Stack Dump, and Debug Port Information.

Know the three methods of memory analysis. The three methods are local debugging, remote debugging, and crashdump.

Understand the CrashDump process. Upon encountering a fatal error, the NT server will copy the contents of memory into the PAGEFILE.SYS file. When the system is restarted the information is copied into another file. This file can be sent to Microsoft for analysis.

Know what options are available when configuring the recovery options for an NT Workstation. Options include:

- Writing an error to the event log
- Sending an administrative alert
- Writing the contents to a file
- Having that file overwrite any existing memory dump file
- Restarting the server automatically

Know the three logs in the Event viewer. The three logs are System, Security, and Application.

Understand the type of information you might find useful in an Event log message. The date and time the event occurred, the Event ID, the name of the service that generated the event message, and the short description of the error.

Know the use of the Event ID. The Event ID can be used during research of a problem. When using Microsoft TechNet, for instance, you can query the database for articles that contain the Event ID.

Key Terms and Concepts

CrashDump: A process in which the contents of memory is dumped into a file for later analysis.

DUMPCHK.EXE: A utility designed to verify the contents of a memory dump file.

DUMPEXAM.EXE: A utility design to analyze a memory dump file and extract any pertinent information into a small text file.

Host computer: When debugging a fatal error, the host is a machine running the debugging software.

Link Time Stamp: The creation date and time of a driver.

Preferred Load Address: The base memory address a driver requests when loaded.

Target computer: When debugging a fatal error, the target is the computer that is encountering the error.

Sample Questions

1. In the driver information section of a stop screen, which of the following are included in the data shown?

   A. The IRQ of the offending device

   B. Preferred load address

   C. Creation date

   D. Name of the driver

   Answer: B, C, D. The driver information section shows information about drivers loaded—not the hardware they might control.

2. Into which file is memory written during memory dump?

   A. MEMORY.DMP

   B. PAGEFILE.SYS

   C. MEMDUMP.TXT

   D. WINNT.CFG

   Answer: B. This is really a trick question because memory is dumped into the paging file first, and then transferred to MEMORY.DMP on the next restart. Read the questions carefully!

Index

NOTE: Page numbers in *italics* refer to figures or tables; page numbers in **bold** refer to significant discussions of the topic.

Q

R

NETWORK PRESS® PRESENTS
MCSE TEST SUCCESS®

THE PERFECT COMPANION BOOKS TO THE MCSE STUDY GUIDES

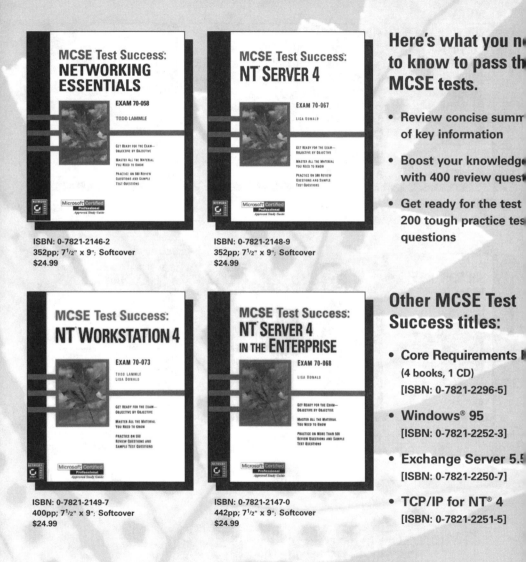

MCSE Test Success: NETWORKING ESSENTIALS
EXAM 70-058
TODD LAMMLE

GET READY FOR THE EXAM—OBJECTIVE BY OBJECTIVE
MASTER ALL THE MATERIAL YOU NEED TO KNOW
PRACTICE ON 500 REVIEW QUESTIONS AND SAMPLE TEST QUESTIONS

Microsoft Certified Professional Approved Study Guide

ISBN: 0-7821-2146-2
352pp; 7¹/₂" x 9"; Softcover
$24.99

MCSE Test Success: NT SERVER 4
EXAM 70-067
LISA DONALD

GET READY FOR THE EXAM—OBJECTIVE BY OBJECTIVE
MASTER ALL THE MATERIAL YOU NEED TO KNOW
PRACTICE ON 500 REVIEW QUESTIONS AND SAMPLE TEST QUESTIONS

Microsoft Certified Professional Approved Study Guide

ISBN: 0-7821-2148-9
352pp; 7¹/₂" x 9"; Softcover
$24.99

MCSE Test Success: NT WORKSTATION 4
EXAM 70-073
TODD LAMMLE
LISA DONALD

GET READY FOR THE EXAM—OBJECTIVE BY OBJECTIVE
MASTER ALL THE MATERIAL YOU NEED TO KNOW
PRACTICE ON 550 REVIEW QUESTIONS AND SAMPLE TEST QUESTIONS

Microsoft Certified Professional Approved Study Guide

ISBN: 0-7821-2149-7
400pp; 7¹/₂" x 9"; Softcover
$24.99

MCSE Test Success: NT SERVER 4 IN THE ENTERPRISE
EXAM 70-068
LISA DONALD

GET READY FOR THE EXAM—OBJECTIVE BY OBJECTIVE
MASTER ALL THE MATERIAL YOU NEED TO KNOW
PRACTICE ON MORE THAN 500 REVIEW QUESTIONS AND SAMPLE TEST QUESTIONS

Microsoft Certified Professional Approved Study Guide

ISBN: 0-7821-2147-0
442pp; 7¹/₂" x 9"; Softcover
$24.99

Here's what you need to know to pass the MCSE tests.

- Review concise summaries of key information

- Boost your knowledge with 400 review questions

- Get ready for the test with 200 tough practice test questions

Other MCSE Test Success titles:

- **Core Requirements**
  (4 books, 1 CD)
  [ISBN: 0-7821-2296-5]

- **Windows® 95**
  [ISBN: 0-7821-2252-3]

- **Exchange Server 5.5**
  [ISBN: 0-7821-2250-7]

- **TCP/IP for NT® 4**
  [ISBN: 0-7821-2251-5]

Microsoft Certified
Professional
Approved Study Guide

NETWORK PRESS®
SYBEX

MCSE EXAM NOTES®

MCSE Exam Notes:
NT SERVER 4

EXAM 70-067

FULL COVERAGE OF EACH
EXAM OBJECTIVE

KNOW WHAT YOU NEED TO
KNOW—AND NAIL THE EXAM

INCLUDES EXAM-TAKING
STRATEGIES

Microsoft Certified
Professional
Approved Study Guide

ISBN: 0-7821-2289-2
384 pp; 5⁷/₈" x 8¹/₄"; Softcover
$19.99

MCSE Exam Notes:
NT SERVER 4
IN THE ENTERPRISE

EXAM 70-068

FULL COVERAGE OF EACH
EXAM OBJECTIVE

KNOW WHAT YOU NEED TO
KNOW—AND NAIL THE EXAM

INCLUDES EXAM-TAKING
STRATEGIES

Microsoft Certified
Professional
Approved Study Guide

ISBN: 0-7821-2292-2
416 pp; 5⁷/₈" x 8¹/₄"; Softcover
$19.99

THE FASTEST AND MOST EFFECTIVE WAY TO MAKE SURE YOU'RE READY FOR THE MCSE EXAMS:

- Unique, innovative approach helps you gain and retain the knowledge you need, objective by objective.

- Essential information is arranged for quick learning and review.

- Exam tips and advice are offered by expert trainers.

OTHER TITLES INCLUDE:

MCSE Exam Notes™: NT® Workstation 4
MCSE Exam Notes™: Networking Essentials
MCSE Exam Notes™: Windows® 95
MCSE Exam Notes™: TCP/IP for NT® Server 4
MCSE Exam Notes™: Exchange Server 5.5
MCSE Exam Notes™: Internet Information Server 4
MCSE Exam Notes™: SQL Server 6.5 Administration
MCSE Exam Notes™: Proxy Server 2
MCSE Exam Notes™: Systems Management Server

CORE BOX SET ALSO AVAILABLE:

MCSE Exam Notes™: Core Requirements box set
- 4 books:
    MCSE Exam Notes™: Networking Essentials
    MCSE Exam Notes™: NT® Workstation 4
    MCSE Exam Notes™: NT® Server 4
    MCSE Exam Notes™: NT® Server 4 in the Enterprise
- Bonus CD
- Only $64.99—Save $15.00

www.sybex.com

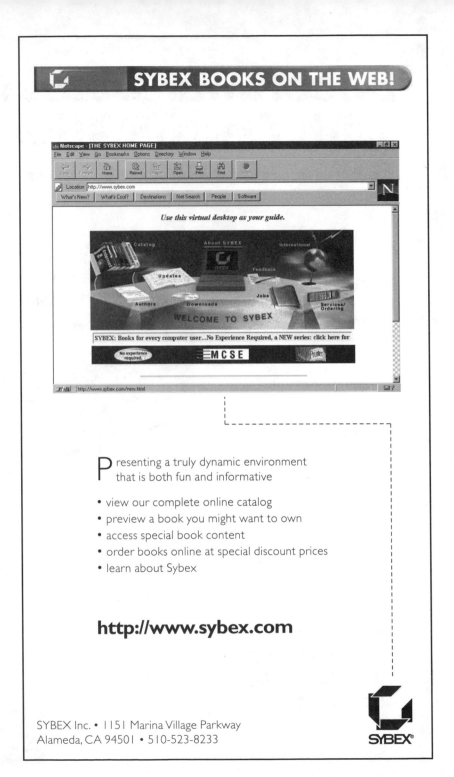